汉英对照·汉语100点实用系列手册

汉语常用100字
100 Chinese Characters Commonly Used

主编：谭春健
编著：任丽丽　杨慧真　张　劼
翻译：张　劼
审译：Jennifer Liu

图书在版编目(CIP)数据

汉语常用100字 /谭春健主编. —北京：北京大学出版社，2013.10
(汉英对照·汉语100点实用系列手册)
ISBN 978-7-301-23155-5

Ⅰ．汉… Ⅱ．谭… Ⅲ．汉字—对外汉语教学—教学参考资料
Ⅳ．H195.4

中国版本图书馆CIP数据核字(2013)第209848号

书　　　　名：	汉语常用100字
著作责任者：	谭春健　主编　任丽丽　杨慧真　张　劼　编著
责 任 编 辑：	沈　岚
标 准 书 号：	ISBN 978-7-301-23155-5/H·3391
出 版 发 行：	北京大学出版社
地　　　　址：	北京市海淀区成府路205号　　100871
网　　　　址：	http://www.pup.cn　　新浪官方微博：@北京大学出版社
电子信箱：	zpup@pup.pku.edu.cn
电　　　　话：	邮购部 62752015　　发行部 62750672
	编辑部 62767349　　出版部 62754962
印　刷　者：	三河市博文印刷厂
经　销　者：	新华书店
	650毫米×980毫米　16开本　27.25印张　390千字
	2013年10月第1版　2013年10月第1次印刷
定　　　　价：	80.00元

未经许可，不得以任何方式复制或抄袭本书之部分或全部内容。
版权所有，侵权必究
举报电话：010-62752024　　电子信箱：fd@pup.pku.edu.cn

目 录

▶▶▶▶▶▶▶▶

前言 ·· 1

Preface ··· 4

一、作数词的汉字 Characters as Numerals ················· 1
   1. 一 one ··· 1
   2. 十 ten ··· 5
   3. 百 hundred ·· 9

二、作代词的汉字 Characters as Pronouns ················ 13
   4. 你 you ·· 13
   5. 我 I ··· 17
   6. 他 he ·· 20
   7. 这 this ·· 23
   8. 谁 who ··· 27
   9. 几 how many ·· 30

三、作名词的汉字 Characters as Nouns ······················ 34
   10. 天 sky ·· 34
   11. 年 year ·· 38
   12. 月 month ··· 42
   13. 日 day ··· 46
   14. 星 star ··· 50
   15. 东 east ·· 54
   16. 中 middle ·· 58
   17. 前 front ··· 63
   18. 左 left ·· 67
   19. 王 king ·· 71

汉语常用100字

20. 男 man ·· 75
21. 岁 age ·· 78
22. 国 country ·· 81
23. 市 city ·· 86
24. 家 family ··· 89
25. 人 person ··· 93
26. 口 mouth ··· 97
27. 手 hand ·· 101
28. 爸 father ·· 105
29. 水 water ··· 109
30. 饭 meal ·· 113
31. 菜 vegetable ·· 117
32. 酒 liquor ·· 121
33. 钱 money ·· 125
34. 元 yuan ·· 129
35. 衣 clothes ··· 133
36. 楼 a storied building ······························· 137
37. 室 room ·· 140
38. 路 road ·· 143
39. 店 shop ·· 147
40. 车 vehicle ··· 151

四、作量词的汉字 Characters as Measure Words ············ 155

41. 个 a measure word ·································· 155
42. 件 piece ··· 159
43. 斤 jin ··· 163
44. 米 meter ··· 167
45. 次 time ·· 171

五、作动词的汉字 Characters as Verbs ·················· 174

46. 有 have ·· 174
47. 是 be ··· 178

目 录

48. 听 listen ·················· 181
49. 说 say ··················· 185
50. 看 look ·················· 188
51. 吃 eat ··················· 192
52. 喝 drink ················· 196
53. 做 do ···················· 200
54. 打 hit ··················· 204
55. 学 study ················· 208
56. 买 buy ··················· 212
57. 给 give ·················· 215
58. 来 come ················· 218
59. 去 go ···················· 221
60. 出 out ··················· 224
61. 上 go up ················ 229
62. 走 walk ················· 232
63. 开 open ················· 235
64. 能 can ··················· 238
65. 会 be able to ············ 241

六、作形容词的汉字 Characters as Adjectives ·········· 244

66. 大 big ··················· 244
67. 多 many ················· 248
68. 早 early ················· 251
69. 高 tall ··················· 254
70. 胖 fat ··················· 258
71. 老 old ··················· 261
72. 长 long ·················· 265
73. 白 white ················· 268
74. 甜 sweet ················ 272
75. 饿 hungry ··············· 275
76. 热 hot ··················· 278
77. 好 good ················· 281

78. 新 new ·········· 285
79. 对 correct ·········· 288
80. 美 beautiful ·········· 291

七、作虚词的汉字 Characters as Function Words ·········· 294

81. 不 no ·········· 294
82. 没 not have ·········· 297
83. 很 very ·········· 301
84. 也 also ·········· 304
85. 都 all ·········· 307
86. 就 just ·········· 311
87. 才 only ·········· 314
88. 和 and ·········· 318
89. 在 indicating the position of a person or thing ·········· 321
90. 向 toward ·········· 324
91. 从 from ·········· 327
92. 比 indicating difference in manner, degree or quantity by ·········· 331
   comparison
93. 为 for ·········· 334
94. 的 auxiliary word ·········· 337
95. 得 auxiliary word ·········· 341
96. 了 auxiliary word ·········· 345
97. 着 auxiliary word ·········· 349
98. 过 auxiliary word ·········· 353
99. 呢 auxiliary word ·········· 356
100. 吗 auxiliary word ·········· 360

答案 Key to Exercises ·········· 363

前言

欢迎使用《汉语常用100字》。这是一本为汉语学习者编写的汉字学习手册。我们希望本手册能为汉语教师教授汉字、编写汉字教材提供一些参考。

据2006年国家语委发布的《中国语言生活状况报告》，最常用的581个汉字即可覆盖80%的报纸、广播电视、网络等媒体。本手册以常用581个汉字为基础，根据第一线教学经验，按照该汉字作为单音节词时的常用语法功能，筛选了作为数词的汉字3个，作为代词的汉字6个，作为名词的汉字31个，作为量词的汉字5个，作为动词的汉字20个，作为形容词的汉字15个，作为虚词的汉字20个，共100个汉字，供汉语初学者学习。

学习汉语，当然要学好汉字。汉字具有"1个字·1个音节·1个概念"的特点（徐通锵，1998）。汉字从构形上看是汉语中一个完整的书写单位，字形分为笔画、部件、整字三个层次；从读音上看，汉字无论其内部构形差异有多大，但都代表一个声、韵、调相拼而成的音节，是一个完整清晰的发音、听觉单位；从功能上看，绝大多数汉字不仅能直接表达意义单独使用，更可以参与构词和造句，因此汉字也是汉语书面语的结构单位。汉字的上述特点决定了汉字的教与学，形、音、义之间要互相通达，识、写、用之间要互相支撑，这样才能使学习者逐步了解汉字独特的内在规律，为进一步学习汉语打下基础。

根据以上思路，本手册的编排体例如下：

第一，以大字体展示汉字本身，标出读音，使学习者首先对汉字有一个音形匹配的认知，并通过字源演变吸引学习者对汉字外观的注意，培养其识字敏感。

第二，英文简单释义，使学习者明了该字的基本意义和常用语法

汉语常用100字

功能。

第三，书写。通过示范、描红、空书等书写练习,使学习者掌握汉字的基本笔顺、笔画,感知汉字上下、左右、内外三种基本位置排列组合而成的方块结构。

第四，选词例句。"字不离词、词不离句。"有些字条也给出了一些相关汉字,扩大学习者的汉字量和词汇量,使学习了解所学汉字的运用情况。

第五，练习。训练学习者见字形能读出音,明白其意思；想到或听到音义,能写出字形；并由字到词,到句,再到篇,把所学汉字当作可以构词造句、灵活使用的基本单位去操练。

第六，汉字常识简介。配合学习100个汉字,手册筛选了汉字常识100点。通过这些汉字常识,学习者可以了解汉字的构形特点、构造原理；掌握一些常用偏旁、部件；理解偏旁、部件提供的字义信息或字音信息；领悟一些汉字的理据性和历史文化内涵；学会一些汉字构词造句的规律等等,从而使学习者能尽快改变原有的拼音文字观念,获得对汉字的整体感受。

《汉语常用100字》具有如下特点：

第一，突出了汉字的语法功能。手册按照词性筛选100个汉字,便于汉语初学者建立起这些汉字作为单音节词与其语法功能上的联系,尽快掌握汉字构词造句的使用规律。

第二，突出了汉字形、音、义三位一体的特点,学用结合。以往的汉字教学,通常只把汉字当作一种书写符号,过多关注汉字字形辨识和书写,忽视了字形和字音、字义之间的联系,更忽视了单个汉字和相关汉字以及与词汇、句子之间的关系。本手册在体例编排上注重汉字形、音、义互相沟通的反复操练,"字不离词,词不离句,句不离篇。"提高学习者使用汉字的能力。

第三，字、词、句、篇的语义内容贴近日常生活。手册中所选的字,所构的词,所示例的句子,所阅读的篇章,内容都是学习者身边的事物和熟悉的场景,让学习者在表达需求的引领下辨识、认读、书写和使用汉字,增加学习者对汉字的敏感和语感。

前　言

　　学习汉字千万不能急于求成。依照本手册所给的100个汉字，你每天学习几个，认一认，读一读，写一写，用一用。只要坚持不懈，过一段时间，你就会发现，你不仅仅能掌握这100个汉字，更能慢慢地领悟到学习汉语的窍门，获取提高汉语水平的钥匙。现在就拿起这本书来试一试吧。

谭春健

2013年1月

Preface

Thank you for choosing *100 Chinese Characters Commonly Used*. This handbook is specially designed for beginners to learn Chinese characters; it can also serve as a reference book and provide teaching materials for Chinese teachers.

According to the *Report on Language Use in China* published by the State Language Commission of China in 2006, the 581 most common Chinese characters comprise about 80% of newspapers, broadcasts and internet reports, etc. Based on our teaching experience, we have selected 100 characters from the 581 most common Chinese characters, and introduce the Chinese character system to beginners, according to their grammatical function, they are classified into 20 verbs, 31 nouns, 15 adjectives and 6 pronouns, along with 3 numerals, 5 quantifiers and 20 function words.

Learn Chinese, if successful, a mastery of the characters is necessary. It can be summed up in the following formula: "one character, one syllable and one concept" (Xu Tongqiang, 1998). In structure, each character forms a complete written unit. The pattern of the character is composed in three levels: strokes, components and the single character as a unit. No matter how different the characters are, they are all syllables combined with initials, finals and tones. Most of the characters can not only represent a meaning, but also make up words and sentences. The characteristics require us to understand the relations of their structure, pronunciation and meaning. Thus, learners can understand the unique system of Chinese characters and build a firm foundation for learning the Chinese language.

Preface

Layout

The stylistic rules and layout of the handbook is as follows:

Firstly, each character is showcased in large font with its pinyin given. In this way, we help our readers to develop the notion of matching the pronunciation with the form of the character. Through tracing the evolutionary process of the characters, we can also help our readers to become more responsive to the form of the characters.

Secondly, readers are given a brief English explanation of the character, through which they can become familiar with its basic meaning and common grammatical functions.

Thirdly, we offer practice in writing Chinese characters through exercises which allow readers to trace over coloured characters or fill in hollow characters. These exercises enable readers to grasp the basic strokes and their order, as well as developing a feeling for the structure of characters— upper/ lower, left/ right and inside/ outside.

Fourthly, we encourage readers to use characters to make first phrases and then sentences, as we believe that characters are best learnt within a language context. We also list some related characters as a means of enlarging the vocabulary of learners. In this manner, we aim to help readers learn how to use the characters they acquired in this book.

Fifthly, we offer many drills. Through practice, the readers will come to pronounce the characters accurately and grasp their meaning; similarly, they will be able to write them when they think of or hear the characters. From characters to phrases, sentences and paragraphs, the learners can learn to use the characters.

Lastly, some basic items of background knowledge about Chinese characters are introduced. Readers can thus come to understand the principles, acquire information on the meaning and pronunciation of the characters through analysis of radicals and components. As a result, they will gradually form a more comprehensive concept of Chinese characters.

Key Features

100 Chinese Characters Commonly Used has the following key features:

It highlights the grammatical functions of Chinese characters. The authors carefully selected 100 Chinese characters in order to help learners connect these characters with their respective grammatical functions. Therefore, readers will quickly come to grasp the rules and usages of characters.

It also underscores that the form, pronunciation and meaning of the Chinese characters are integrated. In teaching the characters, in the past we used to treat them simply as written symbols, paying attention to the identification and script of the characters while neglecting the relations between their form, pronunciation and meaning. The relations between single characters, related characters, phrases and sentences are neglected as well. Drills are emphasized in terms of the relation of form, pronunciation and meaning. In this way, we do our best to improve readers' ability to use Chinese characters.

Finally, characters and descriptions are from daily life. The learners will thus have a strong incentive to recognize, read, speak, write and use the characters, increase their language sense of Chinese characters.

Do not rush to learn Chinese characters. Each day, try to learn several of the 100 Chinese characters given in this handbook. Try to recognize, read, write and use them. After persistent effort for a period of time, you will not only come to master the 100 Chinese characters but also unlock the secret of learning Chinese, obtaining the key for improving your Chinese. So why not pick up this book and have a go now?

Tan Chunjian
Jan 2013

一、作数词的汉字
Characters as Numerals

1. 一 one

yī

字源演变　The etymology of Chinese characters

| 甲骨文 | 金文 | 小篆 | 楷体 |

1. 释义　Meaning

one (num.)

2. 书写　Writing

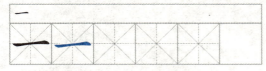

3. 相关词语或表达　Related words or expressions

èr
二（two）2

sān
三（three）3

sì
四（four）4

wǔ
五（five）5

1

汉语常用100字

liù
六（six） 6 　六 六 六 六 六

qī
七（seven） 7 　七 七 七

bā
八（eight） 8 　八 八 八

qiǔ
九（nine） 9 　九 九 九

shí
十（ten） 10 　十 十 十

líng
零（zero） 0 　零 零 零 零 零 零 零 零 零 零 零 零

4. 练习　Exercises

(1) 连线 Link the corresponding pronunciations and meanings of words

七	2	wǔ
三	9	sì
十	1	bā
四	7	shí
八	3	èr
一	5	liù
六	10	líng
二	4	yī
五	0	qī
九	8	jiǔ
零	6	sān

(2) 抄写下列汉字 Copy the following characters

三（　　　）　八（　　　）　六（　　　）
十（　　　）　四（　　　）　五（　　　）
七（　　　）　九（　　　）　一（　　　）

一、作数词的汉字 Characters as Numerals

5. 汉字知识　The knowledge of Chinese characters

汉字的基本笔画

　　汉字是记录汉语的书写符号系统,是形音义的统一体。现代汉字的形体结构可以分为汉字、部件、笔画三个层次。汉字的最小构件是笔画,笔画依照一定的规则组合成部件,部件依照一定的规则组合成合体字。最基本的笔画有八种:

Basic Strokes of Chinese Characters

　　Chinese characters constitute a writing system that records Chinese language by symbols. It is a combination of form, pronunciation and meaning. The morphological type of modern Chinese characters can be divided into three levels: character, component and stroke. The essential part of a Chinese character is stroke, which form components according to the established rules. These components then combine to create a compound character. There are eight types of basic strokes:

笔画 Stroke	名称 Name	写　法 Way of writing	例字 Examples
一	héng 横 horizontal	从左到右,要平 From left to right, keep it level	一(yī) 二(èr) 三(sān)
丨	shù 竖 vertical	从上到下,要直 From top to bottom, keep it straight	十(shí)
丶	diǎnr 点儿 dot	向右下方,顿笔 Falling to the right, make a pause	六(liù)
丿	piě 撇 left-falling	向左下,由重到轻 Falling to the left, from heavy to light	八(bā) 六(liù) 九(jiǔ) 千(qiān)
㇏	nà 捺 right-falling	向右下,有弧度 Falling to the right with a curve	八(bā) 人(rén)
𠃍	zhé 折 turning	先横后竖,连续 First horizontal and then vertical, no pause	四(sì) 五(wǔ)

汉语常用100字

	gōu 钩 hook	拐个钩 With a hook	七(qī) 九(jiǔ)
㇀ ㇀	tí 提 rising	从左下到右上 Rising from bottom left to upper right	我(wǒ)

2. 十 ten

字源演变　The etymology of Chinese characters

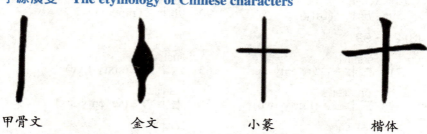

甲骨文　　　　　金文　　　　　小篆　　　　　楷体

1. 释义　Meaning

ten (num.)

2. 书写　Writing

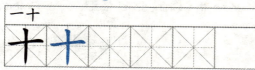

3. 相关词语或表达　Related words or expressions

(1) 11～19

11　十一 shíyī（eleven）　　16　十六 shíliù（sixteen）

12　十二 shí'èr（twelve）　　17　十七 shíqī（seventeen）

13　十三 shísān（thirteen）　　18　十八 shíbā（eighteen）

14　十四 shísì（fourteen）　　19　十九 shíjiǔ（nineteen）

15　十五 shíwǔ（fifteen）

汉语常用100字

(2) 20 ~ 90

20	èrshí 二十	(twenty)		60	liùshí 六十	(sixty)
30	sānshí 三十	(thirty)		70	qīshí 七十	（seventy）
40	sìshí 四十	(forty)		80	bāshí 八十	(eighty)
50	wǔshí 五十	(fifty)		90	jiǔshí 九十	（ninety）

(3) 21 ~ 99

21	èrshíyī 二十一	（twenty-one）		65	liùshíwǔ 六十五	(sixty-five)
32	sānshíèr 三十二	(thirty-two)		76	qīshíliù 七十六	(seventy-six)
43	sìshísān 四十三	(forty-three)		87	bāshíqī 八十七	(eighty-seven)
54	wǔshísì 五十四	(fifty-four)		98	jiǔshíbā 九十八	(ninety-eight)

4. 练习　Exercises

（1）写出汉字并朗读 Write down the Chinese characters and read them aloud

10

17

28

59

43

66

80

91

一、作数词的汉字 Characters as Numerals

（2）在空格处填写相应的汉语数字 Fill the blanks with the correct numbers in Chinese

如：十一 十二 十三____ 十五 十六 （十四）

① 三十二 三十四 三十六 _____

② 五十 六十 _____ 八十 九十

③ 九十九 八十八 七十七 六十六 _____

④ 二十一 二十三 二十五 _____ 二十九

5. 汉字知识　The knowledge of Chinese characters

汉字的书写笔顺（1）

笔顺是指汉字笔画的书写先后顺序。按照合理的笔顺书写汉字，不仅能提高书写的速度，还能使写出来的汉字美观。多数字的写法是以上规则的综合运用。汉字笔顺的基本规则如下：

Order of Strokes of Chinese Characters (1)

Order of strokes refers to the sequence in writing a Chinese character. Writing in a proper order of strokes not only can increase writing speed, but also make characters look neat and beautiful. Most characters are written in accordance with an integration of the following rules. There are some basic rules in order of strokes:

基本规则 Basic rule	例字 Examples	笔顺 Order of strokes
先横后竖 first horizontal and then vertical	shí 十	一 十
先撇后捺 From left-falling to right-falling	rén 人	ノ 人

汉语常用100字

从上到下 From top to bottom	èr 二	一 二
	sān 三	一 二 三
	liù 六	丶 亠 六 六
从左到右 From left to right	bā 八	丿 八
	hàn 汉	丶 氵 汉
从外到内 From outside to inside	tóng 同	丨 冂 冂 同 同 同
从外到内后封口 From outside to inside, then seal the gap	huí 回	丨 冂 冂 回 回 回
先中间后两边 First the middle then the two sides	xiǎo 小	亅 小 小
	shuǐ 水	亅 刁 水 水

3. 百 hundred

bǎi
百

字源演变 The etymology of Chinese characters

甲骨文　　　　　金文　　　　　小篆　　　　　楷体

1. 释义　Meaning

hundred (num.)

2. 书写　Writing

3. 相关词语或表达　Related words or expressions

(1) 100　一百 yībǎi （one hundred）　　200　二百 èrbǎi （two hundred）

　　500　五百 wǔbǎi （five hundred）　　900　九百 jiǔbǎi （nine hundred）

(2) 101　一百零一 yībǎi líng yī （one hundred and one）

　　110　一百一十 yībǎi yī shí （one hundred and ten）

　　111　一百一十一 yībǎi yī shí yī （one hundred and eleven）

　　120　一百二十 yībǎi èrshí （one hundred and twenty）

汉语常用100字

              sānbǎi
300   三百 （three hundred）

              liùbǎi qīshíbā
678   六百七十八 （six hundred and seventy eight）

              jiǔbǎi jiǔshíjiǔ
999   九百九十九 （nine hundred and ninety nine）

              yīqiān èrbǎi sānshísì
1234 一千二百三十四 （one thousand two hundred and thirty four）

     bǎi fēn shù
(3) 百 分 数 （percentage）

            bǎifēn zhīyī
1% 读作：百分之一 （one percent）

            bǎifēn zhī jiǔshíjiǔ
99% 读作：百分之九十九 （ninety-nine percent）

            bǎifēn zhī bǎi
100% 读作：百分之百 （one hundred percent）

(4) 千 （thousand）

    万 （ten thousand）

    亿 （one hundred million）

900，876，054，320 读作：jiǔqiānlíngbāyì qīqiānliùbǎilíngwǔwàn sìqiānsānbǎi'èrshí

4. 练习 Exercises

(1) 写出汉字并朗读 Write down the Chinese characters and read them aloud

103

270

286

591

405

974

3214

一、作数词的汉字 Characters as Numerals

56789

104937

(2) 用汉字写出下列数字 Write down the following numbers in Chinese

100

4210

67893

100054

603609992

5. 汉字知识　The knowledge of Chinese characters

汉字的起源与演变

　　从汉字的起源和发展来看,汉字经历了原始图形文字—古文字—今文字三个阶段,走过了至少五千年漫长的历程。

　　大约在距今六千年的半坡遗址出土的陶器上已经出现了刻画符号,它们有的是具体图形,有的是抽象的符号,这就是汉字的萌芽:

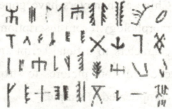

　　汉字形成为系统的文字是在公元前16世纪的商朝。在商朝,国王在做任何事情之前都要占卜,甲骨就是占卜时的用具,而甲骨文则是用刀刻在龟甲和兽骨上的古老文字,用来记录占卜的内容和结果。甲骨文的象形程度较高,如图所示。

　　从商代到今天的三千多年中,汉字主要经过了甲骨文、金文、小篆、隶书、楷书的形体演变过程,在形体上,逐渐由图画变为笔画,由象形变为象征,由复杂变为简单。

汉语常用100字

The Origin and Evolution of Chinese Characters

Judging from the origin and evolutionary history, Chinese characters have gone through over 5000 years of development, which can be divided into three stages: the primitive pictograph, archaic Chinese characters and simpler writing form.

The pottery excavated from the Banpo Site, which dates back to about 6000 year ago, already has some pictures and symbols inscribed on it. This is the beginning of Chinese characters.

It was during Shang Dynasty in 16 B.C. that Chinese characters developed a system. During Shang Dynasty, the king would always resort to divination before doing anything. Oracle bones were the tools when practicing it. Inscriptions on oracle bones are ancient characters inscribed on tortoise shells and animal bones. They are the records of the contents and results of divination. Inscriptions on oracle bones are more pictographic.

From Shang Dynasty to nowadays, in the 3000 years of development, Chinese characters have gone through an evolutionary process in terms of morphology. From inscriptions on oracle bones, inscriptions on bronze, seal characters to official script and regular script, Chinese characters gradually evolved from pictures to strokes, from pictographic to symbolic, and from complicated to simple.

二、作代词的汉字
Characters as Pronouns

4. 你 you

字源演变　The etymology of Chinese characters

篆　　　　　楷体
小篆　　　　楷体

1. 释义　Meaning

you (pron.)

2. 书写　Writing

ノ 亻 亻 仁 仵 佾 你

你 你

3. 相关词语或表达　Related words or expressions

(1) Nǐ hǎo!
　　你好!　　Hello!

　　Xièxie nǐ!
　　谢谢你!　　Thank you!

(2) 你们 you (pron.)

们

13

汉语常用100字

Nǐmen hǎo!
你们 好!   Hello!

Xièxie nǐmen!
谢谢 你们!   Thank you!

(3) 你(们)的 your, yours (pron.)

的												

nǐ de shū
你的 书   your book

nǐ māma
你 妈妈   your mother

nǐmen xuéxiào
你们 学校   your school

zhèxiē shū shì nǐmen de ma?
这些 书 是你们 的 吗?   Are these books yours?

4. 练习   Exercises

(1) 按笔画顺序写出汉字 Write down the Chinese characters in order of strokes

你：

们：

的：

(2) 把下列词和短语的拼音及意思连线 Link the corresponding pronunciations and meanings of words and expressions

你们	nǐ māma	your; yours
你家	xièxie nǐ	your; yours
你们的	nǐmen xuéxiào	you
你们学校	nǐ hǎo	hello
谢谢你	nǐ de	your mother
你的	nǐ jiā	your family
你妈妈	nǐmen	thank you
你好	nǐmen de	your school

二、作代词的汉字 Characters as Pronouns

5. 汉字知识　The knowledge of Chinese characters

汉字的构成：独体字与合体字

　　独体字是指由笔画组成的，不能再分成两部分的汉字，如：八、十、九、人。

　　包含两个或两个以上基本结构的汉字叫合体字，如：你、们、的、妈、好、汉、家、学、校、谢。按照合体字中各个部件之间不同的位置关系，合体字的形体结构类型可以分为以下三种：

　　(1) 上下结构：写、字、零、家；

　　(2) 左右结构：你、们、的、妈、好、汉、校、亿、谢；

　　(3) 内外结构：内外结构又分以下几种：

　　① 四面包围结构：国、图；

　　② 三面包围结构：风、同；

　　③ 两面包围结构：左上包围（在、原）；

　　　　　　　　　　左下包围（这、处）；

　　　　　　　　　　右上包围（可、句）。

Morphology of Chinese Characters: Single Characters and Compound Characters

Single characters refer to the characters that are formed by strokes and cannot be further divided into two parts. For example, 八(bā)、十(shí)、九(jiǔ)、人(rén).

Compound characters refer to the characters that contain two or more than two basic structures. For example, 你(nǐ)、们(men)、的(de)、妈(mā)、好(hǎo)、汉(hàn)、家(jiā)、学(xué)、校(xiào)、谢(xiè). The morphological type of compound characters refers to the relation among the different components of the characters. According to the relations, compound characters can be grouped into the following three morphological types:

　　(1) top-bottom structure: For example, 写(xiě)、字(zì)、零(líng)、家(jiā);

　　(2) left-right structure: For example, 你(nǐ), 们(men), 的(de), 妈(mā), 好(hǎo), 汉(hàn), 校(xiào), 亿(yì), 谢(xiè);

　　(3) inside-outside structure can be divided as follows:

汉语常用100字

① all-side-encircled structure, such as 国(guó), 图(tú);
② three-side-encircled structure, such as 风(fēng), 同(tóng);
③ two-side-encircled structure: left-top-encircled：在(zài), 原(yuán);
　　　　　　　　　　　　　　　left-bottom-encircled：这(zhè), 处(chù);
　　　　　　　　　　　　　　　right-top-encircled：可(kě), 句(jù).

5. 我 I

wǒ
我

字源演变　The etymology of Chinese characters

甲骨文　　　　金文　　　　小篆　　　　楷体

1. 释义　Meaning

I, me (pron.)

2. 书写　Writing

3. 相关词语或表达　Related words or expressions

(1) 我 I; me

Wǒ shì Zhōngguórén.
我 是 中国人。　I am a Chinese.

Nǐ děng wǒ?
你 等 我?　Are you waiting for me?

(2) 我们 we; us

Wǒmen shì hǎo péngyou.
我们 是 好 朋友。　We are good friends.

Lǎoshī bāngzhù le wǒmen.
老师 帮助 了 我们。　Our teacher helped us.

汉语常用100字

(3) 我(们)的 my; our; mine; ours

wǒ de shūbāo
我 的 书包   my bag

Wǒ jiā yǒu sān kǒu rén.
我 家 有 三 口 人。   There are three people in my family.

Wǒmen xuéxiào yǒu hěnduō xuésheng.
我们 学校 有 很多 学生。

There are many students in our school.

Nà xiē shū shì wǒmen de.
那 些 书 是 我们 的。   Those books are ours.

4. 练习 Exercises

(1) 把下列词和短语的拼音及意思连线 Link the corresponding pronunciations and meanings of words and expressions

我们	wǒ māma	our; ours
我家	wǒmen xuéxiào	we; us
我们的	wǒ	our school
我们学校	wǒ de	my family
我妈妈	wǒmen de	I; me
我	wǒ jiā	my; mine
我的	wǒmen	my mother

(2) 选词填空 Fill in the blanks with correct words

你   我   我的   我们

_____好!

你等_____?

_____是好朋友。

这是_____书包。

5. 汉字知识 The knowledge of Chinese characters

"我"字的起源与演变

用来表示第一人称的"我"字在甲骨文中原是一种长柄的兵器,用来

18

二、作代词的汉字 Characters as Pronouns

行刑杀人或肢解牲口,写作"𢦐"。它的右边是"戈",左边是锯齿形的刀刃。其本义是"杀"的意思。这个字形在后来的演变中,锯齿逐渐消失,很难看出是兵器的模样,而它的本义也就被人们忘却了。"我"表示第一人称是在汉、唐以后才开始的,汉、唐之前,第一人称用"吾"、"予"、"余"表示。

The Origin and Evolution of "我"

The character "我" is a first-person pronoun. In its oracle inscription form, it was written as "𢦐" and originally referred to a weapon with a long handle for execution, killing or dissection. Its right part is a spear while the left part is zigzag knife edge. Thus it originally meant "killing". In its later evolution, it lost the saw-tooth gradually, and its original meaning was lost. "我" was used to indicate the first person after the Han Dynasty and Tang Dynasty. Before that, we used "吾(wú)", "予(yú)" and "余(yú)" instead.

6. 他 he

tā
他

字源演变　The etymology of Chinese characters

小篆

楷体

1. 释义　Meaning

he, him (pron.)

2. 书写　Writing

3. 相关词语或表达　Related words or expressions

(1) 他 he, him

　　Tā shì xuésheng.
　　他 是　学生。　　He is a student.

　　Wǒ ài tā.
　　我 爱 他。　　　I love him.

(2) 她 she, her

她									

　　Wǒ yǒu yī ge jiějie, tā měitiān gōngzuò hěn máng.
　　我 有 一个 姐姐，她 每天　工作　很　忙。

I have a sister who is very busy at work every day.

二、作代词的汉字 Characters as Pronouns

Tā bù zài Běijīng, wǒ hěn xiǎng tā.
她不在北京，我很想她。She is out of Beijing and I miss her.

(3) 它(的) tā it, its

它													

Wǒ jiā yǒu yī zhī xiǎo gǒu, tā jiào "Xiǎo bái", tā fēicháng kě'ài.
我家有一只小狗，它叫"小白"，它非常可爱。
I have a dog called "Xiaobai". It is very cute.

(4) 他们 tāmen they, them

Tāmen dōu shì lǎoshī.
他们都是老师。 They are all teachers.

Wǒ xǐhuan tāmen.
我喜欢他们。 I like them.

(5) 他(们)的 tā men de his/their

Tā bàba shì dàifu.
他爸爸是大夫。 His father is a doctor.

Zhè shì tāmen de shū.
这是他们的书。 These are their books.

4. 练习 Exercises

(1) 按笔顺写出汉字，并写出笔画数 Write down the Chinese characters in order of strokes and their numbers of strokes

他：

她：

它：

(2) 把下面的英语翻译成汉语，并用汉字写出来 Translate the following into Chinese and write down the Chinese characters

he   (   )   his   (   )

she   (   )   her   (   )

it   (   )   its   (   )

they (   )   their (   )

5. 汉字知识　The knowledge of Chinese characters

"他"与"她"

"他"是称自己和对方以外的某个人。在现代书面语里,"他"一般只用来指男性。但是在性别不明或没有区分的必要时,"他"是泛指,如若干人有男有女时称"他们"。

"她"是专指除自己和对方以外的某个女性。左边的"女"的古字形是"𠮷",像一个温顺的女人两手交叉身前跪坐在地上。在古代中国,女性的地位低,这个字便表现出了当时社会中女性的形象。

"他" and "她"

"他" refers to someone other than oneself and the person one is talking to. In modern written language, "他" is generally used to indicate the male. But when gender is unknown or there is no need to clarify it, "他" can be used generally. For example, when there are several people, male and female, we refer to them by the word "他们".

"她" refers specifically to a woman other than oneself and the person one is talking to. The left part of its ancient form, written as " 𠮷 ", looks like a dutiful woman sitting down on her heels with her hands crossed in front of her. In ancient China, the female had lower social status. This character reflects the image of women in the society at that time.

7. 这 this

zhè
这

字源演变 The etymology of Chinese characters

小篆

繁体

楷体

1. 释义　Meaning

this (pron.)

2. 书写：(Writing)

3. 相关词语或表达　Related words or expressions

(1) 这 zhè this

Zhè shì Běijīng.
这 是 北京。　　　This is Beijing.

Zhè běn shū shì wǒ de.
这 本 书 是 我 的。　This book is mine.

(2) 那 nà that, those (pron.)

那									

Nà shì shuí?
那 是 谁?　　　Who is that?

汉语常用100字

Nàlǐ de jǐngsè hěn měi.
那里的 景色 很 美。 The scenery is beautiful there.

Nàyàng de xié wǒ yě yǒu yī shuāng.
那样 的鞋 我也有一 双。 I also have a pair of those shoes.

Nàme hǎochī de shuǐguǒ wǒ yě yào mǎi.
那么 好吃 的 水果 我 也 要 买。

I also want to buy such tasty fruit.

Wǒ yījiǔjiǔbā nián lái Běijīng, nà shíhou xué Hànyǔ de rén bú tài duō.
我 1998 年 来 北京，那时(候)学 汉语 的 人不太多。

I came to Beijing in 1998, and there were only a few people who were learning Chinese then.

(3) 这些 zhèxiē these

些

Zhèxiē shū dōu shì zhōngwénshū.
这些 书 都 是 中文书。 These are all Chinese books.

(4) 这里 zhèlǐ here

里

Zhèlǐ xiàtiān hěn rè.
这里 夏天 很 热。 It is pretty hot here in summer.

(5) 这样 zhèyàng like this; this way

样

Wǒ yě xǐhuan zhèyàng de yīfu.
我 也 喜欢 这样 的 衣服。 I also like this kind of clothes.

(6) 这么 zhème such; so

么

Jīntiān zhème rè a!
今天 这么 热啊! It is so hot today.

(7) 这 时候 zhè shíhou at this time; 这时 zhèshí now

Wǒ zhèngzài xiě zuòyè, zhè shíhou diànhuà xiǎngle.
我 正在 写 作业，这 时候，电话 响了。

I was writing my homework when the telephone rang.

Měinián zhè shíhou tā dōu huí lǎojiā kàn fùmǔ.
每年 这 时候 他 都 回 老家 看 父母。

二、作代词的汉字 Characters as Pronouns

He goes back to his hometown to see his parents every year at this time.

4. 练习　Exercises

(1) 按笔顺写出汉字,并写出笔画数 Write down the Chinese characters in order of strokes and their numbers of strokes

这:

那:

些:

里:

么:

(2) 根据图片用所学的汉字完成句子,并写出汉字 Complete the sentences with the Chinese characters you have learned according to the pictures and write down the Chinese characters

(　　)是学校,(　　)是医院。　　(　　)有很多老人,(　　)有很多孩子。

(　　)楼很高,(　　)楼很矮。　　(　　)多水果我吃不完。

汉语常用100字

5. 汉字知识　The knowledge of Chinese characters

汉字的书写笔顺(2)

除了前面已经介绍的基本书写笔顺以外,还有一些补充规则:

Order of Strokes of Chinese Characters (2)

In addition to the basic order of strokes we have already learned, there are also some additional rules:

补充规则 Additional rule	例字 Example	笔顺 Order of strokes
最底下的横后写 The horizontal stroke at bottom is the last stroke.	土(tǔ)	一十土
横在中间,长而且地位重要时后写 When the horizontal stroke is in the middle and is important, it should be the last stroke.	女(nǚ)	ㄑ 女 女
横在竖的一边先写竖 When the horizontal stroke is at one side of the vertical stroke, then the vertical stroke should be written first.	上(shàng) 北(běi)	丨 卜 上 丨 丬 丬 北 北
点在下或右上时后写 When the dot is at the bottom or in the upper right, it should be written later.	点(diǎn) 书(shū)	丨 卜 卜 占 占 占 点 点 点 乛 乛 书 书
从左、下两面或左、下、右三面包围的字先里后外 When encircled by two sides of the left and the bottom or encircled by three sides of the left, the bottom and the right, the inside part should be written before the outside part.	这(zhè) 山(shān)	丶 亠 亍 文 文 这 这 丨 凵 山
从左、下两面以"走"、"是"包围的字先外后里 When encircled by "走" and "是" in the left and at the bottom, the outside part should be written before the inside part.	起(qǐ) 匙(shi)	一 十 土 キ キ 走 走 起 起 丨 冂 日 日 旦 早 旱 昇 是 是 匙

8. 谁 who

shuí
谁

字源演变　The etymology of Chinese characters

小篆　　　　　楷体

1. 释义　Meaning

who, whom (pron.)

2. 书写　Writing

3. 相关词语或表达　Related words or expressions

(1) 谁 shuí who (pron.)

Shuí shì lǎoshī?
谁　是 老师?　　Who's the teacher?

Tā xǐhuan shuí?
他 喜欢　谁?　　Who does he adore?

"谁?" (Somebody is knocking at the door.)
Who's that?

(2) 谁 的 whose (pron.)
　　shuí de

　　Zhè shì shuí de shū?
　　这 是 谁 的 书?　　　　Whose book is this?

4. 练习　Exercises

(1) 写出含有下列笔画的汉字 Write down the Chinese characters with the following strokes in the corresponding brackets

例: 丿（我　　　　　　　）
　　𠃌（　　　　　　　　）
　　乙（　　　　　　　　）
　　㇀（　　　　　　　　）
　　亅（　　　　　　　　）

(2) 用"谁"来提问下列句子中表示人称的词 Make a question with the character "谁" for the following words which indicate people in the following sentences

例: 我是学生。　谁是学生?

① 小王是我的朋友。

　　Xiaowang is my friend.

② 我喜欢她。

　　I like her.

③ 老师是中国人。

　　My teacher is Chinese.

④ 这是妈妈的书。

　　This is my mother's book.

⑤ 他们是我的同学。

　　They're my classmates.

⑥ 我家有三口人,他们是我的爸爸、妈妈和我。

　　There are three people in my family: Dad, Mom and me.

二、作代词的汉字 Characters as Pronouns

5. 汉字知识 The knowledge of Chinese characters

"谁"字的来源

"谁"的右边"隹"在金文中就是一只鸟的形象"🐦";左边的"讠"未简化前是"言",金文写作"🔾",好像开口发出声音。两者合起来就是在短尾鸟"隹"旁加上的"言",写作"🔾"。后来假借为疑问代词。

Origin of the Character "谁"

In bronze inscription, the right part of "谁"—"隹"—depicts the image of a bird "🐦"; the left part "讠" used to be written as "言" before it was simplified. It was written as "🔾" in bronze inscription form, looking like making a sound with mouth open. When combining the two components of "言" and the short-tailed bird "隹". The character was written as "🔾". It was later transformed into an interrogative pronoun.

9. 几 how many

字源演变　　The etymology of Chinese characters

小篆　　　　楷体

1. 释义　Meaning

how many; a few; several (num.)

2. 书写　Writing

3. 相关词语或表达　Related words or expressions

（1）how many

Jīntiān jǐ hào?
今天 几号?　　　　　What's the date today?

Nà ge xiǎo nǚhái jǐ suì le?
那个 小 女孩几岁了?　How old is that little girl?

Nǐ jiā yǒu jǐ kǒu rén?
你家 有 几口 人?　　How many people are there in your family?

Zhè ge xīguā jǐ kuài qián?
这 个西瓜几块 钱?　　How much is this watermelon?

二、作代词的汉字 Characters as Pronouns

(2) a few; several

Wǒ zuótiān mǎi le jǐ běn shū.
我 昨天 买了几本 书。　I bought several books yesterday.

Guò jǐ tiān wǒ qù zhǎo nǐ.
过 几天 我 去 找 你。　I will visit you in a few days.

Tā shíjǐ suì jiù huì shuō sānzhǒng yǔyán.
他 十几 岁就会 说 三种 语言。
He can speak three languages when he's a teenager.

Zuótiān lái kāihuì de rén yǒu jǐ bǎi rén.
昨天 来开会 的人 有 几百 人。
There were hundreds of people present at the meeting yesterday.

4. 练习　Exercises

(1) 抄写下列词组并朗读 Copy the following phrases and read them aloud

几号_____　　几本书_____

几岁_____　　过几天_____

几口人_____　　十几岁_____

几块钱_____　　几百人_____

(2) 用"几"来完成会话 Complete the following conversations with "几"

① A：_____？

　　Zhuōzi shàng yǒu sì běn shū.
　B：桌子 上 有 四 本 书。

There are four books on the table.

② A：_____？

　　Píngguǒ liǎng kuài qián yī jīn.
　B：苹果 两 块 钱 一斤。

The apple is two yuan per Jin (0.5 kg).

③ A：_____？

　　Wǒ qù guo Běijīng sān cì.
　B：我 去 过 北京 三 次。

I've been to Beijing three times.

④ A：北京 的 名胜 古迹 都 去 过 了 吗？
　　　Běijīng de míngshèng gǔjì dōu qù guo le ma?

Have you been to all the places of interests in Beijing?

　B：_____。

⑤ A：_____？

　B：我 的 女儿 三 岁 了。
　　　Wǒ de nǚér sān suì le.

My daughter is three years old.

⑥ A：_____？

　B：我们 班 有 八 名 同学。
　　　Wǒmen bān yǒu bā míng tòngxué.

There're eight students in our class.

5. 汉字知识　The knowledge of Chinese characters

"几"字的起源

"几"(jī)字是从图画变来的，看看古字的"𠘧"，像不像一张桌子呢？"几"本来是一种低矮的桌子，因为在上古时代，人们以跪作为基本的居家姿态。与这种跪姿相应，家具自然也就需要限制高度。而当跪地的居家习惯改变以后，"几"的高度也要加高，人们便给它起了个新的名字"桌(zhuō)"。因此现在摆放在客厅里沙发前的那种低矮的桌子就叫"茶几"。而人们吃饭、看书等用的则叫"饭桌、书桌"。

"几"字还可以表示询问数目，如："来了几个人？"或表示大于一而小于十的数目的意思，如"他买了几本书。"这个时候读音为"jǐ"。

Origin of the Character "几"

The character "几" (jī) was transformed from a picture. Doesn't its ancient form look like a table which was written as "𠘧"? "几" was a low table. In ancient time, people normally took kneeling position at home. Correspondingly, the height of furniture was limited. After this living habit was changed, the height of table was also increased accordingly. People then give it a new name "桌" (zhuō). Therefore, the low tea table in front of couch in living room are called "茶几" (chájī). while the table used to have

二、作代词的汉字 Characters as Pronouns

meals and read books are called "饭桌" (fànzhuō) and "书桌" (shūzhuō) respectively.

"几" can also be used to inquire about number. For example, "来了几个人？" (How many people are here?). In addition, it can indicate number bigger than one but less than ten. For example, "他买了几本书"(He bought a few books). It is pronounced jǐ in this case.

三、作名词的汉字 Characters as Nouns

10. 天 sky

字源演变   The etymology of Chinese characters

甲骨文   金文   小篆   楷体

1. 释义　Meaning

sky, day (n.)

2. 书写　Writing

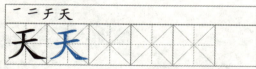

3. 相关词语或表达　Related words or expressions

（1）sky

　　Tiān hěn lán.
　　天 很 蓝。　　The sky is blue.

　　Tiān shàng yǒu yuèliang.
　　天 上 有 月亮。　　The moon is in the sky.

（2）day

　　Wǒ xiūxi le yī tiān.
　　我 休息 了 一 天。　　I had a rest for one day.

三、作名词的汉字 Characters as Nouns

měi tiān
每 天 everyday

Tā měitiān xuéxí Hànyǔ.
他 每天 学习 汉语。 He studies Chinese every day.

jīntiān
今天 today

míngtiān
明天 tomorrow

zuótiān
昨天 yesterday

qiántiān
前天 the day before yesterday

hòutiān
后天 the day after tomorrow

(3) season

chūntiān
春天 spring

xiàtiān
夏天 summer

qiūtiān
秋天 autumn

dōngtiān
冬天 winter

Zhèr chūntiān nuǎnhuo, xiàtiān hěn rè, qiūtiān liángkuai, dōngtiān hěn lěng.
这儿 春天 暖和, 夏天 很热, 秋天 凉快, 冬天 很 冷。
This place is warm in spring, hot in summer, cool in autumn an cold in winter.

tiānqì
(4) 天气 weather

Jīntiān de tiānqì hěn hǎo.
今天 的 天气 很 好。 The weather is pretty fine today.

4. 练习 Exercises

(1) 根据拼音写出汉字,并想想它们的意思 Write down the Chinese characters according to *pinyin* and think about their meanings

zuótiān   (   )   xiàtiān   (   )
měitiān   (   )   tiānqì   (   )

dōngtiān　(　　)　　　jīntiān　　　(　　　)
chūntiān　(　　)　　　xīngqītiān　(　　　)

(2) 请写出带"天"字的词语，写得越多越好 Write down as many words with the character "天" as possible

_____

5. 汉字知识　The knowledge of Chinese characters
"天"字的有关知识

　　天的篆书写作"兲"，像一个正面站立着的人，顶部一横表示人的天灵盖。世间只有人直立行走，是顶天立地的。

　　对大地众生来说，至高无上的地方是天空，古代的帝王自称为"天子"，以此来名正言顺地统治万民。对人体来讲，最高的地方是头顶，所以人的额头又称为"天庭"。以前相士们看相时，常会以"天庭饱满"来形容一个人的面相如何之好。

　　"天"的含义有很多，除了表示天空之外，还有许多用法，例如"一天"指的是时间；"晴天"、"阴天"指的是天气；"天然"指的是大自然。

Knowledge about the Character "天"

　　In seal characters, "天" was written as "兲". It seems like the frontal look of a standing person. The horizontal stroke signifies the top of his head. Since human is the only creature in the world that walk upright, a standing person looks like a giant towering into the sky.

　　For all the creatures on earth, the sky is paramount. The emperors in ancient times called themselves " the Son of Heaven" to justify their ruling of their subjects. Head is the highest place in a human body, so the forehead is also called "天庭(tiāntíng)". In old times, physiognomists often used the phrase "天庭饱满(tiāntíng bǎomǎn)" (a great expanse of forehead) to compliment someone's looks.

三、作名词的汉字 Characters as Nouns

"天" also have many meanings. There are a number of other usages besides indicating the sky. For example, "一天" (yītiān) (one day) indicates time; "晴天 (qíngtiān)" (sunny) and "阴天 (yīntiān)" (cloudy) indicates weather and "天然(tiānrán)" refers to the nature.

11. 年 year

nián
年

字源演变   The etymology of Chinese characters

甲骨文　　　　金文　　　　　小篆　　　　　　楷体

1. 释义   Meaning

year (n.)

2. 书写   Writing

3. 相关词语或表达   Related words or expressions

(1) 年 nián year

Yī nián yǒu sānbǎi liùshíwǔ tiān.
一 年 有 三百 六十五 天。　There're 365 days in a year.

Yī nián yǒu shí'èr ge yuè.
一 年 有 十二 个 月。　There're twelve months in a year.

Měinián wǒ dōu dào Zhōngguó qù xuéxí Hànyǔ.
每年 我 都 到 中国 去 学习 汉语。
I go to China to study Chinese every year.

Jīnnián shì èr líng yī sān nián.
今年 是 2013 年。　This year is 2013.

三、作名词的汉字 Characters as Nouns

Qùnián shì èr líng yī èr nián.
去年 是 2012 年。 Last year was 2012.

Qiánnián shì èr líng yī yī nián.
前年 是 2011 年。 The year before last year was 2011.

Míngnián shì èr líng yī sì nián.
明年 是 2014 年。 Next year is 2014.

Hòunián shì èr líng yī wǔ nián.
后年 是 2015 年。 The year after next year is 2015.

(2) xīnnián
新年 new year

(3) niánlíng
年龄 age

(4) tóngnián
童年 childhood year

shàonián
少年 late childhood (from about ten to sixteen)

qīngnián
青年 youth

zhōngnián
中年 middle age

lǎonián
老年 old age, aged

4. 练习 Exercises

（1）完成句子 Complete the sentences

今年是_____年,去年是_____年,前年是_____年,明年是_____年,后年是_____年。

（2）请用汉语介绍一下你最近几年做些什么;写一写你人生的几个时期都做些什么,或准备做些什么,希望能用上我们学过的表示年份和表示时期的词语 Please introduce in Chinese what you have done for the past few years. Write down the things you have done or prepared to do at each stage of your life. You are expected to use the words and phrases we have learned about years and periods

汉语常用100字

比如：

我的童年在……度过，童年……（过得怎么样？）。

我的少年……

现在我是个青年，我想……

中年以后，我希望……

5. 汉字知识   The knowledge of Chinese characters

"年"的传说与传统习俗

有个传说，古时有一个叫"年"的妖怪，经常杀人放火，无恶不作。后来有一壮士与"年"展开了一场生死搏斗。最后，"年"被杀死，壮士却牺牲了。人们为了怀念这位壮士，便在"年"被杀死的这一天举行各种各样盛大的庆祝活动，而且燃放鞭炮，张贴门神对联以驱赶邪恶，并逐渐形成一种习惯，流传下来，此后，便有了"过年"之说。每年农历正月初一，是中国最重要的一个传统节日——春节，它是亲人团聚的日子。过年的前一夜，叫除夕，在这新旧交替的时候，全家老小都一起熬夜守岁。北方地区在除夕有吃饺子的习俗；南方有过年吃年糕的习惯。千百年来，人们庆祝年俗的活动丰富多彩。节日的热烈气氛不仅洋溢在各家各户，也充满各地的大街小巷，一些地方的街市上还有舞狮子、耍龙灯、逛庙会等习俗。

The Legend of "年" and its Traditional Customs

It is said that there was a monster called "年" who often set places on fire and killed people and stopped at no evil. A man had a life-and-death fight with the monster. In the end, "年" was killed and the heroic man also died. To pay tribute to the heroic man, people hold various grand celebrations on the day "年" was killed. They set off firecrackers and posted up door gods and antithetical couplet to drive evil spirits away. It gradually became a tradition and was passed on from one generation to another. We thus have the tradition of "过年" (guò nián). The first day of the first month in lunar calendar marks the most important traditional festival in China—the Spring Festival, which is a day for family reunion. The day before the festival is called "除夕" (chúxī) eve . The whole family, including the elders and the

三、作名词的汉字 Characters as Nouns

kids, stay up late to witness the beginning of a new year. People from northern region have the habit of having dumplings while people from southern region have sweet steamed glutinous rice pudding. For hundreds of years, people hold various celebrations for the New Year. The festival atmosphere fills every family and every street. In some places, there are lion dancing and dragon-lantern shows and temple fairs.

12. 月 month

yuè
月

字源演变　The etymology of Chinese characters

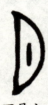   

　　甲骨文　　　　　　金文　　　　　　　小篆　　　　　　　楷体

1. 释义　Meaning

moon; month (n.)

2. 书写　Writing

3. 相关词语或表达　Related words or expressions

(1) yuèliang
月亮 moon

Jīntiān de yuèliang hěn yuán.
今天 的 月亮 很 圆。
Today is a full moon.

(2) yī nián yǒu shí'èr gè yuè, fēnbié shì
一 年 有 12 个 月，分别 是：There're twelve months in a year which are:

yīyuè　　　　　　　qīyuè
一月 January　　　七月 July

三、作名词的汉字 Characters as Nouns

èryuè
二月 February

bāyuè
八月 August

sānyuè
三月 March

jiǔyuè
九月 September

sìyuè
四月 April

shíyuè
十月 October

wǔyuè
五月 May

shíyī yuè
十一月 November

liùyuè
六月 June

shíèr yuè
十二月 December

(3) yī ge yuè
一个月 one month

liǎng ge yuè
两个月 two months

shàng ge yuè
上个月 last month

xià ge yuè
下个月 next month

zhè ge yuè
这个月 this month

Zhè ge yuè shì bāyuè, shàng ge yuè shì qīyuè, xià ge yuè shì jiǔyuè.
这个月是八月，上个月是七月，下个月是九月。

This month is August. Last month was July. Next month is September.

4. 练习 Exercises

(1) 请把下列词语与它们相对应的意思连线 Link the corresponding meanings of words and expressions

五月　　　　　moon

月亮　　　　　the present month

上个月　　　　every month

每个月　　　　May

五个月　　　　next month

这个月　　　　last month

下个月　　　　five months

汉语常用100字

(2) 请用汉字写出下列日期 Please write down the following date in Chinese

例：September/ 2009（二〇〇九年九月）

March/1998　　　（　　　）
January/2005　　　（　　　）
November/1978　　（　　　）
August/1996　　　（　　　）
July/2010　　　　（　　　）
April/1989　　　　（　　　）
February/1993　　（　　　）
October/2008　　 （　　　）
December/2014　　（　　　）

5. 汉字知识　The knowledge of Chinese characters
造字法（1）　象形字

有些汉字是从图画变来的,这些字直接描画事物的形状,用这种方法造的字就是象形字。本课学的"月"字,本义指月亮,甲骨文和金文中的月字,描摹的都是一轮弯月的形状：

甲骨文　金文

类似的象形字还有：

田：这是甲骨文中的"田"字,是不是很像农田呢？

羊：这是用一只羊头来代表羊字。

甲骨文中象形字比较多。象形字一般都是独体字,虽然只占汉字总数的5%左右,但它是汉字形体构造系统的基础。

Method of Character Formation (1)　Pictographic Characters

Some Chinese characters were developed from pictures. These characters depicted the shapes of objects directly, so the characters created in this way were pictographic characters. The character "月" we learn here originally

三、作名词的汉字 Characters as Nouns

meant the moon. Both in oracle inscription and bronze inscription, the character represents the image of a crescent moon.

　　　　𝔇　　　　𝔇
　Oracle inscription　Bronze inscription

There were many similar pictographic characters:

田: This was the character "田(tián)" in oracle inscription, doesn't it look like farmland?

丫: The head of a ram was used to stand for the character "羊(yáng)".

There were many pictographic characters in oracle inscriptions which were generally single characters. Although it only accounted for 5% of the total Chinese characters, they formed the foundation of the morphology of Chinese characters.

13. 日 day

字源演变　The etymology of Chinese characters

甲骨文　　　　　金文　　　　　小篆　　　　　楷体

1. 释义　Meaning

sun; day; date (n.)

2. 书写　Writing

3. 组词造句　Words and sentences formation

（1）day (n.)

Yī nián yǒu sānbǎi liùshíwǔ rì.
一年 有 365 日。 There're 365 days in one year.

rìlì
日历 calendar

rìqī
日期 date

rìzi
日子 day, date

46

三、作名词的汉字 Characters as Nouns

Zhè zhāng rìlì de rìqī shì èr líng yī sān nián yī yuè yī rì, shì xīn nián, shì ge
这　张　日历的日期是　　2013　年　1月1日，是新年，是个
gāoxìng de rìzi.
高兴　的日子。

This calendar shows the date of today is January 1st, 2013. Today is the New Year's Day and it is a happy day.

　　　shēngrì
(2) 生日 birthday

Wǒ de shēngrì shì yī jiǔ bā sān nián qī yuè èrshíliù rì.
我 的 生日 是　 1983　 年 7 月　26 日。

My birthday is on 26th of July,1983.

　　　jiérì
(3) 节日 festival

Chūnjié shì Zhōngguó rén zhòngyào de jiérì.
春节 是　中国　人　重要　的节日。

The spring festival is a very important Chinese festival.

　　　rìjì
(4) 日记 diary

　　　Rìběn
(5) 日本 Japan

Dànèi shì Rìběn rén, tā cóng Rìběn lái, tā huì shuō Rìyǔ.
大内 是 日本 人，她 从　日本 来，她会　说　日语。

Danei is a Japanese. She came from Japan and she can speak Japanese.

4. 练习　Exercises

（1）根据英文意思写出汉字，并加注拼音 Write down the Chinese characters and *pinyin* according to the English meaning

英文　　　　　中文　　　　　　拼音

diary

calendar

date

day

birthday

festivals

Japan

47

（2）请用汉字写出下列日期 Write down the following date in Chinese

例：Sep. 10, 2009　　　（二〇〇九年九月十日）
　　Jan. 1, 2010　　　　（　　　　　　　　　　）
　　Jul. 4, 1776　　　　（　　　　　　　　　　）
　　Nov. 27, 2007　　　（　　　　　　　　　　）
　　Aug. 8, 2008　　　　（　　　　　　　　　　）
　　Mar. 31, 1985　　　（　　　　　　　　　　）
　　Apr. 1, 2003　　　　（　　　　　　　　　　）
　　Dec. 25, 2017　　　（　　　　　　　　　　）
　　Oct. 1, 1949　　　　（　　　　　　　　　　）
　　Feb. 14, 1968　　　（　　　　　　　　　　）

5. 汉字知识　The knowledge of Chinese characters

"日"字的起源和发展

"日"的古字形，就像太阳的形状：⊙。它也是一个象形字，本义就是太阳，圆圈中间的黑点，有人说是代表太阳的光芒，有人说是用来区别"口"字。当太阳升起来，万物都被照亮，当它落下去，黑夜便随之来临。白天与黑夜就这样交替进行着。因此"日"逐渐引申为时间的单位，人们把一昼夜称为一日。在生活中，"日"还特指某一天，比如"生日"、"节日"、"纪念日"等等。"日"字，既可单用，也可作偏旁，凡从"日"字取义的字都与太阳、光阴、时日等义有关，如："晴、旱、时、旦、旧"等。

The Origin and Evolution of "日"

The ancient form of "日" looks like the Sun:⊙. It is also a pictographic character which originally meant the Sun. There is a black dot inside the circle. Some people say it represents sunshine while other people say it is used to differentiate the character of "日" (sun) from the character "口" (mouth). When the sun rises, it illuminates everything. When it falls, the darkness arrives. The day and the night alternate just in this way. Therefore, "日" gradually became a unit of time. One alternation of daytime and nighttime is called "一日" (yīrì) (a day). In daily life, "日" can also refer a specific day,

三、作名词的汉字 Characters as Nouns

such as "生日(shēngrì)" (birthday), "节日(jiérì)" (festival) and "纪念日(jìniànrì)" (commemoration day). "日" can be a single word or a radical. The characters defined by "日" are all related to the Sun, time and day, such as "晴(qíng), 旱(hàn), 时(shí), 旦(dàn), 旧(jiù)" (sunny, drought, time, dawn, old).

14. 星 star

xīng
星

字源演变　The etymology of Chinese characters

甲骨文　　　　金文　　　　小篆　　　　楷体

1. 释义　Meaning

star (n.)

2. 书写　Writing

3. 相关词语或表达　Related words or expressions

(1) xīngxing
　　星星 star

　　Tiānshàng yǒu hěn duō xīngxing.
　　天上　有　很　多　星星。There're a lot of stars in the sky.

(2) xīngqī
　　星期 week

　　xīngqī yī
　　星期 一　　　　Monday

　　xīngqī èr
　　星期 二　　　　Tuesday

　　xīngqī sān
　　星期 三　　　　Wednesday

三、作名词的汉字 Characters as Nouns

xīngqī sì
星期 四   Thursday

xīngqī wǔ
星期 五   Friday

xīngqī liù
星期 六   Saturday

xīngqī rì tiān
星期 日(天)   Sunday

     xīng
(3) ……星 star; famous performer or athlete

gēxīng
歌星   singer

Tā chàng gē chàng de hěn hǎo, tā shì yī ge gēxīng.
他 唱 歌 唱 得 很 好,他 是 一 个 歌星。
He sings very well, he's a singer.

yǐngxīng
影星   movie star

Tā shì hěn yǒumíng de diànyǐngyǎnyuán, tā shì yī ge yǐngxīng.
她 是 很 有名 的 电影演员, 她 是 一个 影星。
She's a very famous movie actress, she's a movie star.

qiúxīng
球星   superstar player

Bèikè hànmǔ shì yī ge qiúxīng.
贝克 汉姆 是 一个 球星。Beckham is a soccer superstar player.

4. 练习　Exercises

(1) 填空 Fill in the blanks

今天是_____年_____月_____日,星期_____。

昨天是_____年_____月_____日,星期_____。

明天是_____年_____月_____日,星期_____。

    歌星 球星 影星

Tā hěn huì chànggē, shì yī ge   tā shì yī ge hǎo yǎnyuán,
她 很 会 唱歌, 是 一个_____;他 是 一个 好 演员,

tā shì yī ge   Yáo Míng lánqiú dǎ de hěn hǎo, shì yī ge
他是一个_____;姚 明 篮球 打得 很 好,是 一个_____。

(2) 请用汉字写出日历中标有下划线的日期（年、月、日、星期）Write down the underlined dates (year, month, day and week) on the calendar in Chinese

10 October 2013						
Sunday	Monday	Tuesday	Wednesday	Thursday	Friday	Saturday
		1	2	<u>3</u>	4	5
6	7	8	9	10	11	12
13	14	15	16	17	18	<u>19</u>
20	21	<u>22</u>	23	24	25	26
27	28	29	<u>30</u>	31		

①
②
③
④

5. 汉字知识　The knowledge of Chinese characters

造字法（2）　形声字

汉字中有很大一部分的合体字，其中有的部件表示字的意义，有的部件表示字的读音，这种造字方法叫做"形声"。大多数汉字是形声字。在形声字里，表示意思的部件叫"形旁"，表示读音的叫"声旁"，声旁的读音与字本身的读音相同或相近。比如："妈"字，"女"表示这个字指的是女性，"马"表示这个字的读音。本课所学的几个汉字大都是形声字。

Method of Character Formation (2)　Pictophonetic Characters

A large number of Chinese characters are compound characters with one component indicates meaning while other components indicates pronunciation. This method of character formation is called pictophonetic. The majority of Chinese characters are pictophonetic characters. In a pictophonetic character, the component that indicates meaning is called "pictograhic radical" and the component that indicates the pronunciation is called "phonetic radical". The

三、作名词的汉字 Characters as Nouns

phonetic radical has the same or similar pronunciation with the character. For example, in character "妈(mā)", "女" shows that this character refer to the female; "马" indicates the pronunciation. The characters we learned in this lesson are mostly of this kind.

汉字 Chinese Character	声旁 Phonetic Radical	形旁 Pictographic Radical
星 xīng	生	日
期 qī	其	月
歌 gē	哥	欠
球 qiú	求	王

15. 东 east

dōng
东

字源演变　The etymology of Chinese characters

甲骨文　　　　　小篆　　　　　繁体　　　　　楷体

1. 释义　Meaning

east (n.)

2. 书写　Writing

3. 相关词语或表达　Related words or expressions

dōngmiàn
东面　　　　east

dōngbiān
东边　　　　east side

dōngbù
东部　　　　the east

dōngfāng
东方　　　　east, the East, the Orient

Shūdiàn zài fànguǎn de dōngbian.
书店　在　饭馆　的　东边。

The bookstore is on the east side of the restaurant.

三、作名词的汉字 Characters as Nouns

(1) xī
西 west (n.)

|西| | | | | | | | | | | | | |

xīběi
西北   northwest

xīnán
西南   southwest

xīcān
西餐   western-style food

Xiànzài Zhōngguó rén yě kāishǐ chī xīcān le.
现在 中国 人也开始 吃 西餐 了。

Nowadays, the Chinese also start to have western-style cuisine.

(2) nán
南 south (n.)

|南| | | | | | | | | | | | | |

nánfāng
南方   the south

dōngnán
东南   southeast

(3) běi
北 north(n.)

|北| | | | | | | | | | | | | |

dōngběi
东北   northeast

Běijīng
北京   Beijing

Tā de jiā zài Běijīng, tā shì Běijīng rén.
他的家在 北京,他是 北京 人。

He came from Beijing and his home is in Beijing.

汉语常用100字

4. 练习　Exercises

（1）根据图示写出他们汉语的方位名称 Write down the name of the directions in Chinese according to the illustrations

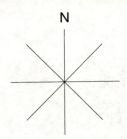

（2）看中国地图，请学生指出以下省份在中国的方位 Take a look at a map of China and ask the students to point out the locations of the following provinces

Xīnjiāng	Guǎngdōng	Yúnnán	Hēilóngjiāng	Běijīng
新疆	广东	云南	黑龙江	北京

5. 汉字知识　The knowledge of Chinese characters

造字法（3）　会意字

　　会意是把两个或两个以上的字组合在一起来表示新的字义的造字法。如"林"字由两个"木"字合成，"木"是树的意思，那"林"就表示树木丛生。由此你可以猜出"森"就表示有很多树的地方。"东"的古字形 🌲 就像太阳升到大树的半腰处，因此古人习惯地把太阳升起的地方称为东方。现在"东方"又指亚洲。古时因为主人的座位在东，宾客的座位在西，所以"东"还可以指主人，如"房东"、"股东"、"东道主"等。如果你打算请别人吃饭，你可以说："今天我做东，请大家吃饭。"

Method of Character Formation (3)　Associative Compound Characters

　　Associative compound refers to the method of combining two or more characters together to express a new meaning. For example, the character "林" (lín) is combined by two "木" (mù, tree) means plenty of trees. Then

三、作名词的汉字 Characters as Nouns

"森" (sēn) signifies a lot of trees. The ancient form of the character "东" looks like the Sun rising to the middle of a tree "🌲". Therefore, the ancient people usually called the place that the sun rises the East. Now "the East" also stands for Asia. In ancient times, host usually sat in the east and guest sat in the west. Thus it can also mean host, such as "房东(fángdōng)" (landlord), "股东(gǔdōng)" (shareholder), "东道主(dōngdàozhǔ)" (host). If you plan to treat someone to dinner, you can say: "今天我做东,请大家吃饭"(I will be the host today. I will treat you).

16. 中 middle

zhōng

字源演变　The etymology of Chinese characters

甲骨文　　　　金文　　　　小篆　　　　楷体

1. 释义　Meaning

centre; middle (n.)

2. 书写　Writing

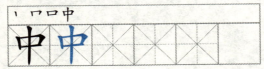

3. 相关词语或表达　Related words or expressions

(1) zhōngxīn
中心 centre

Běijīng shì Zhōngguó de zhèngzhì zhōngxīn.
北京　是　中国　的　政治　中心。
Beijing is the political centre of China.

(2) dà zhōng xiǎo
大　中　小 large; medium; small

gāo zhōng dī
高　中　低 high; mid/intermediate; low

zuǒ zhōng yòu
左　中　右 left; middle; right

58

三、作名词的汉字 Characters as Nouns

shàng zhōng xià
上　中　下　up; middle; down

(3) in

shǒuzhōng
手中　　in one's hand

Tā de shǒuzhōng yǒu yī zhī bǐ.
他的　手中　有一支笔。He has a pen in his hand.

xīnzhōng
心中　　in one's heart; take sth. to heart.

Wǒ de xīnzhōng zhǐ yǒu nǐ.
我的　心中　只有你。You will always be in my heart.

jiāzhōng
家中　　at home

Jiāzhōng yǒu hěn duō shū.
家中　有很多书。There are a lot of books in his house.

注意："……中"的用法比较书面，口语中我们常用"……里"。

Note: "……中" is more formal language while "……里" is usually used in spoken language.

(4) mid/intermediate

zhōngjí
中级　　intermediate; mid-level

Wǒmen xuéxí zhōngjí Hànyǔ.
我们　学习　中级　汉语。
We are learning intermediate level Chinese.

zhōnghào
中号　　medium size

Wǒ chuān zhōnghào de yīfu.
我穿　中号　的衣服。I wear medium size shirt.

zhōngyǔ zhōngxuě
中雨 / 中雪　　rain/snow

Jīntiān yǒu zhōngyǔ (zhōngxuě).
今天　有　中雨　（中雪）。It's raining (snowing) steadily today.

zhōngxué
中学　　middle school

Tā zài nà ge zhōngxué xuéxí.
他在那个　中学　学习。He's studying in that middle school.

zhōngwén
(5) 中文　　Chinese

汉语常用100字

Wǒ xǐhuan xuéxí zhōngwén.
我 喜欢 学习 中文。I like learning Chinese.

zhōngcān
中餐　　Chinese food

Zhōngcān hěn hǎochī.
中餐　很 好吃。Chinese food is delicious.

zhōngyào
中药　　traditional Chinese medicine

Nǐ chī guo zhōngyào ma?
你吃过 中药 吗?
Have you taken traditional Chinese medicine before?

4. 练习　Exercises

(1) 请把下列词语与它们相对应的意思连线 Link the corresponding meanings of words and expressions

中文　　　　Chinese food
中药　　　　Chinese medicine
中心　　　　Chinese language
中号　　　　middle school
中餐　　　　center
中学　　　　medium size
手中　　　　in the hand
心中　　　　in the heart

(2) 请根据提示语标出各组的程度 Mark out the level of each group according to the clues

① A 书很难(nán)　B 书很容易(róngyì)　C 书不太难也不太容易

A 书（　）级
B 书（　）级
C 书（　）级

② 考试(kǎoshì)成绩(chéngjì)：

A : 58分　　B : 100分　　C : 80分

三、作名词的汉字 Characters as Nouns

他们的汉语水平(shuǐpíng)：
A （　　）等
B （　　）等
C （　　）等

③ 小王穿L号的衣服，小李穿M号的衣服，小张穿S号的衣服。
他们穿的衣服号码：
小王　（　　）号
小李　（　　）号
小张　（　　）号

5. 汉字知识　The knowledge of Chinese characters
造字法(4)　指事字

指事就是用象征性符号，比如分别用一条线、两条线和三条线表示"一、二、三"；或者在象形字上加提示符号来表示某个词的造字法，如前边学的"天"字的甲骨文写作" "，它是一个正面站立的人，头上加了一横，表示人头顶着的是天空。用这种方法造的字就是指事字。

"中"字就是指事字，其甲骨文字形是" "，好像旗杆上下有旌旗和飘带，旗杆正中竖立。本义是中心、当中，指一定范围内部适中的位置。过去，中国人觉得自己住在世界的中央，所以自己住的地方就叫"中国"。中国的历史，最早是从"中原"开始的。中原就是中国中部的平原。

Method of Character Formation (4)　Indicative Characters

Indicative refers to a method of character formation which indicates a character through using symbols. For example, using one line, two lines and three lines to signify "一、二、三"(one, two, three). It also refers to a method which adds indicatory symbols to pictographic characters. For example, we have learned that "天" is written as " " in its oracle inscription form. It is the frontal look of a standing person with a horizontal line added above the head, which means the sky is overhead. Characters created in this way are indicative characters.

汉语常用100字

The character "中" is one of this kind. Its oracle inscription form written as "中" seems like there are a flag and a streamer on the upper and lower part of the flagpole which stands up in the middle. Thus the character originally meant center—the middle position of a certain range. In the past, the Chinese believed we were living in the center of the world, so we called the place we lived in "中国 (Zhōngguó)" (the Central Kingdom). The history of China began in the Central Plains "中原 (zhōngyuán)" which are the plains in central China.

17. 前 front

qián
前

字源演变 The etymology of Chinese characters

金文

小篆

楷体

1. 释义　Meaning

front, former, forward, preceding (n.)

2. 书写　Writing

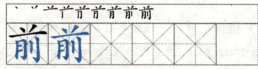

3. 相关词语或表达　Related words or expressions

(1) qián (hòu) biān
　　前（后）边　　　front(behind; back)

Shāngdiàn zài fànguǎn de qiánbiān.
商店　在　饭馆　的　前边。
The store is in front of the restaurant.

qiánmén hòumén
前门 / 后门　　　front door, backdoor

Qiánmén shì Běijīng yī ge hěn yǒumíng de dìfang.
前门　是　北京　一个　很　有名　的　地方。
Qianmen is a very famous place in Beijing.

汉语常用100字

Zhè ge fángzi yǒu qiánmén yě yǒu hòumén, jìn chū hěn fāngbiàn.
这 个 房子 有　前门 也 有 后门，进 出 很　方便。

This house has front and back door, so it's very convenient.

(2) 前天 / 后天　the day before yesterday, the day after tomorrow
　　qiántiān hòutiān

Jīntiān shì xīngqī sān, qiántiān shì xīngqī yī, hòutiān shì xīngqī wǔ.
今天　是 星期　三，前天　是 星期 一，后天　是 星期　五。

Today is Wednesday, the day before yesterday was Monday and the day after tomorrow is Friday.

前者 / 后者　the former, the latter
qiánzhě hòuzhě

Rèn hànzì hé xiě hànzì xiāngbǐ, qiánzhě bǐ hòuzhě róngyì.
认　汉字 和 写 汉字　相比，前者 比 后者　容易。

Comparing recognizing characters with writing them, the former is far easier.

(3) 后 behind; back; after; last; rear;
　　hòu

后													

4. 练习　Exercises

(1) 看图片写出对应的汉语方位词汇并注音 Look at the pictures and write down their corresponding directions in Chinese and their phonetic notations

　　前门在天安门的_____，天安门在前门的_____。

64

三、作名词的汉字 Characters as Nouns

北京医院(hospital)有一个_____和一个_____，医院的_____是车站(bus station)，医院的_____是一个操场(playground)。医院的_____在南面，_____在北面。

(yīyuàn, chēzhàn, cāochǎng)

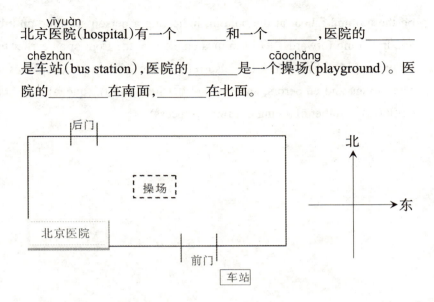

（2）将下列对应的词语用线连接起来 Link the corresponding meanings of words and expressions with their pronunciations

前面	xīmiàn	north
后面	dōngmiàn	in front
北面	qiánmiàn	east
东面	hòumiàn	west
西面	nánmiàn	at the back
南面	běimiàn	south

5. 汉语知识　The knowledge of Chinese characters

"前"与"后"

"前"的古文字写作"𠔉"，上面的部分是脚趾，下面是舟，表示脚踩在船上，乘船前行的意思。它既可以表示位置靠前，也可以指时间比较早，与"前"相对的则是"后"。"后"还可以用来指伺候帝王君主的妻妾，如"皇后、母后"等。

"前" and "后"

In its ancient form, the character "前" was written as "𠔉". It had toes

65

on the top and a boat at the bottom, indicating a person standing on a boat and travelling forward. "前" can mean a place at the front or an earlier time. Its opposite is "后". "后" can also refer to the wives and concubines who serve kings and emperors, such as "皇后(huánghòu)"(queen) and "母后(mǔhòu)"(mother of a king or prince/princess).

18. 左 left

zuǒ
左

字源演变　The etymology of Chinese characters

金文

小篆

楷体

1. 释义　Meaning
left (n.)

2. 书写　Writing

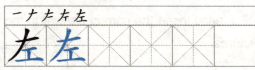

3. 相关词语或表达　Related words or expressions

（1）左(右)边　　　the left side, the right side

Shūdiàn zài fànguǎn de zuǒbiān.
书店 在 饭馆 的 左边。
The bookstore is on the left side of the restaurant.

Dào le qiánbiān de shízìlùkǒu wǎng zuǒguǎi.
到 了 前边 的 十字路口 往 左拐。
Go straight ahead and turn left at the crossing.

zuǒshǒu yòushǒu
（2）左手，右手　　　left hand, right hand

Chī xīcān de shíhou, zuǒshǒu ná dāo, yòushǒu ná chā.
吃 西餐 的 时候，左手 拿刀，右手 拿 叉。

汉语常用100字

Hold the knife in your left hand and the fork in your right hand when having a western meal.

(3) yòu
右 right

右														

4. 练习 Exercises

(1) 根据英文意思写出对应的汉语方位词汇并注音 Write down their corresponding directions in Chinese and their phonetic notations

east   (   )   (   )
left   (   )   (   )
west   (   )   (   )
south   (   )   (   )
north   (   )   (   )
right   (   )   (   )
in front (   )   (   )

(2) 请根据下列图示选择填空 Please insert the correct answer in the blanks according to the pictures

前边　　左边　　后边　　右边　　中间

qīzi　　　　　zhàngfu　　　　　　xiǎogǒu
妻子（wife）在丈夫（husband）_____，小狗（dog）在他们_____。

68

三、作名词的汉字 Characters as Nouns

Lǎoshī zài hēibǎn
老师 在 黑板（blackboard）_____。

A　　　B　　　C

　zài　　　　zài　　　　zài
A在_____,B在_____,C在_____。

5. 汉字知识　The knowledge of Chinese characters
中国人传统观念中的"左"和"右"

在甲骨文中，"左"字"𠂇"和"右"字"𠂇"就像人的左手和右手。左手和右手相对，还可以用来表示方位和方向。中国历史上曾流行过左尊右卑的观念，比如人们一直遵从"男左女右"的习惯；宫殿豪宅门前的一对石狮子，通常也是雄在左，雌在右；古人乘车，尊者坐在左侧，护卫坐在右侧；现代中国人宴请宾客时，最尊贵的客人也一般坐在主人的左侧。尊左的观念据说源于对东方的崇拜，因为对坐北朝南的人来说，左就是东。

汉语常用100字

The Left and the Right in the Traditional Concept of the Chinese

In oracle inscriptions, the characters "𠂇" (左) and "㝢" (右) resemble the left and right hands of a person. The left hand corresponds to the right hand. Both "左" (left) and "右" (right) can indicate position and direction. In Chinese history, people used to have higher regard for the left in comparing with the right. For example, people had been following the tradition of "the male on the left and the female on the right". For the pair of stone lions outside palaces and mansions, the male lion is generally on the left while the female lion on the right. In ancient time, the person of higher status always sat on the left side while his bodyguard sat on the right side when taking a ride. Nowadays, when hosting a banquet, the most distinguished guest often sits to the left of the host. The respect for the left originates from the worship of the east, because the left side is east when people sitting in the north and facing the south.

19. 王 king

wáng
王

字源演变　The etymology of Chinese characters

甲骨文

金文

小篆

楷体

1. 释义　Meaning

king (n.)

2. 书写　Writing

3. 相关词语或表达　Related words or expressions

guówáng
(1) 国王　king

Guòqù de guówáng jiào huángdì.
过去 的 国王 叫 皇帝。
King is also called emperor in ancient times.

Guówáng de qīzi jiào wánghòu.
国王 的妻子叫 王后。King's wife is called queen.

Guówáng de érzi jiào wángzǐ.
国王 的儿子叫 王子。King's son is called prince.

xìng
(2) 姓　surname

汉语常用100字

Nín guì xìng? Wǒ xìng Wáng.
您 贵 姓？我 姓 王。
May I ask your name please? —My surname is Wang.

Zài Zhōngguó xìng Wáng de rén hěn duō.
在 中国 姓 王 的 人 很 多。
There are many people with the family name of "王" in China.

Lǎo Wáng shì wǒ de hǎo péngyou.
老 王 是 我 的 好 朋友。Laowang is my good friend.

XiǎoWáng yǐjing sānshí duō suì le.
小王 已经 三十 多 岁 了。Xiaowang is in his thirties.

Zhōngguó chángyòng xìngshì
中国 常用 姓氏：Common family names in China

Lǐ   Zhāng Zhào   Liú
李   张   赵   刘

4. 练习 Exercises

(1) 认一认并写一写下列常用姓氏（中国人数最多的姓氏）Recognizing and writing the following common family names in China

① 李（Lǐ）
② 王（Wáng）
③ 张（Zhāng）
④ 刘（Liú）
⑤ 陈（Chén）
⑥ 杨（Yáng）
⑦ 赵（Zhào）
⑧ 黄（Huáng）
⑨ 周（Zhōu）
⑩ 吴（Wú）

三、作名词的汉字 Characters as Nouns

（2）请写出你知道的或你熟悉的人的汉字姓氏 Write down the Chinese family names you know

5. 汉字知识　The knowledge of Chinese characters

偏旁与部首

偏旁是指构成合体字的表意或表音的单位。如"明"字就是由"日"和"月"合成的；"字"是由"宀"和"子"合成的。这其中的"日"、"月"、"宀"、"子"都是偏旁。在汉字的偏旁中，有的本身就是一个字，比如"日"、"月"、"子"等；有的偏旁是不成字的，比如"宀"。有的独体字在它作偏旁使用的时候，字形会有一些细微的变化，比如"你"字中把"人"写成"亻"。

部首是具有字形归类作用的偏旁。它是为了满足编排字典的需要，按照汉字的结构而设立的。比如"他、你、们"都有"亻"，这里的"亻"就是部首。应当指出的是：汉字的偏旁和部首是既有联系，又有区别的。所有的部首可以作偏旁，但偏旁不一定都是部首。比如"你"，偏旁有"亻"和"尔"，部首只有"亻"。

Radicals and Indexing Radicals

Radicals are units which indicate meaning and sound of compound characters. For example, the character "明(míng)" is combined by "日" and "月"; the character "字(zì)" is combined by "宀" and "子". In these two characters, "日" and "月", "宀" and "子" are all radicals. Some of the radicals are characters themselves, such as "日", "月" and "子" while others are not, such as "宀". Some single characters, when used as radicals, will have some minor changes. For example, "人(rén)" is written as "亻" in the character "你".

Indexing radicals are radicals that help arrange characters according to their forms. They are created according to the structures of Chinese characters for the purpose of compiling dictionary. For example, the characters "他(tā)", "你(nǐ)" and "们(men)" all contain the radical "亻". In this case, "亻" is the indexing radical. It has to be noted that there are connections and differences between the radicals and indexing radicals. All the indexing

汉语常用100字

radicals can be used as radicals, but only some radicals can be indexing radicals. For example, "亻" and "尔" are both radicals in the character "你", but only "亻" is indexing radical.

20. 男 man

nán
男

字源演变 The etymology of Chinese characters

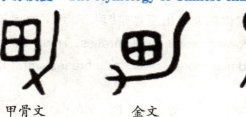

甲骨文　　　　金文　　　　小篆　　　　楷体

1. 释义　Meaning

man, male (n.)

2. 书写　Writing

3. 相关词语或表达　Related words or expressions

(1) nánrén
男人 (man)

nánháir
男孩儿 (boy)

Tā de nán péngyou shì dàifu.
她的 男 朋友 是大夫。 Her boyfriend is a doctor.

nán cèsuǒ
男 厕所 (the Gentlemen's)

(2) nǚ
女　　woman, female

nǚrén
女人 (woman)

汉语常用100字

nǚ péngyou
女 朋友 (girlfriend)

Wǒ de nǚ péngyou shì lǎoshī.
我 的 女 朋友 是 老师。 My girlfriend is a teacher.

nǚ cèsuǒ
女 厕所 (the Ladies')

4. 练习　Exercises

（1）写一写下列词组，想一想你还能写出更多带"男"和"女"的词组吗？Write down the following words and phrases. Think about whether you can write down more words and phrases with the characters "男" and "女"

男人　（　　　　）　　　女人　（　　　　）
男孩儿（　　　　）　　　女孩儿（　　　　）
男朋友（　　　　）　　　女朋友（　　　　）
男厕所（　　　　）　　　女厕所（　　　　）
男老师（　　　　）　　　女老师（　　　　）
……　（　　　　）　　　……　（　　　　）

（2）选择填空 Insert the correct answer in the blanks
① 他　　她
　　_____是男人，_____是女人。
② 男　　女
　　妻子(qīzǐ, wife)是_____的，丈夫(zhàngfu, husband)是_____的
③ 男厕所　女厕所
　　他要去_____，她要去_____。
④ 男　　女
　　爷爷(yéye, grandpa)不喜欢(xǐhuɑn, like)女孩儿，他喜欢____孩儿。

三、作名词的汉字 Characters as Nouns

5. 汉字知识　The knowledge of Chinese characters
常见的偏旁部首(1)　田

"田"就像一块方形的大田,由纵横的田埂分成几块小田。"田"的本义是农田。"田"字既可单用,也可作偏旁。在汉字中凡由"田"取义的字皆与田地等义有关。比如"富"字,古时有很多田地的人被看作富人。

甲骨文、金文中的"力"字都像古人犁地用的一种工具"𠨌",由一块弯曲的木头制成,下部装有一根横梁。人们用它犁出沟垄,然后播种。犁地要用力气,"力"由此引申指体力、力气。

"男"是会意字,上边是田,下边是力,表示用力在田间耕作。因为农耕主要是男子的事。

Common Radicals and Indexing Radicals (1)　田

"田(tián)" resembles a large piece of square farmland which are divided into several small pieces by horizontal and vertical ridges. It originally means farmland and can be used independently or as a radical. The Chinese characters which derive their meaning from it are all related to farmland. For example, the character "富(fù)"(rich). In the old times, people with a large tract of farmland were considered rich.

The character "力" in its oracle inscription and bronze inscription form both look like a tool for plowing a field which is made by a piece of bended wood with a crossbar in the lower part which was written as "𠨌". The ancient people used it to make furrows for sowing. Plowing requires strength, the character "力(lì)" thus gradually developed the meaning of physical strength and force.

"男" (man) is an associative compound character with field on top and strength at bottom. It signifies a man who is plowing a field vigorously because farming was mainly a man's work.

21. 岁 age

suì
岁

字源演变　The etymology of Chinese characters

甲骨文　　　　　小篆　　　　　繁体　　　　　楷体

1. 释义　Meaning

age, year (n.)

2. 书写　Writing

3. 相关词语或表达　Related words or expressions

（1）常用问年龄的用法 (Common ways to ask about age)

Nǐ jǐ suì le?　Wǒ sì suì.
你几岁了？我 四岁。

How old are you? I'm four years old.

Nǐ duō dà le?　Wǒ shíwǔ suì le.
你多 大了？我 十五 岁了。

How old are you? I'm fifteen years old.

Nǐ duō dà suìshù?　Wǒ sìshí sān suì.
你多 大岁数？我 四十三 岁。

How old are you? I'm forty-three years old.

三、作名词的汉字 Characters as Nouns

Nín duō dà niánjì? Wǒ bāshí liù suì le.
您 多 大 年纪？我 八十 六 岁 了。

How old are you? I'm eighty-six years old.

Nín gāo shòu? Wǒ yībǎi líng yī suì le.
您 高 寿？我 一百 零 一 岁 了。

How old are you? I'm a hundred and one years old.

(2) 岁末 the end of the year

Měi dāng nián chū suì mò wǒmen dōu hěn máng.
每 当 年 初 岁末 我们 都 很 忙。

At the beginning and end of the year, we are always very busy.

4. 练习 Exercises

完成下列对话 Complete the following dialogue

A：小朋友，你今年 _____ ?

B：阿姨，我三岁半了。

A：老先生，您今年 _____ ?

B：我都八十多岁了。

A：同学，你今年 _____ ?

B：我二十一岁。

A：小张，你 _____ ? 有女朋友(girlfriend)了吗？

B：三十岁了，还没有呢。

A：老奶奶，您身体(health)真好呀，您 _____ ?

B：我的孙子都有儿子了，我明年就一百岁了。

(My grandson already has a son. I will be 100-year old next year.)

5. 汉字知识　The knowledge of Chinese characters

"岁"的起源和发展

"岁"的古文字写作" "，由三部分组成，中间是代表刑器的"戈"，上下各是一个表示人的脚的"止"。两个当脚讲的"止"跨越，表示今年"过"到明年。夏商时期一年一次祭祀时，杀人作为祭品，因此从夏商时代起，称"年"为"岁"。如古时称呼皇帝为"万岁"。

The Origin and Evolution of "岁"

The character "岁" is written as " " in its ancient form. It is comprised of three components: the middle part represents an instrument of torture—dagger-axe; the upper part and lower part—"止"—both represent one foot of a person. Two feet (止) leaping over means this year transition to the next year. On the annual sacrifice during Xia Dynasty and Shang Dynasty, people were killed to serve as sacred offerings. Therefore, since Xia Dynasty and Shang Dynasty, we use the character "岁" to indicate "年(nián)" (year). For example, emperors were called "万岁(wànsuì)" (Your Majesty) in ancient times.

22. 国 country

guó

字源演变　The etymology of Chinese characters

　小篆　　　　　繁体　　　　　　楷体

1. 释义　Meaning

nation, country, state (n.)

2. 书写　Writing

3. 相关词语或表达　Related words or expressions

guójiā		
国家		country; nation
中国	Zhōngguó	China
美国	Měiguó	United States of America
韩国	Hánguó	South Korea
法国	Fǎguó	France
德国	Déguó	Germany
英国	Yīngguó	United Kingdom
泰国	Tàiguó	Thailand

很多国家的名字在汉语中是以"……国"来表示的,这种情形多为国家

汉语常用100字

名字只有一个汉字时,有时国家的名字比较长时,后边就不加"国"了。
In Chinese, we add the character "国" at the end of the names of many countries. This happens when the names of these countries only have one Chinese character. We don't add "国" to the countries whose names are pretty long.

如:

日本	Rìběn	Japan
印度	Yìndù	India
巴西	Bāxī	Brazil
瑞士	Ruìshì	Switzerland
埃及	Āijí	Egypt
加拿大	Jiā nádà	Canada
意大利	Yìdàlì	Italy
西班牙	Xībānyá	Spain
葡萄牙	Pútaoyá	Portugal
俄罗斯	Éluósī	Russia
澳大利亚	Àodàlìyà	Australia
马来西亚	Mǎláixīyà	Malaysia
印度尼西亚	Yìndùníxīyà	Indonesia

guógē
国歌 national anthem

yī shǒu guógē
一 首 国歌 a national anthem

guóqí
国旗 national flag

yī miàn guóqí
一 面 国旗 a national flag

Guóqìng jié
国庆 节 national day

Zhōngguó de Guóqìng jié shì shí yuè yī rì.
中国 的 国庆 节 是 十 月 一 日。

China celebrates its national day on October 1st.

三、作名词的汉字 Characters as Nouns

4. 练习 **Exercises**

（1）请根据英语写出下列国家的汉语名字 Please insert the Chinese names of the following nations

France

Germany

Thailand

Japan

India

Brazil

Egypt

Italy

Spain

Portugal

Russia

Australia

Malaysia

Indonesia

（2）看国旗写国家名字 Please insert each nation's Chinese name beside its national flag

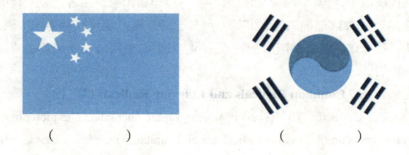

（　　　　）　　　　　　　　（　　　　）

( )　　　　　　( )

( )　　　　　　( )

5. 汉字知识　The knowledge of Chinese characters

常见的偏旁部首(2)　囗部

"囗"（wéi）是个象形字，凡是以囗为偏旁的形声字都是表示周围有界限的字，比如"园"、"围"、"圆"、"圈"等等。

"国"繁体写作"國"。外面的囗表示区域国土，简化时里面的"或"被"玉"代替。玉是一种十分珍贵的石头，需要像保护土地一样保管玉。在现代汉语中，"国"字的含义比较单纯，一般即指国家。在古代，王、侯的封地称为国，如"赵国"、"秦国"等。另外，都城、城邑也可以称为国。因此，在古代著作中，"走出国门"不一定是走出国境，也可能是走出都城或城邑的城门。

Common Radicals and Indexing Radicals (2)　囗

The character "囗" (wéi) is a pictographic character. The pictophonetic characters with "囗" as the radical are all characters with boundaries, such as "园(yuán)" (garden), "围(wéi)" (enclose) "圆(yuán)" (circle) and "圈(quān)" (encircle).

The character "国" was written as "國" in traditional Chinese. The

三、作名词的汉字 Characters as Nouns

"囗" outside indicates national boundaries. In its simplified form, the part inside "或" is replaced by "玉". "玉(yù)"(jade) is a kind of very precious stone which needs to be safely protected as land. In modern Chinese, the character "国" simply means a nation. In ancient times, the fiefs of kings and marquises were called "国", such as "赵国" and "秦国". Moreover, capitals and towns could also be called "国". Therefore, in ancient literature, "走出国门" (go outside) did not definitely mean go across the national boundary. It could also mean get out of the capital or towns.

23. 市 city

shì
市

字源演变　The etymology of Chinese characters

金文　　　　　小篆　　　　楷体

1. 释义　Meaning

city, market (n.)

2. 书写　Writing

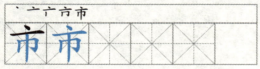

3. 相关词语或表达　Related words or expressions

(1) chéngshì
　　城市 city

　　chéng
　　城

Xiànzài chéngshì lǐ de rénkǒu yuèláiyuè duō.
现在　城市　里的 人口　越来越　多。

Today there are more and more people in the cities.

shìmín
市民 city resident

三、作名词的汉字 Characters as Nouns

(2) 市 shì market

市场 shìchǎng market

场

Chéngshì lǐ yǒu gèzhǒnggèyàng de shìchǎng, rénmen mǎi dōngxi hěn fāngbiàn.
城市 里有 各种各样 的 市场，人们 买 东西 很 方便。

There are many kinds of markets in the cities, and shopping is very convenient.

夜市 yèshì night market

Zhōumò de shíhou wǒ cháng qù yèshì chī dōngxi.
周末 的 时候 我 常 去 夜市 吃 东西。

At the weekends, I often go to the night markets to eat.

黑市 hēishì black market

Yào qù yínháng huàn qián, bù yào qù hēishì huànqián, hěn wēixiǎn.
要 去 银行 换 钱，不 要 去 黑市 换钱，很 危险。

Don't change money on the black market: only change money at the bank.

4. 练习 Exercises

(1) 选词填空 Insert the correct answer in the blanks

城市　夜市　市场　黑市

① 大_____的汽车(qìchē car)越来越(yuèláiyuè more and more)多。

② 别去_____买东西，不安全(ānquán safe)。

③ 下班后我喜欢去_____吃点东西。

④ 我家附近(fùjìn nearby)有个服装(fúzhuāng clothing)_____。

（2）看中国地图朗读中国的省市，并会写重要的城市名称 Look at a map of China and read aloud the provinces and cities of China and learn to write the names of important cities

5. 汉字知识　The knowledge of Chinese characters
"市"字的起源与发展

"市"本义是指定期集中买卖交换货物的固定场所。小篆的写法是"𠔉"，下边的方框是围墙的意思，因为古代的市场是用围墙围起来的；上边"之"字表示到什么地方去。经过隶书的变化，上边成了一点一横，下面变成了"巾"。

The Origin and Evolution of "市"

The character "市" originally refers to a fixed place for trading and exchanging commodities on a regular basis. Its seal character is written as "𠔉". The square frame in the lower part indicates walls because ancient markets were encircled by walls. The "之(zhī)" on the top means going to some place. After the official script period, the upper part was transformed into one dot and one horizontal bar and the lower part became the character "巾(jīn)".

24. 家 family

jiā
家

字源演变 The etymology of Chinese characters

甲骨文　　　　金文　　　　小篆　　　　楷体

1. 释义　Meaning

home, family, expert (n.)

2. 书写　Writing

3. 相关词语或表达　Related words or expressions

(1) jiā
家 family; household; home;

Wǒ jiā yǒu wǔ kǒu rén.
我 家 有 五 口 人。There are five people in my family.

huí jiā
回家 go home

Wǒ měitiān xiàwǔ liù diǎn huíjiā.
我 每天 下午 6 点 回家。I go home at 6 PM every day.

jiātíng
家庭 family

Tā yǒu yī ge xìngfú de jiātíng.
他 有 一个 幸福 的 家庭。He has a happy family.

汉语常用100字

jiāxiāng
家乡 hometown

Wǒ hěn xiǎngniàn wǒ de jiāxiāng.
我 很 想念 我 的 家乡。I miss my hometown very much.

(2) zhuānjiā
专家 expert

Tā shì jìsuànjī zhuānjiā.
他 是 计算机 专家。He is an expert in computer science.

yīnyuèjiā
音乐家 musicians

wénxuéjiā
文学家 literary writer

yìshùjiā
艺术家 artists

kēxuéjiā
科学家 scientists

huàjiā
画家 painter

(3) jiā
家 classifier

yī jiā shāngdiàn yínháng, gōngsī, yóujú, fànguǎn
一家 商店 （银行、公司、邮局、饭馆）

a store(a bank, a company, a post office, a restaurant)

4. 练习 Exercises

(1) 把下列词语和它们相对应的意思连线 Link the corresponding meanings of words and expressions

jiā
家   artist

jiāxiāng
家乡   painter

jiātíng
家庭   scientist

zhuānjiā
专家   family

huàjiā
画家   expert

三、作名词的汉字 Characters as Nouns

yīnyuèjiā
音乐家   home

yìshùjiā
艺术家   musician

kēxuéjiā
科学家   hometown

(2) 填空 Please fill in the blanks

这是一_____银行。

这是我的_____。

她钢琴弹得很好,她是一个_____。

毕加索(Pablo Picasso)是一位_____,他的画很有名。

鲁迅(Lǔ Xùn)写了很多书,是一个_____。

5. 汉字知识　The knowledge of Chinese characters

常见的偏旁部首(3)　宀部

"宀"是一个常见的偏旁,叫宝盖儿,甲骨文中好像一座两边有木柱,上边为尖屋顶的房屋的外形"⌂",其本义指房子,因此用它作形旁的字大多和房间有关。比如"家"字,上面的"宀"代表屋顶,下面是"豕",即猪。在屋顶下有一头猪,住的地方养猪说明人置产于此,要在这里长期居住,繁衍生息。因此"家"的本义指住所。其他带"宀"的汉字还有很多,比如"宫"、"牢"、"宿"、"室"、"寝"、"安"、"定"等等。

Common Radicals and Indexing Radicals (3)　宀

"宀" is a common radical which is called Bǎo gàir (a cover). In oracle inscription form, its top part looks like a house with pitched roof. "⌂" originally means house, thus the characters with it as the ideographic radical are largely related to housing. For example, the upper part of the character "家"—"宀"—represents roof while the lower part—"豕" refers to a pig. The character thus means there is a pig under the roof. Having a pig at the place someone live indicates the person bought the property there and will live here for a long time and have offspring. Therefore, the character originally refers to housing. There are many characters with the radical "宀", for example "宫(gōng)"(palace), "宿(sù)"(living), "室(shì)"(room), "寝 (qǐn)"(sleep), "安(ān)"(safe) and "定(dìng)" (settle).

25. 人 person

字源演变　The etymology of Chinese characters

甲骨文　　　　金文　　　　小篆　　　　楷体

1. 释义　Meaning

human, people, human being, fellow (n.)

2. 书写　Writing

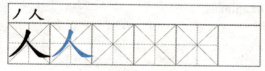

3. 相关词语或表达　Related words or expressions

rén
人 person

Zhōngguó yǒu hěn duō rén.
中国 有 很 多 人。China has a large population.

rénmen
人们 people

Èr shí yī shìjì, rénmen duì wèilái chōngmǎn le xīwàng.
21 世纪, 人们 对 未来 充满 了 希望。
In the 21st century, people are hopeful about the future.

nánrén
男人 man

汉语常用100字

nǚrén
女人 woman

hǎorén
好人 good person

huàirén
坏人 bad person

dàrén
大人 adult

chéngniánrén
成年人 adult; grown-up

niánqīngrén
年轻人 young people

biérén
别人 other people; others

Zǒu zìjǐ de lù ba, bié guǎn biérén shuō shénme.
走自己的路吧,别 管 别人 说 什么。

Walk your own road regardless of what the other people say about you.

rénlèi
人类 humanity

Rénlèi yīnggāi hé dòngwù chéngwéi péngyou.
人类 应该 和 动物 成为 朋友。

Humans should be the friend of animals.

Zhōngguórén
中国人 Chinese

wàiguórén
外国人 foreigner

Wǒ shì Zhōngguó rén, tā shì wàiguó rén.
我 是 中国 人,他是 外国人。

I'm a Chinese and he's a foreigner.

4. 练习 Exercises

(1) 将下列词语和词组与对应的拼音及意思连线 Link the corresponding pronunciations and meanings of words and expressions

好人	huàirén	other people
女人	hǎorén	humanity
男人	dàrén	good person

三、作名词的汉字 Characters as Nouns

大人	nǔrén	woman
坏人	nánrén	man
别人	rénlèi	people
人们	biérén	adult
人类	rénmen	bad person

(2) 用所给词语完成下列一段话 Complete the following paragraph with the given words

女人　年轻人　外国人　人们　人类

Wǒmen xuéxiào yǒu hěnduō rén, nánrén, _____、lǎorén、_____、
我们　学校　有　很多　人，男人，_____、老人、_____、

Zhōngguórén、_____。_____ Měitiān dōu hěn máng, dàjiā wèi _____
中国人、_____。_____ 每天　都　很　忙，大家　为_____

de wèilái ér nǔlì.
的　未来　而 努力。

5. 汉字知识　The knowledge of Chinese characters

"人"、"大"和"夫"

"人"是个象形字，甲骨文写作"𠁽"，像一个站立的人的侧面，手下垂或轻轻举到前面，颈背微微前倾。很多汉字都包含"人"，这也许是因为古老的中国人觉得，"人"是这个世界的中心；当人把他的两臂伸展开，就代表着"大"。再比如表示"成年男子"的"夫"字。古人认为头发是父母所给的，不能损伤，因此是不准剪头发的。古代小孩是披着头发，而成年男子则把长头发束起来并插上一根簪子，"夫"字在"人"字上加了一横就表示束发的簪子。

"人""大"and "夫"

"人"(human) is a pictographic character. In its oracle inscription form "𠁽", it looks like the side view of a standing person who is leaning slightly forward with his hands down or holding in front of him. Many characters contain "人". Maybe it is because the ancient Chinese believe humans are the center of the world; when humans extend their arms, it signifies "大

(dà)" (big). There is another example. The character "夫 (fū)" refers to "adult male". The ancients believed hair was given by parents which can endure no damage. Therefore, the ancients were not allowed to have hair cut. The children at that time had hair hang over shoulders while the adult male had their long hair tied with a hair clasp. The character "夫" thus has a horizontal bar added on top of the character "人" to represent the hair clasp.

26. 口 mouth

kǒu

字源演变　The etymology of Chinese characters

甲骨文　　　　金文　　　　小篆　　　　楷体

1. 释义　Meaning

mouth (n.); oral; a measure word

2. 书写　Writing

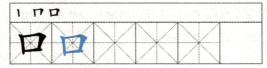

3. 相关词语或表达　Related words or expressions

(1) (classifier for the total number of people in the family)

　　　Nǐ jiā yǒu jǐ kǒu rén?
A: 你家 有几口 人? How many people are there in your family?

　　　Wǒ jiā yǒu sān kǒu rén, bàba māma hé wǒ.
B: 我家 有 三 口 人,爸爸、妈妈 和 我。

There are three people in my family: Dad, Mom and me.

kǒuyǔ
(2) 口语 spoken language

　　Jīntiān wǒmen yǒu kǒuyǔ kè.
　　今天 我们 有 口语 课。

Today we have the course of speaking Chinese.

汉语常用100字

kǒushì
口试 oral examination

Jīntiān de kǒushì bù tài nán.
今天 的 口试 不太 难。Today's oral examination is not too hard.

kǒuyīn
(3) 口音 accent

Tā shuōhuà yǒu Shànghǎi kǒuyīn.
她 说话 有 上海 口音。She has Shanghai accent.

kǒuwèi
(4) 口味 taste

Nǐ xǐhuan shénme kǒuwèi de cài?
A：你 喜欢 什么 口味 的 菜？
What kind of flavor would you prefer?

Wǒ xǐhuan qīngdàn de kǒuwèi.
B：我 喜欢 清淡 的 口味。I prefer food with light flavor.

kǒuhóng
(5) 口红 lipstick

yī zhī kǒuhóng
一支 口红 a lipstick

4. 练习　Exercises

(1) 请写出带"口"字旁的汉字，写得越多越好 Write down as many characters with the radical "口" as possible

例：吃、喝……

_____ _____

_____ _____

(2) 选词填空 Insert the correct answer in the blanks

　　　　口　　口红　　口味　　口语　　口音　　口试

Tāmen jiā yǒu wǔ　　　rén.
① 他们 家 有 五_____人。

Nǐ xǐhuan zhè zhǒng　　　de cài ma?
② 你 喜欢 这 种_____的 菜 吗？

98

三、作名词的汉字 Characters as Nouns

③ 明天 有_____课。
　　Míngtiān yǒu　　　kè.

④ 他 有 广东_____。
　　Tā yǒu Guǎngdōng

⑤ 昨天 的_____难 吗?
　　Zuótiān de　　　nánma?

⑥ 我 买 了 一 支_____。
　　Wǒ mǎi le yī zhī

5. 汉字知识 The knowledge of Chinese characters

"口"字的有关知识

"口"字是个象形字,它的形状就好像人的嘴"廿",其本义就是嘴的意思。一个人只有一张嘴,而且在古代要让所有的人都吃饱是很困难的,想到人,自然想到填饱口。因此人们习惯了以"口"作为统计人数的单位,在中国经常有人问你家有几口人;丈夫和妻子可以叫"两口子";现在中国有十多亿人口。由口的形状和功能,人们自然而然地用它来表示出入通过的地方,比如"门口"、"路口"、"出口"、"入口"、"瓶口"、"碗口"、"井口"、"洞口"、"入海口"、"火山口"等等。

Knowledge about the Character "口"

"口" (mouth) is a pictographic character, written as "廿". It resembles the mouth of a person and originally just means it. People only have one mouth and it was difficult in the old times to have enough food for all people. People naturally thought of filling the stomach when thinking of people. Therefore, people got used to take "口" as a unit for measuring population. In China, people often ask "你家有几口人" (how many people are there in your family). Husband and wife can be called "两口子(liǎng kǒuzi)". So far China has a population (人口) of over 10 billion. For its shape and function, people naturally use it to represent the place for entry, exit and passage, such as "门口 (ménkǒu)" (doorway), "路口 (lùkǒu)" (intersection), "出口 (chūkǒu)" (exit), "入口 (rùkǒu)" (entrance), "瓶口

(píngkǒu)"(bottleneck), "碗口(wǎnkǒu)"(bowl rim)、"井口(jǐngkǒu)"(wellhead), "洞口(dòngkǒu)"(mouth of a cave), "入海口(rùhǎikǒu)"(mouth of a river), "火山口(huǒshānkǒu)"(crater).

27. 手 hand

shǒu

字源演变   The etymology of Chinese characters

金文   小篆   楷体

1. 释义   Meaning

hand (n.)

2. 书写   Writing

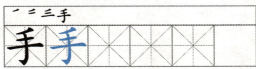

3. 相关词语或表达   Related words or expressions

shǒu
(1) 手 hand

Wǒmen yǒu yīshuāng shǒu, zuǒshǒu hé yòushǒu.
我们 有 一双 手，左手 和 右手。
We have a pair of hand, left hand and right hand.

Tā shǒu lǐ ná zhe yī zhī bǐ.
他 手 里拿着一支笔。He is holding a pen in his hand.

shǒuzhǐ
(2) 手指 finger

Tā de shǒuzhǐ hěn cháng.
他的 手指 很 长。His fingers are pretty long.

(3) shǒubiǎo
　　手表 wrist-watch

　　Māma mǎi le yī kuài shǒubiǎo.
　　妈妈 买了一块 手表。My mother bought a wrist-watch.

(4) shǒujī
　　手机 mobile cell phone

　　Zhè shì nǐ de shǒujī ma?
　　这 是你的 手机吗? Is this your cell phone ?

(5) shǒutíbāo
　　手提包 handbag

(6) expert in a certain skill or getting sth. done

　　néngshǒu
　　能手 skilled hand

　　Tā shì yī ge zhòng huā néngshǒu.
　　他是一个 种 花 能手。

　　He is a good hand at cultivating flowers.

　　gēshǒu
　　歌手　　singer

　　shuǐshǒu
　　水手　　sailor

(7) Classifier for skill or dexterity

　　Tā néng zuò yī shǒu hǎocài.
　　她 能 做一手 好菜。She is good at cooking.

4. 练习　Exercises

(1) 根据英文翻译写出相应的词语 Write down the corresponding Chinese words according to the translations

　　mobile (　　)　　　　watch (　　)
　　hand (　　)　　　　　sailor (　　)
　　handbag (　　)　　　singer (　　)
　　skilled hand (　　)　finger (　　)

(2) 回答问题 Answer the following questions

　① 你常常用左手还是右手?
　　Do you often use your left hand or right one?

102

三、作名词的汉字 Characters as Nouns

我常常_____。

② 你有手表吗？

Do you have a wrist watch?

我_____。

③ 你的妈妈有手机吗？

Does your mother have a cell phone?

我的妈妈_____。

④ 你的手指长吗？

Are your fingers long?

我的_____。

⑤ 你喜欢哪一个歌手？

Which singer do you like?

我喜欢_____。

5. 汉字知识　The knowledge of Chinese characters

"手"字的有关知识

最初刻在青铜器上的"手"字都是一只伸出五指的手的形状。带手的汉字比如"拿"，手合起来才能握持住东西。"手"的构词能力很强。人劳动主要靠手，所以有"手"的词常常表示劳动。比如，开始做一件事情叫"入手"；干活儿干得好的人叫"能手"；协助别人进行工作的人叫"助手"；此外，手又引申为拥有专门技能的人，如"歌手"、"多面手"。花钱没有节制叫"大手大脚"。

Knowledge about the Character "手"

The character "手" resembled the shape of a hand with extended fingers when first inscribed on bronze ware. "手" can easily form another character. The character with the radical "手" such as "拿" means people can only hold something with the hand closed. People do labor work mainly by hand, thus phrases with the character "手" are often related to labor. For example, starting something is called "入手(rùshǒu)"; a good hand in his specialty area is called "能手(néngshǒu)"; the person who assists someone in doing some work is called "助手(zhùshǒu)"(assistant). In addition, "手" also extended to indicate people with special skills, such as "歌手(gēshǒu)" (singer) and "多面手(duōmiànshǒu)" (an expert at many things). A prodigal who squander money is called "大手大脚(dà shǒu dà jiǎo)".

28. 爸 father

bà
爸

字源演变　The etymology of Chinese characters

楷体

1. 释义　Meaning

dad, father (n.)

2. 书写　Writing

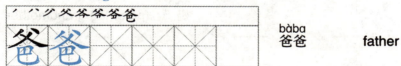

bàba
爸爸　　father

3. 相关词语或表达　Related words or expressions

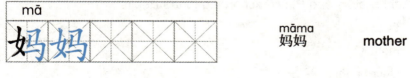

māma
妈妈　　mother

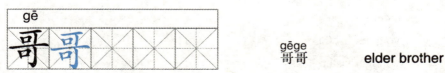

gēge
哥哥　　elder brother

汉语常用100字

jiě
姐姐

jiějie
姐姐 elder sister

dì
弟弟

dìdi
弟弟 younger brother

mèi
妹妹

mèimei
妹妹 younger sister

yé
爷爷

yéye
爷爷 (paternal) grandfather

nǎi
奶奶

nǎinai
奶奶 (paternal) grandmother

4. 练习 **Exercises**

（1）根据英文意思写出相应的汉字及拼音 Write down the Chinese characters and Pinyin according to the English

father (　　) (　　)
mother (　　) (　　)
elder brother (　　) (　　)
elder sister (　　) (　　)
younger brother (　　) (　　)
younger sister (　　) (　　)
(paternal) grandfather (　　) (　　)
(paternal) grandmother (　　) (　　)

三、作名词的汉字 Characters as Nouns

(2) 请根据图片描述一下这个家庭 Describe the family according to the picture

6. 汉字知识　The knowledge of Chinese characters
常见的偏旁部首(4)　父部

"父"的古文字写作"⿱"、"⿰"等。据考证,这个字形是一只手拿着石斧的形象。远古石器时代的成年男子以石斧作为主要生产工具,因此以"父"作形旁的字大多表示男性长辈。"父"字旁在字的上部,位置比较固定。比如"爸"、"爷"等。在正式的称呼中,"爸爸"又叫"父亲"。所谓"祖父、叔父、舅父",所指的都是亲族中的男性长辈;爸爸的父亲或者年岁与祖父相仿的男子,我们叫他"爷爷"。在中国古代父权制度下,男性家长主宰其他家庭成员,因此父亲具有绝对的权威,这也体现在汉语中一些涉及父亲的词语:一些神仙的称呼后加上一个"爷"以示虔诚,如"阎王爷、灶王爷";地方官又被称为"父母官"。"父"亦作声旁,如"斧"。

Common Radicals (4) 父

The character "父(fù)" is written as "⿱" or "⿰" in its ancient form. According to research, it depicts an image of a hand holding a stone axe. In remote Stone Age, stone axe is the major instruments of production for adult male, so the characters with "父" as the pictographic radical are largely related to male elders. "父" is always placed at the top, such as "爸" and "爷". "爸爸" (Dad) is formally addressed as "父亲(fùqin)" (father). "祖父(zǔfù)(grandfather)", "叔父(shūfù)(paternal uncle)" and "舅父(jiùfù)" (maternal uncle) are all refer to male elders in a family. We call the father of a person's dad or male elders who are of the same age as our grandfather "爷爷". In ancient patriarchy, male elders held domination over other family members, so father had absolute authority. This is also reflected in some Chinese characters that are connected with father: the title of some gods are added with "爷(yé)" to show piety, such as "阎王爷(yánwangyé)"(King of Hell) and "灶王爷(zàowangyé)"(Kitchen God); local officials are also called "父母官(fùmǔguān)". "父" also serves as phonetic radical such as "斧(fǔ)".

29. 水 water

shuǐ
水

字源演变 The etymology of Chinese characters

 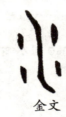  

甲骨文　　　　金文　　　　小篆　　　　楷体

1. 释义　Meaning

water (n.)

2. 书写　Writing

亅 亅 氵 水

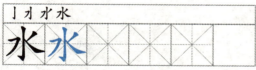

3. 相关词语或表达　Related words or expressions

(1) shuǐ
　　水 water

　　yī bēi shuǐ
　　一杯 水 a glass of water

　　bēi
　　杯 cup

　　kuàngquánshuǐ　　　　qìshuǐ
　　矿泉水 mineral water　汽水 aerated water; soft drink; soda water

　　Wǒ yào yī píng kuàngquánshuǐ hé yī píng qìshuǐ.
　　我 要 一 瓶　矿泉水　和一 瓶 汽水。

汉语常用100字

I want a bottle of mineral water and a bottle of aerated water.

píng
瓶 bottle

hēshuǐ
喝水 drink water

Gǎn mào de shíhou yào duō hē shuǐ.
感冒的时候要多喝水。

People who have a cold need to drink more water.

　　　hǎishuǐ　　héshuǐ　　jiāngshuǐ　　húshuǐ　　quánshuǐ
(2) 海水 sea 河水 river 江水 river 湖水 lake 泉水 spring water

shuǐmiàn
水面 surface of the water

Xiǎochuán zài shuǐmiàn shàng piāozhe.
小船　在　水面　上　漂着。

The boat is floating on the water surface.

　　yàoshuǐ
(3) 药水 liquid medicine

píngguǒ shuǐ
苹果　水 apple juice

júzi shuǐ
橘子水 orange juice

　　shuǐguǒ
(4) 水果 fruit

Xiàtiān de shíhou, zhèlǐ yǒu gèzhǒnggèyàng de shuǐguǒ.
夏天　的 时候，这里 有　各种各样　的 水果。

In summer, there're many kinds of fruits here.

4. 练习　Exercises

（1）将下列词语和词组与对应的拼音及意思连线 Link the corresponding pronunciations and meanings of words and expressions

水果	shuǐmiàn	mineral water
海水	yàoshuǐ	liquid medicine
喝水	shuǐguǒ	the surface of the water
矿泉水	háishuǐ	apple juice

110

三、作名词的汉字 Characters as Nouns

药水	hēshuǐ	fruit
水面	píngguǒshuǐ	drink water
苹果水	kuàngquánshuǐ	seawater

（2）写出带有水或偏旁氵的字 Write down as many characters with "水" or "氵"as possible

_____ _____ _____ _____

5. 汉字知识　The knowledge of Chinese characters
常见的偏旁部首(5)　水部

　　水在字的左边作偏旁时写作"氵"，称为三点水。凡由"氵"所构成的字大都与水流等义有关，比如"河"、"海"、"江"、"湖"、"泪"、"汗"。

　　无论在甲骨文、金文或小篆中，水的形体都是弯弯曲曲的流水之形，"氺"，其中几点，表示激流中溅起的水花。"水"的本义是河流，有很多古老的河流至今仍称为水，如"汉水"、"渭水"、"泗水"等等。"水"后来泛指江、河、湖、海、洋等一切水域，如"万水千山"中的"水"。由水的液体性质，"水"字又被用来泛指汁、液，比如"药水"、"汗水"、"汽水"、"墨水"、"泪水"等。

Common Radicals and Indexing Radicals (5)　水

When on the left, the radical "水" is written as "氵" and is called three drops of water. The characters containing this radical are mostly related to water, such as "河(hé)" (river), "海(hǎi)"(sea), "江(jiāng)"(river), "湖(hú)" (lake), "泪(lèi)"(tear) and "汗(hàn)" (sweat).

In oracle inscription, bronze inscription or sealed characters, the shape of water is winding: "氺". Several dots signify splashes of rushing water. "水" originally means river. Many ancient rivers are still called "水" today, such as 汉水(Hànshuǐ), 渭水(Wèishuǐ), and 泗水(Sìshuǐ). "水" later generally refers to all waters including "江, 河, 湖, 海 and 洋(yáng) (ocean)". For example, the character "水" in the phrase "万水千山(wàn shuǐ qiān shān)" (ten thousand mountains and rivers). Since water is liquid, the character is used extensively to indicate juice and liquid, such as "药水 (yàoshuǐ)" (liquid medicine), "汗水 (hànshuǐ)" (sweat), "汽水 (qìshuǐ)" (an aerated water), "墨水 (mòshuǐ)" (ink) and "泪水 (lèishuǐ)" (tear).

30. 饭 meal

fàn
饭

字源演变 The etymology of Chinese characters

小篆　　　　　繁体　　　　　楷体

1. 释义　Meaning

meal, cooked rice (n.)

2. 书写　Writing

3. 相关词语或表达　Related words or expressions

mǐfàn
米饭　　cooked rice

Tā chī le yī wǎn mǐfàn.
他 吃了一 碗　米饭。He ate a bowl of rice.

chī fàn
吃 饭　　have dinner (breakfast, lunch, etc.)

zǎofàn
早饭　　breakfast

wǔfàn
午饭　　lunch

wǎnfàn
晚饭　　supper

汉语常用100字

Wǒ měitiān chī sān dùn fàn, zǎofàn, wǔfàn hé wǎnfàn.
我 每天 吃 三 顿 饭，早饭、午饭 和 晚饭。

I usually eat three meals every day: breakfast, lunch and supper.

fànguǎnr
饭馆儿　　　　restaurant

Zài Zhōngguó de yǐnshí zhōng, fàn yī bān zhǐ zhǔshí,
在 中国 的 饮食 中，"饭"一般 指 主食（In Chinese cooking,
fàn.　　　　　　　　　　　　　　Rú mǐfàn miàntiáo　　　mántou
"饭" usually refers to staple food）。如：米饭、面条(noodles)、馒头(steamed
　　　　bāozi　　　　　　　　jiǎozi　　　děng.
bread)、包子(steamed stuffed buns)、饺子(dumpling)等。

4. 练习　Exercises

(1) 选择填空 Insert the correct answer in the blanks

　　　　米饭　　吃饭　　晚饭　　饭馆　　面条

Měitiān wǒ chī sān dùn fàn, zǎofàn, wǔfàn, wǎnfàn. Zǎoshang wǒ cháng
每天 我 吃 三 顿 饭，早饭、午饭、晚饭。早 上 我 常
cháng zài jiā　　　　zǎofàn wǒ chī bāozi. Kěshì xiàbān yǐhòu, wǒ yǒu
常 在 家_____，早饭 我 吃 包子。可是 下班 以后，我 有
shíhòu qù　　　　chī　　　　nà jiā fànguǎn de　　　hé　　　dōu
时候 去_____吃_____，那家 饭馆 的_____和_____都
hěn hǎochī.
很 好吃。

(2) 看图片认一认这些都是什么饭 Please insert the Chinese name beside its picture

　　（　　）　　　　　（　　）　　　　（　　）

三、作名词的汉字 Characters as Nouns

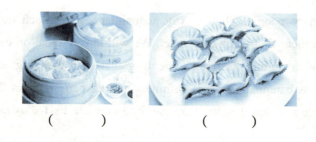

(　　)　　　　(　　)

5. 汉字知识　The knowledge of Chinese characters
常见的偏旁部首(6)　食部

"食"是个象形字：🍚，甲骨文的下部是一个食器装着丰盛的食物，两侧的两个点表示已经装满外流了，上部的三角形是食器的盖子。"食"的本义就是食物，又引申作动词用，表示"吃"。食字旁在左侧时简化为"饣"，在其他部位时仍写作"食"。带食部的字大多和吃的东西或者吃的动作有关，比如"饭馆"、"饿"、"饱"、"饼"、"饮"、"餐"等。中国有句古话叫"民以食为天"，在以前，对老百姓来说填饱肚子是最重要的事情，这也就是为什么以前熟人见面第一句话常常问："吃饭了吗？"逢年过节要吃饭，老朋友聚会要吃饭，遇到婚丧嫁娶等这些大事都要吃饭，在商业宴请中，吃饭更是必不可少的一项重要环节。难怪有人说，最能代表中国文化的就是中国的饮食。

Common Radicals and Indexing Radicals (6)　食

"食" is a pictographic character written as "🍚". In its oracle inscription form, its lower part depicts a food vessel with plenty of food; the two dots at two sides indicate the vessel is too full that the food is flowing over the top; and the triangle at the top stands for the cover of the food vessel. The primary meaning of the character is food. When on the left, the radical "食" is simplified as "饣" such as "饭馆(fànguǎn)"(restaurant), "饿(è)"(hungry), "饱(bǎo)"(full), "饼(bǐng)"(pastry) and "饮(yǐn)"(drink). It is still written as "食" on the right and at the bottom such as "餐(cān)"(meal). There is an old saying in China—"food is the paramount necessity of the people". In the old times, filling the stomach is the most important thing for the ordinary people. That's why acquaintances ask each other whether they had a meal first when they meet. We will have a meal on each important occasion including festivals, friend gatherings, wedding and funerals. For business banquet, dinner is definitely an indispensable part. No wonder some people say that it is the Chinese food that can best showcase the Chinese culture.

31. 菜 vegetable

cài
菜

字源演变 The etymology of Chinese characters

小篆

楷体

1. 释义 Meaning

vegetable, dish (n.)

2. 书写 Writing

3. 相关词语或表达 Related words or expressions

(1) shūcài
    蔬菜 vegetable

Shìchǎng shàng yǒu gèzhǒnggèyàng de shūcài.
市场   上   有   各种各样   的 蔬菜。

There're all kinds of vegetables in the market.

báicài
白菜   Chinese cabbage

xiǎobáicài
小白菜   pakchoi

bōcài
菠菜   spinach

汉语常用100字

	yóucài 油菜	rape green rape; colza
	kòngxīncài 空心菜	water spinach
	juǎnxīncài 卷心菜	cabbage
	yóumàicài 油麦菜	leaf lettuce
	xiāngcài 香菜	coriander
	qíncài 芹菜	celery
	jiǔcài 韭菜	Chinese chive
	càihuā 菜花	cauliflower
(2)	diǎn cài 点 菜	to order a dish
	càidān 菜单	menu
	Zhōngguó cài 中国 菜	Chinese dish
	chǎocài 炒菜	stir-fry
	hūncài 荤菜	meat dish
	sùcài 素菜	vegetable dish
	rècài 热菜	hot dish; main dish
	liángcài 凉菜	cold dish
	chuāncài 川菜	Sichwan dish; Sichwnan cuisine; (the Sichwan style of cooking or cuisine featuring liberal use of hot pepper and strong seasonings)
	náshǒucài 拿手菜	specialty

三、作名词的汉字 Characters as Nouns

4. 练习　Exercises

(1) 看图片，说出下列蔬菜的名字 Say the names of the following vegetables in the pictures

(2) 大声朗读下列点菜的句子 Please read aloud the following sentences for ordering dishes

　　　Wǒ kàn yīxià càidān.
① 我　看一下　菜单。

　　May I see the menu, please?

　　　Wǒ yào yī ge hūncài hé yī ge sùcài.
② 我　要一个　荤菜　和一个　素菜。

　　I'd like a meat dish and a vegetable dish.

　　　Zhè shì chuāncài.
③ 这是　川菜。

　　This is Sichuan cuisine.

　　　Wǒ xiǎng diǎn yī ge liángcài.
④ 我　想　点一个　凉菜。

　　I'd like to have a cold dish.

　　　Qǐng jièshào　yīxiàr nǐmen de náshǒucài.
⑤ 请　介绍　一下儿 你们 的　拿手菜。

　　What's your specialty?

汉语常用100字

5. 汉字知识　　The knowledge of Chinese characters

常见的偏旁部首(7)　　艹部

"艹"俗称"草字头",本是一个象形字"艸",好像两棵并排长着的植物的样子,凡是以"艹"为偏旁的字大都和草本植物有关,"艹"字旁都在字的上部,比如:"菜"、"茶"、"草"、"花"等等。

"菜"是一个形声字,"艹"代表意思,"采"表示读音。上古时期"菜"只指蔬菜,到了中古以后,肉类、蛋类等熟食也叫做菜了。

Common Radicals and Indexing Radicals (7)　艹

The radical "艹" is commonly referred to as "草字头(cǎozìtóu)" (the top of the character "草"—grass). It is originally a pictographic character, appearing like two plants growing side by side. "艸", the characters containing this radical are mostly connected with herbals. It is always on the top, such as "菜(cài)"(dish), "茶(chá)"(tea), "草(cǎo)"(grass) and "花(huā)" (flower).

The character "菜" is pictophonetic character with "艹" indicating the meaning and "采" indicating the pronunciation. In ancient times it only referred to vegetable, but after medieval times, it also means meat, egg and cooked food.

32. 酒 liquor

jiǔ
酒

字源演变   The etymology of Chinese characters

甲骨文

小篆

楷体

1. 释义   Meaning

alcoholic drink; spirits; wine; liquor (n.)

2. 书写   Writing

丶 丶 氵 氵 沂 沂 洒 洒 洒 酒

酒 酒

3. 相关词语或表达   Related words or expressions

báijiǔ
白酒   white spirit

píjiǔ
啤酒   beer

pútaojiǔ
葡萄酒   wine

jīwěijiǔ
鸡尾酒   cocktail

hē jiǔ
喝酒   drinking

Nǐ hē shénme jiǔ? Báijiǔ, píjiǔ, pútaojiǔ háishi jīwěijiǔ?
你喝 什么 酒？白酒、啤酒、葡萄酒 还是 鸡尾酒？

汉语常用100字

What would you like to drink: white spirit, beer, wine or cocktail?

jiǔ bā
酒 吧　　　　bar

jiǔguǎnr
酒馆儿　　　pub

jiǔdiàn
酒店　　　　hotel

Zhè ge jiǔdiàn tài guì le.
这 个 酒店 太 贵 了。 This hotel is too expensive.

4. 练习　Exercises

(1) 把下列汉字写在相应的结构后 Write the following Chinese characters next to their corresponding structures

酒　你　这　男　岁　国　左

zuǒyòu jiégòu
左右　结构（　　　）(left-right structure）

shàngxià jiégòu
上下　结构（　　　）(top-bottom structure）

zuǒ xià bāowéi jiégòu
左 下 包围 结构（　　　）(left-bottom-encircled structure）

zuǒ shàng bāowéi jiégòu
左 上 包围 结构（　　　）(left-top-encircled structure）

sìmiàn bāowéi jiégòu
四面 包围 结构（　　　）(all-side-encircled structure）

(2) 看图片认一认这些都是什么酒 What are these alcohols in the picture

（　　）

（　　）

三、作名词的汉字 Characters as Nouns

(   )

(   )

5. 汉字知识   The knowledge of Chinese characters

中国的酒文化

古汉字的"酒"字写作"㊂",左边是表示液体的水字旁,右边是一个装酒的酒坛子。酒渗透于整个中华五千年的文明史中,从文学艺术创作、文化娱乐到饮食烹饪、养生保健等各方面,酒在中国人生活中都占有重要的位置。中国有句俗话"无酒不成席",酒在我们的社会生活中无所不在;从古到今,中国人一向敦于友谊,友人相逢,无论是久别重逢,还是应邀而逢,都要把酒叙情,喝个痛快。中国人把婚礼的筵席称"喜酒",生了孩子办满月称"满月酒",祝捷要喝"庆功酒",婚礼中夫妻喝"交杯酒"。此外,敬神、祭祖、开业等等都要喝酒,酒已成为中国人际交往的桥梁和纽带,在日常生活中发挥着重要的作用。

The Culture of Chinese Liquor

In its ancient form, "酒" was written as "㊂", the left part of the character is the radical "水" which indicates liquid and the right part is a jar holding liquor. Liquor permeates throughout the 5000 years of Chinese civilization— literature, art, culture, entertainment, food, cooking, keeping fit and all other aspects of civilization. It has great significance in the life of Chinese people. There is a popular saying that "it can not be a banquet without liquor." Liquor is everywhere in our social life. From the ancient times to the present, the Chinese people value friendship. When friends get together either after a long time or at an invitation, we will chat over liquor

汉语常用100字

and have a good drink. The Chinese people call the banquet of a wedding "喜酒(xǐjiǔ)", the banquet for celebrating a one-month old baby "满月酒 (mǎnyuèjiǔ)" and the celebration of success "庆功酒(qìnggōngjiǔ)". Wife and husband drink "交杯酒(jiāobēijiǔ)" during a wedding ceremony. In addition, we drink liquor when worshiping gods and ancestors and at an opening ceremony. Liquor has become the bridge and bond in the social in the social life of the Chinese people. It plays a very important role in daily life.

33. 钱 money

qián
钱

字源演变　**The etymology of Chinese characters**

　　小篆　　　　　　繁体　　　　　　楷体

1. 释义　Meaning

money (n.)

2. 书写　Writing

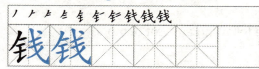

3. 相关词语或表达　Related words or expressions

yuán
元　yuan

jiǎo
角　jiao

kuài
块　(same as yuan)

máo
毛　(same as jiao)

fēn
分　fen

　　　duōshao qián
① 多少　钱　　　how much

汉语常用100字

　　　　Zhè běn shū duōshao qián?
　　A:这 本 书 多少 钱？How much is this book?

　　　　Sān kuài wǔ máo
　　B:3 块 5（毛）。￥3.5.

　　　　Xīhóngshì duōshao qián yī jīn?
　　A:西红柿 多少 钱一斤？How much is this tomato per jin?

　　　　Yī kuài wǔ máo èr fēn.
　　B:1 块 5 毛 2（分）。￥1.52.

　　　　Kělè yīpíng duōshao qián?
　　A:可乐一瓶 多少 钱？How much is a bottle of coke?

　　　　Sān yuán wǔ jiǎo.
　　B:3 元 5 角。￥3.5.

　　　huā qián
② 花　钱　　　spend money

　　　Jīntiān wǒ huā le sān bǎi kuài qián.
　　今天 我 花了 300 块 钱。Today I spent 300 yuan.

　　　qiánbāo
③ 钱包　　　wallet

　　　Wǒ de qián zài qiánbāo lǐ.
　　我 的 钱 在 钱包 里。My money is in my wallet.

4. 练习　Exercises

(1) 请读出下列钱数 Say the following amount of money

0.05元	yuán wǔfēn 五分	
0.20元	liǎngmáo 两毛	liǎngjiǎo 两角
1.00元	yī kuài 一块	yī yuán 一元
2.30元	liǎngkuàisān 两块三	liǎng kuài sān máo 两 块 三 毛
3.46元	sān kuài sì máo liù 三 块 四 毛 六	sān kuài sì máo liù fēn 三 块 四 毛 六 分
6.05元	liù kuài líng wǔ 六 块 零 五	liù kuài líng wǔ fēn 六 块 零 五 分
28.55元	èr shí bā kuài wǔ máo wǔ 二十八 块 五 毛 五	èr shí bā kuài wǔ máo wǔ fēn 二十八 块 五 毛 五 分
100.50元	yī bǎi kuài líng wǔ máo 一 百 块 零 五 毛	

三、作名词的汉字 Characters as Noun

        yuán   èr bǎi sān shí jiǔ kuài qī máo bā fēn
239.78元   二 百 三 十 九 块 七 毛 八（分）

（2）跟朋友互相询问并说出身边物品的价格 Practice with your friends and ask each other about the prices of the things around you

例如：书

A：你的书多少钱？
    How much is your book?

B：25块。

   bǐ
① 笔   pen; pencil

   shǒujī
② 手机   mobile, cellphone

   shǒubiǎo
③ 手表   watch

   kuàngquánshuǐ
④ 矿泉水   mineral water

5. 汉字知识　The knowledge of Chinese characters

常见的偏旁部首(8)　金部

    "金"的本义不是指黄金，在商周时期，人们使用的金属器具都是青铜制造的，"金"特指青铜，这也是为什么人们把刻在青铜器上的铭文称为"金文"。随着生产技术的不断发展，人们开采冶炼的金属越来越多，"金"字就被用作各种金属的统称。因此大部分表示金属的汉字都有"金"作形旁，金字旁在字的左侧时写作"钅"，比如"钢"、"铁"、"铜""铝"、"钟"等等。后来"金"字慢慢被用来专指黄金，又引申指钱。

    "钱"是个形声字，左形右声。它本义是铁铲，一种金属农具。上古时期曾以农具作为交易的媒介，后来铸造货币又仿照它的样子，因此引申指货币、钱财。

Common Radicals and Indexing Radicals (8)　金

    Originally, the character "金(jīn)" did not refer to gold. During Shang Dynasty and Zhou Dynasty, people used bronze instruments instead of metal ones. "金" specifically indicates bronze. That's why people called the inscription on bronze "金文(jīnwén)". With the continuous development of the means of production, people were able to exploit and smelt more metals. The character thus was used generally to mean all kinds of metals. As a result, most of the Chinese characters which indicate metals have the character "金" as the pictographic radical. When on the left, it is written as "钅", such as "钢(gāng)" (steel), "铁(tiě)" (iron), "铜(tóng)" (copper), "铝(lǚ)" (aluminum), "钟(zhōng)" (bell). Later the character "金" gradually became used to indicate gold, specifically with the extended meaning of money.

"钱" is a pictophonetic character with pictographic radical on the left and phonetic radical on the right. It originally meant shovel which is a metal farming instrument. In ancient times, farming instruments were used as a medium of exchange. Later coins were cast in the shape of farming instruments so that the character also means currency and money.

34. 元 yuan

yuán
元

字源演变 The etymology of Chinese characters

甲骨文　　　　　金文　　　　　小篆　　　　　楷体

1. 释义　Meaning

yuan

2. 书写　Writing

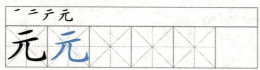

3. 相关词语或表达　Related words or expressions

　　　yuán
(1) 元

　　Wǒ yǒu yīzhāng wǔyuán de rénmínbì. Tóng kuài.
　　我 有 一张　五元　的 人民币。同"块"。
　　I have a five yuan note.

　　　　yuán　　dú zuò   èr bǎi sān shí kuài
　　230元　　读 作：二 百 三 十 块

　　　　yuán　　dú zuò   bā kuài sì máo wǔ
　　8.45元　　读 作：八 块 四 毛 五

　　　　yuán　　dú zuò èr shí yī kuài líng bā fēn
　　21.08元　　读 作：二 十 一 块 零 八 分

305.70元 　　读作：三百零五块七
　　　　　　　　dú zuò sān bǎi líng wǔ kuài qī

6.99元 　　　读作：六块九毛九
　　　　　　　　dú zuò liù kuài jiǔ máo jiǔ

7.5元 　　　　读作：七块五
　　　　　　　　dú zuò qī kuài wǔ

Yī měiyuán kěyǐ huàn liù kuài'èr rénmínbì.
一 美元 可以 换 六 块 二人民币。($1=￥6.2)

One US Dollar equaled to 6.2 Chinese Yuan.

　　　　yuáncháo
(2) 元朝　　Yuan Dynasty

Yuáncháo jiàn yú gōngyuán yī èr qī yī nián, yuáncháo zuì yǒumíng de
元朝　　建于　　公元　　1271　年，元朝　最　有名　的

shīgē shì yuánqū.
诗歌 是 元曲。

Yuan Dynasty was established in 1271. The most famous poetry of Yuan Dynasty is Yuan Qu.

　　　　yuándàn
(3) 元旦　　　New Year's Day

Yī yuè yī rì shì yuándàn, shì xīnnián.
一 月 一 日 是　元旦，是　新年。

January the first is New Year's Day.

　　　　dānyuán
(4) 单元　　　unit

　　　　yuányīn
(5) 元音　　　vowel

4. 练习　Exercises

(1) 请读出下列钱数并写出汉字 Say the following amount of money and write them down in Chinese

74.56元

8324.8元

207.09元

43.06元

100.8元

三、作名词的汉字 Characters as Nouns

50.07元
99.16元

(2) 看图片识别钱币 Identify the currency in the pictures

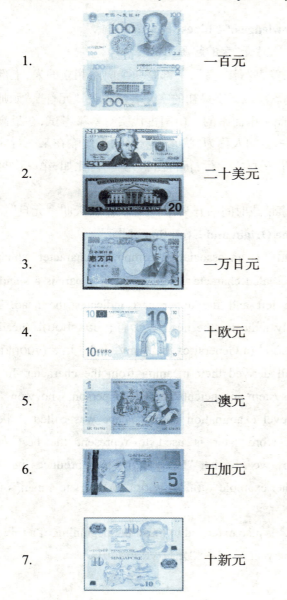

1. 一百元

2. 二十美元

3. 一万日元

4. 十欧元

5. 一澳元

6. 五加元

7. 十新元

汉语常用100字

8.  一千韩元

5. 汉字知识　The knowledge of Chinese characters

"元"字的起源和发展

元是一个会意字,篆书写作"𠄞",下部是一个向左侧立的人,上部表明人体的部位,即头部。所以元字最初的字义表示人头。"元首"、"元帅"、"元老"的含义都是由此引申而来的。中国古代实行科举考试,在最高等级的殿试中考取的第一名的人称为"状元";后来用来比喻在某一行业中成绩最好的人,正所谓"三百六十行,行行出状元"。再比如,第一次娶的妻子称"元配"。

"元"字又引申为事情或时间的开头,如一年的第一天叫"元旦"。

The Origin and Evolution of "元"

The character "元" is an associative compound character which is written as "𠄞" in its sealed character form. The lower part is a standing person who faces the left and the upper part indicates the head. The character thus originally indicates the head. "元首(yuánshǒu)" (head of state), "元帅(yuánshuài)" (a General of the Army) and "元老(yuánlǎo)" (a senior statesman) all derived their meaning from the character. In the imperial examination system in ancient China, the person who won first place in the highest level examination in the palace was called "状元(zhuàngyuán)". This word later is used to represent the best in a profession. That's why we say that "Every profession produces its own topmost master." Another example "元配" (yuánpèi) refers to a man's first wife.

The character "元" is also extended to mean the beginning of a thing or time. The first day of the year is called "元旦(yuándàn)".

35. 衣 clothes

字源演变　The etymology of Chinese characters

甲骨文　　　　　小篆　　　　　楷体

1. 释义　Meaning

clothes (n.)

2. 书写　Writing

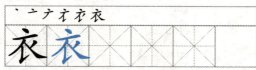

3. 相关词语或表达　Related words or expressions

(1) 衣服 yīfu　　clothes
Wǒ mǎi le yī jiàn yīfu.
我 买 了一件衣服。I bought a coat.

上衣 shàngyī　　coat, jacket

大衣 dàyī　　overcoat

外衣 wàiyī　　outer clothing

毛衣 máoyī　　a woolen sweater

汉语常用100字

　　chènshān
　　衬衫　　　　shirt

　　kùzi
　　裤子　　　　pants, trousers

　　qúnzi
　　裙子　　　　skirt

Zuótiān wǒ mǎi le yī jiàn máoyī, liǎng jiàn chènshān, yī tiáo kùzi hé yī tiáo
昨天　我 买了一件 毛衣、两 件　衬衫、一条 裤子和一条

qúnzi.
裙子。 I bought a sweater, two shirts, a pair of trousers and a skirt.

　　　chuānyī
（2）穿衣　　　　dress

　　xǐ yīfu
　　洗衣服　　　wash clothes

Zhōumò wǒ zài jiā xǐ yīfu.
周末　我 在 家洗衣服。I'll wash clothes at weekend.

4. 练习　Exercises

（1）将下列词语和词组与对应的拼音及意思连线 Link the corresponding pronunciations and meanings of words and expressions

毛衣	máoyī	skirt
裙子	wàiyī	clothes
上衣	shàngyī	coat, jacket
衣服	dàyī	wash clothes
外衣	yīfu	dress
穿衣	chuān yī	wool sweater
洗衣服	chènshān	shirts
裤子	kùzi	overcoat
大衣	qúnzi	outer clothing
衬衫	xǐ yīfu	pants, trousers

134

三、作名词的汉字 Characters as Nouns

(2) 看图片识别各种衣服并写在图片下边 Identify different kinds of clothes in the pictures and write down their names below the pictures

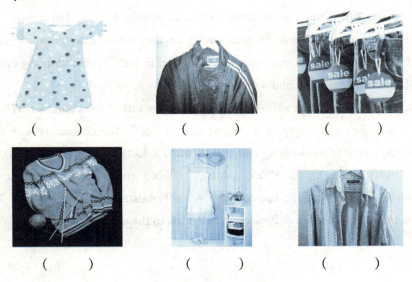

( )　　　　　　( )　　　　　　( )

( )　　　　　　( )　　　　　　( )

5. 汉字知识　The knowledge of Chinese characters
常见的偏旁部首(9)　衣部

"衣"是一个象形字,古文字中的"衣"字都很像古代的衣服" 🜊 "。现在,中国人在口语中常把"衣服"说成"衣裳",可是在古代这是两个词,"衣"专指上衣,"裳"指下身穿的裙子。裤子是后来才出现的,是北方游牧民族带给汉族的礼物,因为游牧民族生活在草原上,裤子更适合骑马的生活。裤子的出现,方便了人们的日常生活和工作,是中国服饰文化的一次革命。

"衣"部作形旁放在字的左边时写作"衤",放在字的下边或右边仍写成"衣"。带衣字旁的汉字多跟衣服有关,比如"裙"、"裤"、"衬"、"衫"、"袄"、"袍"、"装"等。"衤"容易与 表示祭祀义的偏旁"礻"相混,注意区别。

Common Radicals and Indexing Radicals (9)　衣

"衣" is a pictographic character and written as " 🜊 " in its ancient form which resembles ancient clothes. Nowadays, we call "衣服(yīfu)" "衣裳

(yīshang)" in our colloquial language. But in the old times, these are two words. "衣(yī)" referred specifically to tops while "裳(shang)" referred to dresses for the lower part of body. Trousers did not appear until later, which are the gift from the northern nomadic people to the Han people. The nomadic people lived on grasslands, so they needed trousers for riding horses. Trousers brought about a revolution in the Chinese clothing culture, facilitating daily life and work.

"衣" is written as "衤" when put on the left of the character. When at bottom or on the right, it is still written as "衣". The characters with it are largely related to clothes, such as "裙(qún)"(skirt), "裤(kù)"(trousers), "衬(chèn)"(lining), "衫(shān)"(shirt), "袄(ǎo)"(jacket), "袍(páo)"(robe) and "装(zhuāng)"(costume). "衤" is easily mistaken with the radical "礻" which means sacrifice. Please pay attention to the differences.

36. 楼 a storied building

lóu
楼

字源演变　The etymology of Chinese characters

  楼

小篆　　　　　繁体　　　　　楷体

1. 释义　Meaning

a storied building, floor (n.)

2. 书写　Writing

3. 相关词语或表达　Related words or expressions

（1）a storied building

lóufáng
楼房

fáng
房

Zhōngguó hěn duō nóngcūn yě dōu gàiqǐ le lóufáng.
中国　　很多　农村　也　都　盖起了　楼房。

Many multi-storey houses are also built in villages of China.

（2）floor

Wǒ jiā zhù zhè ge dānyuán de sānlóu.（jí dì sān céng）
我 家 住 这 个 单元　的 三楼。（即第三　层）

汉语常用100字

I live on the third floor of this entrance.

(3) 楼梯 stairs

tī
梯

lóudào
楼道 corridor

bàngōnglóu
办公楼 office building

gāolóu dàshà
高楼 大厦 high buildings and large mansions

mótiān dàlóu
摩天 大楼 a skyscraper

(4) yínlóu (mài jīnyín shǒushi de dìfang)
银楼（卖 金银 首饰 的 地方）silverware shop; shop that sells gold and silver ornaments

shǒushì lóu
首饰 楼 jewellery shop, shop that sells ornaments

yǐng lóu zhuānyè zhàoxiàng shèyǐng de dìfang
影 楼（ 专业 照相 摄影 的 地方）Photography Studio

chá lóu hē chá de dìfang
茶 楼（喝 茶 的 地方）tea house

4. 练习 Exercises

选择填空 (Insert the correct answer in the blanks)

三楼　　楼道　　三层　　楼房　　高楼大厦　　楼梯

Wǒ de dàxué lǐ dōu shì _____, bàngōnglóu yǒu liù céng, lǎoshī de
我 的 大学 里 都 是_____，办公楼 有 六 层，老师 的

bàngōngshì zài yǒu yě yǒu diàntī hěn
办公室 在_____，有_____也 有 电梯(elevator)，_____很

kuānchang. Jiàoxuélóu yǒu sì zuò, měi zuò lóu dōu shì, zài zhōuwéi
宽敞。 教学楼 有 4 座，每 座 楼 都 是_____，在 周围

de zhīzhōng, xiǎnde yǒuxiē dī'ǎi.
的_____之中， 显得 有些 低矮。

三、作名词的汉字 Characters as Nouns

5. 汉字知识　**The knowledge of Chinese characters**

常见的偏旁部首(10)　木部

"木"的古字形就是树木的形状"米"，上面是枝，中间是干，下面是根。因此用"木"作形旁的字多与树木、木材或木制品有关。比如"椅"、"树"、"桌"、"棵"、"样"等。

"楼"是一个形声字，左形右声，本义指两层以上的木楼。

Common Radicals and Indexing Radicals (10)　木

The character "木" looks like a tree with branches on top, trunk in the middle and roots at bottom "米" in its ancient form. Thus the characters with "木" as the pictographic radical are largely related to trees, wood or wood products, such as "椅(yǐ)"(chair), "树(shù)"(tree), "桌(zhuō)"(desk), "棵(kē)"(a classifier for trees) and "样(yàng)"(shape).

"楼" is a pictophonetic character with the pictographic radical on the left and phonetic radical on the right. It originally meant wooden house with two or more floors.

37. 室 room

shì
室

字源演变　The etymology of Chinese characters

甲骨文　　　　　金文　　　　　小篆　　　　　楷体

1. 释义　Meaning

room (n.)

2. 书写　Writing

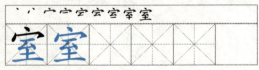

3. 相关词语或表达　Related words or expressions

(1) 教室　　classroom
jiàoshì

Xuésheng zài jiàoshì shàng kè.
学生　在 教室　上　课。
The students are having classes in the classroom.

(2) 办公室　　office
bàngōngshì

Lǎoshī de bàngōngshì zài nàr.
老师　的 办公室　在 那儿。The professor's office is over there.

(3) 卧室　　bedroom
wòshì

三、作名词的汉字 Characters as Nouns

Dìdi zài wòshì shuì jiào.
弟弟在 卧室 睡 觉。

My younger brother is sleeping in his bedroom.

shìwài
（4）室外　　　outdoor

shìnèi
室内　　　indoor

Xià yǔ le, wǒmen zài shìnèi kàn diànshì ba.
下 雨 了，我们 在 室内 看 电视 吧。
It is raining outside. Let's watch TV inside.

Wǒ xǐhuan qù shìwài yùndòng.
我 喜欢 去 室外 运动。 I like outdoor sports.

4. 练习　Exercises

（1）把下列词语及其相对应的拼音和意思连线 Link the corresponding pronunciations and meanings of words and expressions

教室	wòshì	office
卧室	shìnèi	classroom
室内	shìwài	bedroom
室外	bàngōngshì	indoor
办公室	jiàoshì	outdoor

（2）选词填空　Insert the correct answer in the blanks

　　　　室内　　室外　　办公室　　教室　　卧室

Xuésheng qù　　　shàng kè.
①学生 去_____上 课(attend class)。

Jīnglǐ zài　　　gōngzuò.
②经理 在_____工作(to work)。

Wǒ zài　　　shuì jiào.
③我 在_____睡 觉(sleep)。

Gēge zài　　　kàn diànshì.
④哥哥 在_____看 电视(watch TV)。

Dìdi zài　　　tī zúqiú.
⑤弟弟 在_____踢足球(play football)。

5. 汉字知识　The knowledge of Chinese characters

"室"与"宫"

"室"是个会意字,由"宀"(宝盖儿)和"至"组成。"宝盖儿"代表居住的房屋;在甲骨文、金文、小篆中的"至"字形状都像一支倒立在地上的箭。二者组合起来,"室"就表示人到了这里就可以住下来,把它当成居室了。

"室"的本义是内屋,如卧室。在古代,女子结婚后也多在室中,所以"妻子"又可以称为"妻室"。后来"室"的含义有所发展,像"教室"、"候车室"这些场所也称"室"。

另外一个表示居住房屋的字是"宫",长期以来,只有帝王住的地方才能叫"宫",如北京的故宫以及故宫里面后妃居住的地方,大都称为"宫"。但现在一些公共活动场所也可以称为"宫",如"少年宫"、"文化宫"。

"室" and "宫"

The character "室" is an associative compound character, which is composed of "宝盖儿" (cover) and "至". The cover stands for the room a person lives in. In oracle inscription, bronze inscription and sealed character, the character "至" is shaped like an arrow that stands upside down in the floor. Combining the two, "室" indicates that when a person comes into the room, he can live in it.

The character originally meant inner room such as bedroom. The ancient women would stay mostly in the room after they got married, so "妻子(qīzi)" (wife) can also be called "妻室(qīshì)". Later, it also refers to other places like "教室(jiàoshì)" (classroom) and "候车室 (hòuchēshì)" (waiting room).

The character "宫(gōng)" can also indicate the room people live in. But this character has long been used only for the place where emperors lived in. For example, the Imperial Palace and the palaces the queen and concubines lived in are mostly called "宫". However, there are many public places that can be called a palace nowadays such as ,"少年宫(shàonián gōng)"(youth palace) and "文化宫(wénhuàgōng)"(culture palace).

38. 路 road

lù
路

字源演变　The etymology of Chinese characters

金文　　　　　小篆　　　　楷体

1. 释义　Meaning

road; street (n.)

2. 书写　Writing

3. 相关词语或表达　Related words or expressions

(1) 路 lù　street

Wǒ jiā qiánbiān yǒu yī tiáo lù.
我家前边有一条路。There is a road in front of my house.

Wǒmen xuéxiào zài xuéyuàn lù èr shí wǔ hào.
我们学校在学院路 25 号。

Our school is on No.25 of Xue Yuan Road.

(2) 马路 mǎlù　road; street

Guò mǎlù yào xiǎoxīn.
过马路要小心。Look out when you're crossing the street.

汉语常用100字

gōnglù
公路　highway

(3) lùkǒu
路口　street intersection; crossroads

Qiánbiān yǒu ge lùkǒu.
前边　有　个　路口。There is one intersection ahead.

(4) zǒulù
走路　walk; go on foot (v.)

Tā zǒu lù huí jiā.
他 走 路回家。He walks home.

(5) xiànlù
线路　route（n.）

sān qī wǔ lù gōnggòng qìchē
375　路　公共　汽车 bus No. 375

4. 练习　Exercises

(1) 根据拼音写出相应的词或短语 Write down the corresponding words and expressions according to Pingyin

yì tiáo lù　　　（　　　）

lù kǒu　　　　（　　　）

guò mǎlù　　　（　　　）

zǒu lù　　　　（　　　）

(2) 看图写句子　Complete the sentences according to the pictures

① 小明家前边有_____。　② 前边有_____。

三、作名词的汉字 Characters as Nouns

③ _____要小心。

④ 我_____去教室。

5. 汉字知识　The knowledge of Chinese characters

　　　　　　常见的偏旁部首(11)　　足部

"足"的古字形是"🦶"，下部是脚的形状，上面的"口"形至今众说纷纭。有的说是膝盖的象形，两部分合起来正好是古代"足"所指的范围，即自膝盖到脚趾这一部分。带"足"部的字多表示脚或脚的动作，例如："跑"、"跳"、"踢"、"蹦"、"跟"。

"路"是一个形声字，左形右声。"足"作形旁表示"路"是脚走的，所以"路"的本义是"道路"，即来往的通道。此义稍引申，指"路程"，如"走了五里路"。由"路程"再引申出"路线"这一词义，如"坐8路公共汽车"。

Common Radicals and Indexing Radicals (11)　足

The ancient form of the character "足" which was written as "🦶" has a lower part that resembles a foot. But people still have different opinions about the "口" on the top. Some people say it stands for knee, so the two parts represent "足" in the old times. This covered the part from the knees to the toes. The characters with "足" are mostly related to the foot or activities of the foot such as "跑(pǎo)"(run), "跳(tiào)"(jump), "踢(tī)"(kick), "蹦(bèng)"(jump) and "跟(gēn)"(follow).

The character "路" is a pictophonetic character with the pictographic radical on the left and phonetic radical on the right. "足" as the pictographic radical indicates travelling on road by foot. The originally meaning of "路" thus is "道路(dàolù)" (road), i.e. passage for travel. The character can also mean "路程(lùchéng)" (distance to be covered). For example, "走了五里路" (travel 5 miles). We can also develop another meaning from the phrase "路程"—"路线(lùxiàn)" (route). For example, "坐8路公共汽车" (take bus No.8).

39. 店 shop

diàn
店

字源演变　The etymology of Chinese characters

楷体

1. 释义　Meaning

shop, store, hotel (n.)

2. 书写　Writing

3. 相关词语或表达　Related words or expressions

(1) shāngdiàn
　　商店 shop, store

　　Wǒ cháng qù nà jiā shāngdiàn mǎi dōngxi.
　　我　常　去那家　商店　买　东西。
　　I always go shopping in that store.

　　shūdiàn
　　书店　　　　book store

　　yàodiàn
　　药店　　　　pharmacy

　　huādiàn
　　花店　　　　flower shop

汉语常用100字

      yǎnjìngdiàn
      眼镜店   optical shop

      fàndiàn
(2) 饭店 hotel, restaurant

      Tā zhù zài Běijīng fàndiàn.
      他 住 在 北京 饭店。He is staying at the Beijing Hotel.

      Zhè ge fàndiàn de cài hěn hǎochī.
      这 个 饭店 的 菜 很 好吃。This restaurant has delicious food.

      lǚdiàn
      旅店   hotel

      Qǐng bāng wǒ zhǎo yī jiā lǚdiàn, hǎoma?
      请 帮 我 找 一家 旅店, 好吗?

      Please help me find a hotel, would you?

4. 练习 Exercises

(1) 回答问题 Answer the following questions

   ① 你去哪儿买东西?

      Where do you go shopping?

   ② 你去哪儿吃饭?

      Where do you have your meals?

   ③ 你去哪儿买书?

      Where do you buy books?

      lǚxíng
   ④ 旅行(travel)的时候, 你住在哪儿?

      Where do you live when you go on a trip?

   ⑤ 你在哪儿买药?

      Where do you get medicine?

   ⑥ 你常去哪儿买花?

      Where do you usually go to buy flowers?

三、作名词的汉字 Characters as Nouns

(2) 请写出下列各种商店的名称 Please write the names of the following stores

(　　　)　　　(　　　)　　　(　　　)

(　　　)　　　(　　　)　　　(　　　)

5. 汉字知识　The knowledge of Chinese characters
常见的偏旁部首(12)　广部

广部称为广字旁。它看上去好像房子的纵断面,其本义是房屋。早期人类只是模仿动物栖身于山洞或依树而构巢。"广"是这一阶段较为常见的人类居室类型。现在在黄土高原上还可见到的窑洞,应当是这种原始的建筑形式的孑遗。在造字的时候,由于这种建筑形式极为人们所熟悉,因此"广"也就被赋予了"房屋建筑"的意义。"广"作形旁的字多和房屋、殿堂有关。作偏旁的"广"的位置很固定,比如"店"、"床"、"庙"、"庵"、"府"、"库"、"座"等等。

"店"的"广"是形符,"占"为声符,其本义为放货物的房屋。

Common Radicals and Indexing Radicals (12)　广

"广" is also a radical called "广字旁(guǎnzìpáng)". It looks like the longtiudinal profile of a house, so it originally meant house. In early days, humans lived in caves or build their nests next to trees as animals did. "广" resembles the dwellings of humans at that time. Now we can still see caves in the Loess Plateau which may be traced back to the primitive constructions. In creating this character, "广" was given the meaning of "residence" because people are very familiar with this kind of construction. The characters with "广" as the pictographic radical are largely related to housing and palace. As a radical, it has a fixed position, such as "店(diàn)" (shop), "床(chuáng)"(bed), "庙(miào)"(temple), "庵(ān)"(nunnery), "府(fǔ)" (Official residence; seat of a government), "库(kù)"(warehouse) and "座(zuò)"(seat).

In the character "店", "广" serves as the pictographic radical while "占" as the phonetic radical. It originally means room for storing goods.

40. 车 vehicle

chē
车

字源演变　The etymology of Chinese characters

甲骨文　　　　小篆　　　　繁体　　　　楷体

1. 释义　Meaning

vehicle; bike; car; bus; train (n.)

2. 书写　Writing

3. 相关词语或表达　Related words or expressions

（1）chēliàng
　　 车辆 vehicle

　　 qìchē
　　 汽车 automobile

　　 jiàochē
　　 轿车 car

　　 diànchē
　　 电车 tram; trackless trolley

　　 kǎchē
　　 卡车 truck

　　 kèchē
　　 客车 bus; coach

汉语常用100字

huòchē
货车 van

mǎchē
马车 carriage

huǒchē
火车 train

zìxíngchē
自行车 bike

gōnggòng qìchē
公共　汽车 bus

chūzū qìchē
出租　汽车 taxi

kāi chē
(2) 开 车 to drive

sàichē
赛车 racing car

tíngchē
停车 to park

kuàichē
快车 express train or bus

mànchē
慢车 bus or passenger train that stops at every station along a route

zǎobānchē
早班车 morning train

mòbānchē
末班车 night train

yèchē
夜车 night train; work late into the night

Tā de gōngzuò hěn máng, chángcháng yào kāi yèchē. Zhǐ wǎnshàng bú
他的　工作　很忙，　常常　要开夜车。(指　晚上　不

shuìjiào (gōngzuò)
睡觉　工作) He is very busy. He often works late into the night.

liàng
(3) 辆　　(classifier)

yī liàng qìchē
一 辆 汽车 a car

yī liàng zìxíngchē
一　辆　自行车 a bicycle

三、作名词的汉字 Characters as Nouns

4. 练习　Exercises

（1）看图写出汉语，并加注拼音 Write down the corresponding Chinese expressions and their phonetic notations according to the pictures

_____

_____

_____

_____

_____

_____

汉语常用100字

5. 汉字知识　The knowledge of Chinese characters

常见的偏旁部首(13)　车部

　　车是陆地上的交通工具。古文字写成"车""󰀀"，"󰀀"等，画的都有马车的车轮、车轴和车厢。"车"在古代是重要的战斗工具，战车的多少成为一个国家强弱的标志。乘车人的身份不同，车子的级别也有很大差异。凡从"车"取义的字多与车辆有关。例如"轮"、"辆"、"轨"、"辙"、"轴"、"转"等。在生活中还有一些有轮子可以转动的东西我们也叫做"车"，比如"风车"、"水车"、"纺车"。

Common Radicals and Indexing Radicals (13)　车

　　"车" refers to vehicle on land. In its ancient form, it was written as "󰀀" or "󰀀" which depicted wheels, axles and the carriage of a cart. "车" is an important combat tool and its number reflects the strength of a country. The level of the complicacy of a cart changes with the rider's social status. The characters which derive their meanings from "车" are largely related to vehicles, such as "轮(lún)"(wheel), "辆(liàng)"(classifier for land vehicles), "轨(guǐ)"(rail), "辙(zhé)"(track of wheels), "轴(zhóu)"(axle) and "转(zhuàn)"(revolve). There are other things with rotating wheels called "车" also. For example, "风车(fēngchē)"(windmill), "水车(shuǐchē)"(water wagon)and "纺车(fǎngchē)"(spinning wheel).

四、作量词的汉字
Characters as Measure Words

41. 个 a measure word

gè
个

字源演变　The etymology of Chinese characters

繁体　　　　　楷体

1. 释义　Meaning

Classifier. (It is the most frequently used classifier in Chinese for people, places and most objects.)

2. 书写　Writing

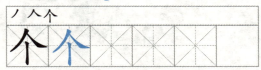

3. 相关词语或表达　Related words or expressions

yī ge rén
一 个 人　　　　a person

liǎng ge xuésheng
两 个 学生　　　two students

sān ge píngguǒ
三 个 苹果　　　three apples

汉语常用100字

<pre>
sì ge mántou
四个 馒头   four steamed breads

yī ge zì
一个 字   a character

yī ge yuè
一个 月   a month

wǔ ge xīngqī
五 个 星期   five weeks

yī ge jiā
一个 家   a family

yī ge guójiā
一个 国家   a country

yī ge dìfang
一个 地方   a place

Nǐ yǒu jǐ ge péngyou?
你 有 几个 朋友？   How many friends do you have?

Nǐmen bān yǒu duōshǎo ge xuésheng?
你们 班 有 多少 个 学生？
</pre>

How many students are there in your class?

4. 练习　Exercises

（1）看图片说出东西的数量 Say the numbers of the things in the pictures

这是＿＿＿包子。

这儿有＿＿＿人。

四、作量词的汉字 Characters as Measure Words

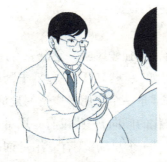

图上有_____人。　　　　一_____月有_____星期

(2) 读短文并回答问题 Read the following passage and answer question

我家有五口人,爸爸、妈妈、一个哥哥、一个妹妹和我。我们家还有一个小狗(xiǎogǒu dog),小狗每天要吃三个包子。我有一个好朋友,她常来我家,她喜欢吃苹果,今天就吃了两个。我们两个家庭(jiātíng family)很友好(yǒuhǎo friendly),常常一起玩。

问:

① 她家有几口人?

How many people are there in her family?

② 她有几个哥哥,几个妹妹?

How many elder brothers and younger sister does she have?

③ 她家有小狗吗? 有几个? 小狗每天吃几个包子?

Does she have dogs at home? How many? How many steamed buns do they have one day?

④ 今天她的好朋友吃了几个苹果?

How many apples does her best friend eat today?

⑤ 她们两个家庭怎么样?

How is the relationship between their two families?

5. 汉字知识　The knowledge of Chinese characters

量词

　　汉语的量词丰富多彩，在世界各种语言中独领风骚。它既有专用的，如"一本书"、"一匹马"，也有临时借用的，如"一桌菜"、"一包瓜子"，还有通用的，如"一种语言"、"一类学生"等。"个"是一个使用很广泛的量词，能够和它组合的名词越来越多，表现出通用化的倾向，一些没有专用量词的名词经常用它，如"一个人"、"一个想法"、"一个星期"。有专用量词的名词有时也用它。另外，它还表示单独，如"个人"、"个体"、"个案"。

Classifier

　　Chinese language abounds in classifier, more than all the other languages in the world. Some of the classifier are special, such as in the phrases "一本书(yī běn shū)" (a book) and "一匹马(yī pǐ mǎ)" (a horse). Some of them are borrowed temporarily, such as in the phrase "一桌菜(yī zhuō cài)" (a table of dishes) and "一包瓜子(yī bāo guāzǐ)" (a pack of melon seeds). Some others are for common use, such as "一种语言(yī zhǒng yǔyán)" (a language) and "一类学生(yī lèi xuésheng)" (a kind of students). "个" is used extensively and can be combined with increasingly more nouns. It tends to be used generally to add to the nouns without special classifiers. For example, "一个人(yī ge rén)" (a person), "一个想法(yī ge xiǎngfǎ)" (an idea) and "一个星期(yī ge xīngqī)" (a week). Some nouns with special classifier also use it. In addition, it also indicates being single. For example, "个人(gèrén)" (individual), "个体(gètǐ)" (single) and "个案(gè'àn)" (a case).

42. 件 piece

jiàn
件

字源演变　The etymology of Chinese characters

小篆　　　　　　楷体

1. 释义　Meaning

Classifier for items such as clothing, luggage, furniture, ect.

2. 书写　Writing

3. 相关词语或表达　Related words or expressions

(1)　yī jiàn dàyī
　　一件 大衣 an overcoat

　　liǎng jiàn xíngli
　　两　件 行李 two pieces of luggage

　　sān jiàn jiājù
　　三　件 家具 three pieces of furniture

　　yī jiàn shì
　　一件 事 a matter; a problem; an issue

(2)　wénjiàn
　　文件 official documents, letters, etc.

xìnjiàn
信件 letters

yóujiàn
邮件 mail

kuàijiàn
快件 (of postal service) express mail; express package

zhèngjiàn
(3) 证件 credentials, papers, certificate

Zuò fēijī de shíhou yào dài shàng zìjǐ de zhèngjiàn, rú shēnfènzhèng,
坐飞机的时候要带上自己的证件，如 身份证、

hùzhào děng.
护照 等。

When traveling by airplane, you must take your certificates with you, such as your identification card, passport, and etc.

4. 练习　Exercises

看图片认识和熟悉下列证件 Look at the pictures and get familiar with the following certificates

hùzhào
1. 护照 passport

Zhōngguó de shēnfènzhèng
2. 中国 的 身份证 Chinese identity card

xuéshengzhèng
3. 学生证 student ID

gōngzuòzhèng
4. 工作证 employee's card

四、作量词的汉字 Characters as Measure Words

5. 交通卡 jiāotōng kǎ traffic card

6. 驾驶证 jiàshǐzhèng driving license

5. 汉字知识　Knowledge of Chinese Characters

"件"字的起源与演变

　　按照古书《说文解字》中的解释，其本义是"分隔开"。这是因为"人"和"牛"在中国传统的文化观念中都是具有特殊地位。毋庸置疑，"人"是最能与其他生灵相区分的种类。与人的这种特有地位相似，"牛"在牲畜中的地位也同样最为特异，这是由它在古代社会中的地位作用决定的。它在农耕生产中成为人们最得力的助手，而农业生产又是当时人类社会存在的基础，因此，牛在古代社会中的地位要远远超过现代。同时，祭祀是古代社会中的头等大事，而牛则是古代用来祭祀的牲畜中等级最高的一种，这也大大提升了牛的地位。事物一经分别，往往也就具备可以计数的量，所以它终于演化为一个常见的量词也是在情理之中的。有形之物可以用"件"来数，如"一件衣服"，无形之事也可用"件"来算，如"一件事"。由于这个量词使用频率极高，它又干脆被人们用来表示——计算的事物本身，如"零件"、"配件"、"案件"、"文件"等等。

The Origin and Evolution of "件"

　　According to the explanation in the classic *SHUO WEN JIE ZI*, the original meaning of the character "件" was to distinguish human and cattle. Both have a special position in traditional Chinese culture. There is no doubt that humans are the most distinct from other living creatures. Corresponding to this uniqueness, cattle also occupy a special position within livestock because of their position and function in ancient society.

汉语常用100字

　　Meanwhile, sacrifice was a paramount event in ancient society and cattle were the highest level among the livestock for sacrifice. This also greatly improved the position of cattle. Things can be counted after they are distinguished. So the character "件" naturally developed into a common classifier for tangible and intangible things such as "一件衣服(yī jiàn yīfu)" (a piece of clothes) and "一件事(yī jiàn shì)" (a matter) respectively. Since this classifier is used most frequently, it is also used to indicate the things, which have to be counted separately, such as "零件(língjiàn)" (part), "配件(pèijiàn)" (fittings of machine), "案件(ànjiàn)" (case) and "文件 (wénjiàn)" (document).

43. 斤 jīn

字源演变　The etymology of Chinese characters

　甲骨文　　　　　金文　　　　　　小篆　　　　　楷体

1. 释义　Meaning

half kilo; unit of weight and 1 jin is equal to 500g

2. 书写　Writing

3. 相关词语或表达　Related words or expressions

yī jīn shuǐguǒ
一斤 水果　　　half kilo of fruit

yī jīn cài
一斤 菜　　　　half kilo of vegetable

yī jīn ròu
一斤 肉　　　　half kilo of meat

yī jīn jīdàn
一斤 鸡蛋　　　half kilo of egg

Wǒ yào mǎi yī jīn píngguǒ, liǎng jīn ròu, yī jīn jīdàn.
我 要 买一斤 苹果，两 斤 肉，一斤 鸡蛋。

I want to buy 0.5kg apples, 1kg meat and 0.5kg eggs.

汉语常用100字

Nǐ mǎi jǐ jīn cài?
你买几斤菜？How much vegetable would you like to buy?

Yī jīn jīdàn duōshao qián?
一斤鸡蛋多少钱？How much is the eggs per Jin?

Jīdàn duōshao qián yī jīn?
鸡蛋多少钱一斤？How much is the eggs per Jin?

gōngjīn
公斤　　　　kilogram

　gōngjīn　jīn　　kè
1公斤=2斤=1000克

kè
克　　　　　gram

4. 练习　Exercises

(1) 请按笔画顺序写出下面的汉字，并写出笔画数 Write down the Chinese characters in order of strokes and write down their numbers of strokes

斤(　　　　)

件(　　　　)

衣(　　　　)

水(　　　　)

男(　　　　)

个(　　　　)

元(　　　　)

家(　　　　)

年(　　　　)

几(　　　　)

四、作量词的汉字 Characters as Measure Words

(2) 当你在市场买下列东西时，试试自己问价钱 Try to ask about the prices of the following things when you go shopping in a market

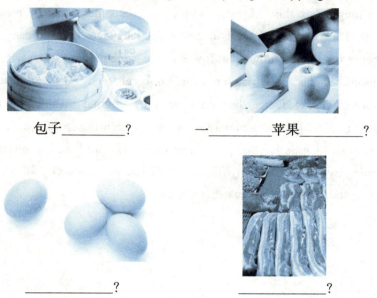

包子_____？　　　一_____苹果_____？

_____？　　　_____？

5. 汉字知识　The knowledge of Chinese characters

"斤"字的起源与演变

"斤"本来是一个象形字，甲骨文""像一把刃朝左的斧子。金文""是一把宽刃大斧。它是古代砍伐树木的一种工具，跟斧相似。在现代汉语中，这一原始的含义已经不用了，变成了表示重量的单位。这是为什么呢？实际上在最初的口语里已有了当重量讲的字，读音与"斤"相同，然而在笔下却没有这个字，所以就把"斤"字借来用上了。而"斤"字索性将自己的本义交给与它同义的"斧"字表示，自己专门表示重量单位。不过凡是从"斤"取义的字还是能看出与斧砍有关的意思，比如"斧"、"断"、"斩"、"折"等。

The Origin and Evolution of "斤"

The character "斤" primarily is a pictographic character. Its oracle inscription form looks like an axe with the edge in the left "". In bronze inscription form, "斤" was a broad axe. It resembles an axe and was used for chopping down trees in the ancient times. In Modern Chinese language, it no longer has this original meaning and becomes unit for measuring weight. The reason is in fact in colloquial language, there already was a character for expressing weight. It was of the same pronunciation with "斤", but it did not exist in written language. So the character "斤" was used as a substitute. The character thus transferred its original meaning to the its synonym "斧(fǔ)" (axe) and only serves as a measuring unit for weight. The characters which derive their meanings from "斤" all have the meaning of chopping by axe, such "斧(fǔ)" (axe), "断 (duàn)" (break), "斩 (zhǎn)" (cut off) and "折(zhé)" (break; fracture).

44. 米 meter

字源演变　The etymology of Chinese characters

甲骨文　　　　小篆　　　　楷体

1. 释义　Meaning

   meter; rice

2. 书写　Writing

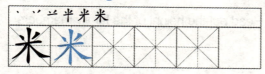

3. 相关词语或表达　Related words or expressions

   (1) meter

   　　mǐ　　　límǐ
   　1米=100厘米(cm)

   　Tā shēngāo yī mǐ bā wǔ.　　　huò
   　他　身高　一米　八　五。(1.85m 或 185cm)

   　He is 185 centimeters tall.

   (2) rice

   　大米

   　Wǒ mǎi wǔ jīn dàmǐ, yī jīn xiǎomǐ, zài yào liǎng jīn Tàiguó xiāngmǐ.
   　我　买　五斤　大米，一斤　小米，再要　两　斤　泰国　香米。

   　I want to buy 2.5kg rice, 0.5 kg millet and 1kg Thailand fragrant rice.

mǐfàn
米饭 cooked rice

Qǐng lái yī wǎn mǐfàn.
请 来一 碗 米饭。Please give me a bowl of rice.

mǐcù
米醋 rice vinegar

Wǒ yào mǎi yī píng mǐcù.
我 要 买 一 瓶 米醋。Give me a bottle of rice vinegar please.

mǐfěn
米粉 rice flour; rice-flour noodles

mǐjiǔ
米酒 rice wine

mǐsè
米色 cream-colored

Wǒ hěn xǐhuan zhè jiàn mǐsè de dàyī.
我 很 喜欢 这 件 米色 的大衣。

I like this cream-colored overcoat.

mǐ huáng sè
米 黄 色 beige; very light yellowish brown

4. 练习　Exercises

(1) 读出下面一家人的身高 Read out the height of the family members

yéye   mǐ
爷爷 1.74 米

nǎinai   mǐ
奶奶 1.58 米

bàba   mǐ
爸爸 1.80 米

māma   mǐ
妈妈 1.65 米

érzi   mǐ
儿子 1.87 米

nǚér   mǐ
女儿 1.73 米

四、作量词的汉字 Characters as Measure Words

（2）看图片写出汉字和拼音 Write down the corresponding names in Chinese and *pinyin* according to the pictures

1. _____   2. _____

3. _____   4. _____

5. 汉字知识　The knowledge of Chinese characters

常见的偏旁部首(14)　米部

"米"是一个象形字，甲骨文写作"米"，上下四个点儿像谷物的颗粒，"十"像谷物的秸秆，起衬托的作用。米字旁的字大多和粮食有关，比如"粉"字，左形右声，其本义是指化妆用的粉；"粗"的本义是还没经过加工的谷物；"精"则是经过筛选后不含杂物的纯米；"粒"的本义是一颗颗的谷物，现在经常作量词使用，用于粒状的东西，如"一粒米"。

Common Radicals and Indexing Radicals (14)　米

The character "米" is a pictographic character which is written as "米" in its oracle inscription form. The four dots at the top and the bottom look like grains and the "十" resembles a straw of cereals for holding the grains. The characters with "米" are largely related to food, such as the character "粉(fěn)" (powder). The left part serves as the pictographic radical while the right as the phonetic radical. And it originally referred to powder for make-up. "粗(cū)" primarily means unprocessed grains while "精(jīng)" refers to pure rice after sifting. "粒(lì)" originally meant grains. Now it is often used as a classifier for granular things, such as "一粒米" (a grain of rice).

45. 次 time

cì
次

字源演变 The etymology of Chinese characters

金文　　　　　小篆　　　　　楷体

1. 释义　Meaning

Classifier for occurrence; time

2. 书写　Writing

3. 相关词语或表达　Related words or expressions

yī cì huìyì
一次会议　　　　a meeting

dì yī cì
第一次　　　　　the first time

dì yī cì shìjiè dàzhàn
第一次 世界 大战　First World War

Zhè shì wǒ dì yī cì lái Zhōngguó.
这 是 我第一次来　中国。It's my first time to come to China.

shàng yī cì
上 （一）次　　　last time

zhè yī cì
这（一）次　　　this time

汉语常用100字

xià yī cì
下(一)次　　　　　next time

Wǒmen shàng cì jiàn miàn shì zài qùnián.
我们　上 次见 面　是 在　去年。Our last meeting was in last year.

Xià cì zài shuō.
下 次再　说。We can talk it later.

4. 练习　Exercises

(1) 大声朗读下面一段话，并想想它们的意思 Read aloud the following passage and think about the meanings

Wǒ dì yī cì lái Zhōngguó shì zài èr líng líng bā nián, zhè yī cì yǐjing
我 第一次来　中国　是在　2008　年，这 一 次 已经

shì dì sān cì lái le. Shàng yī cì wǒ shì lái lǚxíng de, zhè yī cì shì lái xuéxí
是 第 三 次来了。上 一次我 是 来 旅行 的，这 一 次是来 学习

Hànyǔ, wǒ xīwàng xià yī cì néng qù Shànghǎi kànkan.
汉语，我　希望　下一次　能 去　上海　看看。

(2) 选择填空 Insert the correct answer in the blanks

　　　件　　米　　个　　斤　　次

① 我去过三_____西安。

② 妈妈买了两_____肉。

③ 他的身高是一_____八。

④ 我喜欢这_____国家。

⑤ 这_____毛衣真漂亮(piàoliang beautiful)。

5. 汉字知识　The knowledge of Chinese characters

常用偏旁部首(15)　冫部

冫部称为"两点水"，它来源于"冰"。"冰"的篆书为"𣲃"，表示"零度以下的水凝结成的固体"。"冰"字左边的"冫"就是由"仌"隶变而来。因此带两点水的汉字大都表示寒冷之意，比如"冷"、"冻"、"凛"、"冽"等等。在写两点水的时候注意和三点水的区别。

四、作量词的汉字 Characters as Measure Words

Common Radicals and Indexing Radicals (15)　冫

冫 is called "两点水 (liǎng diǎn shuǐ)" (two drops of water). It originates from the character "冰(bīng)" (ice) which is written as "㳌" in its sealed character form, indicating water will freeze into solid when falls below zero degree. The left part of the character "冰" evolved from "仌". Therefore, the characters with two drops of water mostly indicate cold, such as "冷(lěng)" (cold), "冻(dòng)" (freezing), "凛(lǐn)" (cold) and "冽(liè)" (chilly). Pay attention to the difference between characters with two drops of water and the one with three drops of water in writing.

五、作动词的汉字 Characters as Verbs

46. 有 have

yǒu
有

字源演变 The etymology of Chinese characters

金文

小篆

楷体

1. 释义　Meaning

have, exist (v.)

2. 书写　Writing

一ナ才冇有有

有 有

3. 相关词语或表达　Related words or expressions

（1）have (v.)

Wǒ yǒu yī běn Zhōngwénshū.
我 有 一 本 中文书。I have a Chinese book.

Tā méiyǒu Zhōngwénshū.
他 没有 中文书。He doesn't have a Chinese book.

（2）exist; there is

Jiàoshì lǐ yǒu hěn duō zhuōzi.
教室 里 有 很 多 桌子。There're many desks in the classroom.

五、作动词的汉字 Characters as Verbs

    Xuéxiào pángbiān yǒu yī jiā shāngdiàn.
    学校　旁边　有一家　商店。There's a store by our school.

(3) indicator of degree, often used for measurements.

    Tā yǒu yī mǐ bā gāo le.
    他 有 一米 八 高 了。He is now 180 centimeters tall.

    Chángjiāng yǒu duōcháng?
    长江　　 有　多长？How long is the Changjiang river?

(4) used in comparative sentences to mean A is up to B.

    Tā yǒu māma nàme gāole.
    她 有　妈妈　那么　高了。She is as tall as her mother.

    Wǒ de Yīngyǔ méiyǒu gēge nàme hǎo.
    我 的　英语　没有　哥哥　那么　好。

    My English is not as good as my elder brother.

(5) indicate occurrence or emergence

    Àoyùnhuì zhīhòu, Běijīng yǒu le biànhuà.
    奥运会　 之后，北京　有了　变化。

    There are many changes in Beijing after the Olympics.

(6) one day

    yǒu yī tiān
    有 一天，…… One day, ...

(7) sometimes; at times; now and then

    yǒu shíhòu　　yǒu shíhòu
    有　时候……，有　时候…… Sometimes... and sometimes...

(8) somebody

    yǒu de rén　　yǒu de rén
    有　的人……，有　的人…… Some people ... and some people ...

4. 练习　Exercises

熟读下面的句子并记住它们的用法 Read aloud the following sentences and remember their usages

        Túshūguǎn lǐ yǒu hěn duō Hànyǔ shū.
(1) 图书馆　里有　很 多　汉语 书。

    There're a lot of Chinese books in the library.

       Wǒ yǒu yī ge xìngfú de jiā.
(2) 我　有 一个　幸福　的 家。

I have a happy family.

(3) 中国 有 很多 美丽的 地方。
Zhōngguó yǒu hěn duō měilì de dìfang.

There're a lot of beautiful places in China.

(4) 这 几年，北京 有了 很 大的 变化。
Zhè jǐ nián, Běijīng yǒu le hěn dà de biànhuà.

Great changes have taken place in Beijing in recent years.

(5) 我 汉语 学 得 没有 哥哥 那么 好。
Wǒ Hànyǔ xué de méiyǒu gēge nàme hǎo.

My Chinese is not as good as my elder brother.

(6) 刚 到 北京 我 没有 很 多 朋友。
Gāng dào Běijīng wǒ méiyǒu hěn duō péngyou.

I do not have many friends since I just arrive in Beijing.

(7) 学 汉语 的 时候 我 有 时候 写，有 时候 读。
Xué Hànyǔ de shíhou wǒ yǒu shíhòu xiě, yǒu shíhòu dú.

When learning Chinese, sometimes I write and the other time I read.

(8) 这些 苹果 有 三 斤 吗？
Zhèxiē píngguǒ yǒu sān jīn ma?

Are these apples 1.5 kg?

5. 汉字知识　The knowledge of Chinese characters

"有"字的介绍

"有"是一个会意字，古代汉字写作"𠂇"，上面是一只手，下面是一块肉，用手拿着一块肉，是"持有、占有"的意思。那时候能吃上肉也是一种比较富有的表现。

"有"的用法越来越多，也可以表示拥有、具有等含义。有形的东西可以说有，无形的东西也可以说有，如"有时间"、"有脾气"、"有意思"等等。

The Introduction of Character "有"

The character "有" is an associative compound character which was written as "𠂇" in ancient Chinese. The top part is a hand and the lower part is a piece of meat. Holding a piece of meat by hand suggests the meaning of "possessing and taking". Back then, having meat to eat indicates wealth.

五、作动词的汉字 Characters as Verbs

With increasing usages of "有" and it also expresses the meaning of having and possessing. It can be used for tangible things as well as intangible things, such as "有时间(yǒu shíjiān)" (have time), "有脾气(yǒu píqi)" (have a bad temper) and "有意思(yǒu yìsi)" (interesting).

47. 是 be

shì
是

字源演变   The etymology of Chinese characters

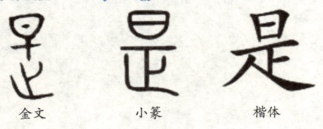

金文   小篆   楷体

1. 释义   Meaning

Used like "be" before nouns or pronouns to identify, describe or amplify the subject; used after a noun to indicate position or existence. (v.)

2. 书写   Writing

3. 相关词语或表达   Related words or expressions

        zhǔ yǔ shì míng
(1) 主 语+是+ 名

Wǒ shì Zhōngguó rén.
我 是   中国 人。I am Chinese.

Zhè běn shū de zuòzhě shì/bùshì Lǔ Xùn.
这 本 书 的 作者 是/不是 鲁迅。
The writer of this book is/is not Lu Xun.

Wǒ jiā qiánbiān shì yī jiā shūdiàn.
我 家 前边   是 一家 书店。
There's a bookstore in front of my house.

五、作动词的汉字 Characters as Verbs

(2) 是……的 It is used to emphasize the doer, time, place, manner in the occurrence of the event.

Zhè běn shū shì shuí de?　　Shì wǒ de.
这 本 书 是 谁 的?——是 我 的。

Whose book is this? —It's mine.

Nǐ shì shénme shíhou lái de?　　Wǒ shì zuótiān lái de.
你 是 什么 时候 来 的?——我 是 昨天 来 的。

When did you come? —I came here yesterday.

Nǐ shì cóng nǎlǐ lái de?　　Wǒ shì cóng Shāndōng lái de.
你 是 从 哪里 来 的?——我 是 从 山东 来 的。

Where are you from? —I come from Shangdong province.

Nǐ shì zěnme lái de?　　Wǒ shì zuò fēijī lái de.
你 是 怎么 来 的?——我 是 坐飞机 来 的。

How did you get here? —I came here by plane.

4. 练习　Exercises

(1) 熟读下面的句子并记住它们的用法 Get familiar with the following sentences and remember their usages

Wǒ shì xuésheng, tā shì lǎoshī.
我 是 学生，他 是 老师。

I'm a student and he's a teacher.

Tāmen dōu shì Zhōngguó rén.
他们 都 是 中国 人。

They are all Chinese.

Wǒ jiā hòubiān shì yìjiā shāngdiàn.
我 家 后边 是 一家 商店。

There's a store behind my house.

Zhè shì wǒ de shū.
这 是 我 的 书。

This is my book.

Tā shì qùnián lái Zhōngguó de.
他 是 去年 来 中国 的。

He came to China last year.

(2) 选择填空 Insert the correct answer in the blanks

有　　　　是

① 我_____两个哥哥。

② 他_____中国人。

③ 这_____我的衣服。

④ 我没_____很多朋友。

⑤ 他不_____老师。

5. 汉字知识　The knowledge of Chinese characters

"是"字的相关知识

"是"的小篆写作"昰",由"日"和"正"上下组合而成,是一个会意字。它是怎样会意的呢?古代的文字学家解释说:天下万物,日是最正直的。仔细想想,也确有道理。比如"是非"中的"是"就表示"正确的"。

在现代汉语中,"是"是一个很常用的判断词。在书面语中还保留了少量的文言用法,如"共商国是"("国是"即国家大计,与"国事"有别)。

Knowledge about the Character "是"

The character "是" is written as "昰" in sealed character form. It is an associative compound character with "日(rì)(the sun)" on the top and "正(zhèng)" (upright) at the bottom. How did the meaning get combined? Ancient linguists explained: for all the things, the Sun is the most upright one. It does stand to reason after careful consideration. For example, "是" in "是非(shìfēi)"(right and wrong) just means correct.

In modern language "是" is a common defining word. It retains some classical Chinese usages in modern written Chinese. For example, "共商国是"("国是" means national strategy, which differs from "国事"—national affairs).

48. 听 listen

tīng
听

字源演变　The etymology of Chinese characters

繁体

楷体

1. 释义　Meaning

listen to; hear (v.)

2. 书写　Writing

3. 相关词语或表达　Related words or expressions

（1）verb.

tīng gēqǔ
听 歌曲　　　listen to songs

tīng shōuyīnjī
听 收音机　　listen to the radio

tīng kè
听 课　　　 attend a lecture

tīng jiǎng
听 讲　　　 listen to a talk; attend a lecture

（2）verb.＋complement

tīngjiàn　tīngdào
听见 （听到）　hear

汉语常用100字

Wǒ tīngjiàn tā shuō huà le.
我 听见 他 说 话 了。I heard his words.

tīngdǒng
听懂 understand

Tā shuō de huà wǒ tīngdǒng le.
他 说 的 话 我 听懂 了。I understood his words.

tīng de jiàn
听 得 见 can hear

tīng bu jiàn
听 不 见 cannot hear

Nǐ shuō huà de shēngyīn tài xiǎo le, wǒ tīng bu jiàn.
你 说 话 的 声音 太 小 了,我 听 不 见。
Your voice is too low and I cannot hear you.

Shēngyīn hěn dà, wǒ tīngjiàn le, kěshì hěn nán, wǒ tīng bu dǒng.
声音 很 大,我 听见 了,可是 很 难,我 听 不 懂。
The sound was quite loud. I heard it, but it is too difficult to understand.

tīng dé dǒng
听 得 懂 can understand

Wǒ jiǎng de nǐ néng tīngdǒng ma? Lǎoshī jiǎng de hěn qīngchu, wǒ tīng
我 讲 的你 能 听懂 吗? 老师 讲 的 很 清楚,我 听

de dǒng.
得 懂。 Can you follow me? —It is quite clear. I can get it.

(3) noun.

tīnglì
听力 hearing (ability); aural comprehension(in language teaching)

tīngjué
听觉 sense of hearing;

tīngtǒng
听筒 (telephone) receiver; head-phone; earphone

tīngzhòng
听众 audience; listeners

(4) classifier

Wǒ mǎi le yī tīng kěkǒukělè, hái mǎi le liǎng tīng Běijīng píjiǔ.
我 买 了一 听 可口可乐,还 买 了 两 听 北京 啤酒。
I bought a can of Coca Cola and two cans of Beijing beer.

五、作动词的汉字 Characters as Verbs

4. 练习　Exercises

(1) 用"听"完成句子 Complete the sentences with "听"

① 他的 汉语 说 得太 快 了，我 听_____。
　　Tā de Hànyǔ shuō de tài kuài le, wǒ tīng

② 电话 的 声音 太小 了，我 听_____。
　　Diànhuà de shēngyīn tàixiǎo le, wǒ tīng

③ 唱　中国　歌 也可以 学　中文，所以 我　常常　在
　　Chàng Zhōngguó gē yě kěyǐ xué Zhōngwén, suǒyǐ wǒ chángcháng zài
　　家里 听_____。
　　jiālǐ tīng

④ 老师　讲　的话 你都 听_____ 吗？
　　Lǎoshī jiǎng de huà nǐ dōu tīng　　　ma?

⑤ 在_____课 上，我们 老师会 让 我们 练习发音。
　　Zài　　　　kè shàng, wǒmen lǎoshī huì ràng wǒmen liànxí fāyīn.

(2) 用有关听的词语回答下列问题 Answer the following questions with words for listening

① 你 每天 能 听懂 老师 讲课 吗？
　　Nǐ měitiān néng tīngdǒng lǎoshī jiǎng kè ma?
　　Can you understand the lessons of the teachers every day?

② 你 在 电梯里 能 听清 手机里的 说 话 声音 吗？
　　Nǐ zài diàntī lǐ néng tīngqīng shǒujī lǐ de shuō huà shēngyīn ma?
　　Can you hear the voice in your cellphone clearly when you are in an elevator?

③ 你 能 听见 邻居 看 电视 的 声音 吗？
　　Nǐ néng tīngjiàn línjū kàn diànshì de shēngyīn ma?
　　Can you hear the sound of your neighbor's television?

④ 你 汉语 的 听力 水平 怎么样？
　　Nǐ Hànyǔ de tīnglì shuǐpíng zěnmeyàng?
　　How's your Chinese listening ability?

⑤ 应该 怎样 保护 小孩子 的 听力？
　　Yīnggāi zěnyàng bǎohù xiǎoháizi de tīnglì?
　　How should we protect the hearing of kids?

5. 汉字知识　The knowledge of Chinese characters

"听"与"闻"

小篆的"听"字用"䎽"代表发出的声音为"耳"所闻。它的意思也就是"声音入耳"。只是后来随着时间的推移,"耳"旁讹变成了"斤"旁。另外一个表示听的字是"闻",但"闻"是听到、听清的意思,而"听"只是个动作。比如中医的诊断方法就是"望、闻、问、切"。

"听" and "闻"

The sealed character form of the character "听" is written as "䎽" which signifies that the sound we make is heard by "耳(ěr)" (ear). It means sound going into ears. However, with the passage of time, "耳" radical was corrupted and became "斤" radical. The other character which also indicates listening is "闻(wén)". But "闻" means hear something clearly while "听" is simply an action. For example, the diagnostic methods of traditional Chinese medicine is "望(wàng)", "闻(wén)", "问(wèn)" and "切(qiè)" (look, listen, question and feel the pulse).

49. 说 say

shuō
说

字源演变 The etymology of Chinese characters

小篆　　　　　繁体　　　　　楷体

1. 释义　Meaning

say, speak (v.)

2. 书写　Writing

3. 相关词语或表达　Related words or expressions

shuō huà
说 话　say, speak, talk

Tā bù xǐhuan shuōhuà.
他不 喜欢 说话。He doesn't like to talk.

Bié shuō huà, háizi gāng shuìzháo.
别 说 话，孩子 刚 睡着。Keep quiet, the kids just fell asleep.

shuō　yǔ
说……语

shuō Hànyǔ
说 汉语　　　speak Chinese

shuō Yīngyǔ
说 英语　　　speak English

汉语常用100字

shuō Rìyǔ
说 日语　　　　　speak Japanese

shuō Fǎyǔ
说 法语　　　　　speak French

Tā huì shuō Hànyǔ, Yīngyǔ, Rìyǔ, bù huì shuō Fǎyǔ.
他 会 说 汉语、英语、日语，不 会 说 法语。
He can speak Chinese, English and Japanese, but he cannot speak French.

shuō yi shuō
说 一 说　　　　say a few words

Qǐng nǐ shuō yi shuō nǐ de àihào.
请 你 说一 说 你的 爱好。
Please say a few words about your hobbies.

shuō yīxiàr
说 一下儿　　　　say a few words

Nǐmen yǒu shénme jiànyì, qǐng shuō yīxiàr.
你们 有 什么 建议，请 说 一下儿。
If you have any suggestion, please say it.

4. 练习　Exercises

（1）看拼音写出下列词和短语并记住它们的意思 Write down the words and expressions in Chinese according to *pinyin* and remember their meanings

shuō huà　　（　　）　　shuō yi shuō（　　）

shuō Yīngyǔ　（　　）　　shuō Fǎyǔ　（　　）

shuō Hànyǔ　（　　）　　shuō Rìyǔ　（　　）

shuō yíxià'r　（　　）

（2）用上边学习过的词和短语完成句子 Complete the sentences with the words and expressions learned in this lesson

① 去年我去日本了，可是我不会_____。

② 请_____你的名字，好吗？

③ 我要多练习_____，因为我要在中国工作。

④ 我想休息一下儿，请你们别_____了，好吗？

⑤ 请你们_____你们的家庭。

五、作动词的汉字 Characters as Verbs

5. 汉字知识　The knowledge of Chinese characters
常见的偏旁部首(16)　言部

"言"的甲骨文是在"舌"的上面加了一横"🐚",表示从口中,由舌头发出的声音。凡是用"言"作偏旁的字多和说话有关。言字旁在左侧时写作"讠"。比如"话"、"讲"、"语"、"诉"、"谢"、"请"、"让"、"谁"等等。再比如,"认识"一个人当然要从跟他讲话开始了。

Common Radicals and Indexing Radicals (16)　言

The character "言" is written as "🐚" in oracle inscription form. It adds a horizontal stroke on top of "舌" indicating that sound is made by tongue in mouth. The characters with "言" are mostly related to speaking. When it is on the left, it is written as "讠", such as "话(huà)"(word), "讲 (jiǎng)" (speak), "语(yǔ)"(language), "诉(sù)"(tell), "谢(xiè)"(thank), "请(qǐng)" (please), "让 (ràng)"(let) and "谁(shuí)"(who). Here is another example: "认识(rènshi)" (knowing) someone starts by talking with him/her.

50. 看 look

kàn
看

字源演变　The etymology of Chinese characters

小篆　　　　　楷体

1. 释义　Meaning

look; see (v.)

另：看 kān look after; take care of

2. 书写　Writing

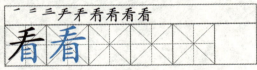

3. 相关词语或表达　Related words or expressions

(1) 看+noun.
　　kàn
　　
　　kàn shū
　　看 书 read (a book)
　　
　　kàn diànshì
　　看 电视 watch TV
　　
　　kàn diànyǐng
　　看 电影 see a film; go to the movies
　　
　　kàn
　　看+complement

五、作动词的汉字 Characters as Verbs

kànjiàn
看见 catch sight of; see

kàn de/bù jiàn
看 得/不 见 can see; cannot see

kàndǒng
看懂 understand

kàn de/bù dǒng
看 得/不 懂 can or cannot understand

kànshàng
看上 take a fancy to; settle on

Wǒ qù shāngchǎng de shíhou kàn shàng le yī jiàn hóngsè de yīfu.
我 去 商场 的 时候 看 上 了一件 红色 的衣服。

I was attracted by a red dress in the shopping mall.

dòngcíchóngdié
动词重叠 (Duplication of the verb is a colloquial speech pattern, indicating the action takes place within a short time)

kànkan
看看 have a quick look

kàn yi kàn
看 一看 have a quick look

kàn yīxiàr
看一下儿 have a quick look

kàn bìng
(2) 看 病 (of a patient)to see a doctor;(of a doctor)see a patient

Wǒ gǎn mào le, xiàwǔ qù yīyuàn kàn bìng.
我 感 冒 了,下午 去 医院 看 病。

I'm going to see a doctor tomorrow.

kàn péngyou
(3) 看 朋友 to visit a friend

kànwàng
看望 call on; visit; see

Jiàoshījié de shíhou wǒ huì qù kànwàng wǒ de lǎoshī.
教师节 的 时候 我 会去 看望 我的 老师。

I will visit my professor in Teacher's Day.

kàn
(4) 看着 zhe

Nǐ kàn zhe wǒ jiāo nǐ huà.
你看 着 我 教 你 画。

You watch while I show you how to paint this.

kān zhe
看 着 look after; take care of; tend

Nǐ kān zhe háizi, wǒ qù zuò fàn.
你看 着孩子,我去 做饭。
Keep an eye on the kids while I cook the dinner.

4. 练习　Exercises

(1) 看拼音写出下列词语并记住它们的意思 Write down the words and expressions in Chinese according to *pinyin* and remember their meanings

kān jiā　　　　　　　kàn shū

kànbujiàn　　　　　　kànwàng

kànzhe　　　　　　　kànjiàn

kànshang　　　　　　kànbìng

(2) 解释下列句子中"看"的意思 Explain the meaning of "看" in the following sentences

　Wǒ māma bù zài jiā, tā qù kàn wǒ lǎolao qù le.
①我 妈妈不 在家,她去看 我 姥姥 去了。　　(　　)

　Nǐ kànshàng nà tái diànnǎo le, nà shì xiànzài zuì hǎo de.
②你 看上　那台 电脑 了,那是 现在 最好 的。(　　)

　Kàn yi kàn zhè dào tí, nǐ kàndedǒng ma?
③看一看 这 道题,你 看得 懂 吗?　　　　　(　　)

　Tā de yǎnjing bù hǎo, tā qù yīyuàn kàn yǎnjing qù le.
④他 的 眼睛不 好,他去 医院 看 眼睛 去了。(　　)

　Nǐ kān zhe háizi, wǒ qù mǎi cài.
⑤你看 着孩子,我 去 买 菜。　　　　　　　(　　)

5. 汉字知识　The knowledge of Chinese characters
　　　　　　常见的偏旁部首(17)　 目部

　　古汉字的"目"字,就好像一个人的眼睛的形状"⌒⌒",因此"目"字作形旁的字也多和眼睛或者动作"看"有关,比如"瞧"、"看"、"睡"、"瞪"、

五、作动词的汉字 Characters as Verbs

"盯"等。"目"字作形旁多半在左侧。

"看"的小篆写作"看",就像一个人把手搭在眼睛上四处观望,至今人们向远处看去时还往往使用这种动作。"相"字与"看"意思有共同之处,是更仔细地看,如"相面"、"相亲"。甲骨文的"相"写作" ",像是人的眼睛观看树木的样子,其本义是指观察事物的外表来判断它的好坏。

Common Radicals and Indexing Radicals (17) 目

"目" in ancient Chinese characters resembles the shape of a person's eye " " signifying the eye. Thus the characters with "目" as the pictographic radical are largely related to eyes or the action of looking, such as "瞧(qiáo)"(look)、"看(kàn)"(look;see)、"睡(shuì)"(sleep)、"瞪(dèng)" (glare) and "盯(dīng)"(stare). As the pictographic radical, "目" is always on the left.

The character "看" was written as " " in sealed character, which looks like a person who is looking around with his hand cupped above this eyes. Until now, people still do this when looking afar. "相(xiàng)" has some overlapping with "看" in meaning, but it refers to more careful observation. For example, "相面(xiàng miàn)"(tell fortune by reading facial features) and "相亲(xiāng qīn)"(blind date). It is written as " " in oracle inscription form. It resembles the eye of a person that is looking at a tree. It originally meant judging something by its appearance.

51. 吃 eat

chī
吃

字源演变　The etymology of Chinese characters

小篆　　　　　　楷体

1. 释义　Meaning

eat (v.)

2. 书写　Writing

3. 相关词语或表达　Related words or expressions

chī fàn
吃 饭 have one's meals

chī zǎofàn
吃 早饭 have breakfast

chī bāozi
吃 包子 eat dumplings

chī wǔfàn
吃 午饭 have lunch

chī mǐfàn
吃 米饭 eat rice

chī wǎnfàn
吃 晚饭 have dinner

chī miàntiáo
吃 面条 eat noodle

Wǒ měitiān chī sān dùn fàn, zǎofàn chī bāozi, wǔfàn chī mǐfàn, wǎnfàn chī
我 每天 吃 三 顿 饭，早饭 吃 包子，午饭 吃 米饭，晚饭 吃

miàntiáo.
面条。

五、作动词的汉字 Characters as Verbs

I have three meals a day: steamed bun for breakfast, rice for lunch and noodle for dinner.

chī shuǐguǒ
吃 水果 eat fruit

chī píngguǒ
吃 苹果 eat an apple

chī pútao
吃 葡萄 eat grapes

chī xiāngjiāo
吃 香蕉 eat a banana

chī xīguā
吃 西瓜 eat watermelon

　　　Nǐ xǐhuan chī shénme shuǐguǒ?
——你 喜欢 吃 什么 水果？What fruit would you like?

　　　Wǒ xǐhuan chī píngguǒ hé xiāngjiāo.
——我 喜欢 吃 苹果 和 香蕉。I like apple and banana.

chī cài
吃 菜 have dish

Nǐ xiǎng chī shénme cài? Māma gěi nǐ zuò.
你 想 吃 什么 菜？妈妈 给 你 做。

What dishes would you like to have? Let Mom cook for you.

chī yào
吃 药 take medicine

Nǐ bìng le, yīnggāi chī yào.
你 病 了，应该 吃 药。You are sick. You need to take some medicine.

4. 练习　Exercises

(1) 把下列短语与其相对应的拼音连线 Link the corresponding pronunciations and meanings of words and expressions

吃饭　　　　　　chī mǐfàn

吃饺子　　　　　chī píngguǒ

吃面条　　　　　chī yào

吃药　　　　　　chī xīguā

吃苹果　　　　　chī jiǎozi

吃西瓜　　　　　chī cài

吃菜　　　　　　chī miàntiáo

吃米饭　　　　　chī fàn

汉语常用100字

(2) 你喜欢吃什么饭？什么水果？什么菜？请在下边写一写，写得越多越好，可以模仿给出的句式来写 What would you like for dinner? What fruit would you like? What dishes would you prefer? Write down as much as possible, and you can follow the given sentence pattern

Fàn wǒ xǐhuan chī
饭，我 喜欢 吃……

①
②
③

Shuǐguǒ, wǒ xǐhuan chī
水果， 我 喜欢 吃……

①
②
③

Cài, wǒ xǐhuan chī
菜，我 喜欢 吃……

①
②
③

(3) 读短文并回答问题 Read the passage and answer questions

中国人一般一天吃三顿饭，早饭、午饭和晚饭。早饭 年轻人(niánqīngrén)（young people）常常吃面包(miànbāo)(bread)或包子，老人有时吃 面条(miàntiáo)(noodles)。午饭一般吃米饭和菜。晚饭常常在家吃，所以吃得比较多。有的人吃菜、米饭或者馒头(mántou)(steamed bun)，有的人吃面条，有的人吃饺子(jiǎozi)(dumpling)。水果一般也是晚饭以后吃，因为晚上有时间。

194

五、作动词的汉字 Characters as Verbs

问题：
① 中国人一般一天吃几顿饭？
② 早饭年轻人吃什么？
③ 晚饭常常在哪儿吃？
④ 水果一般什么时候吃？

5. 汉字知识　The knowledge of Chinese characters
常见的偏旁部首(18)　口部

我们知道古文字中的"口"字的形状就好像人或者动物的嘴"ᄇ"，因此以"口"为偏旁的字多与口的形状、动作、功能有关，比如"嘴"、"叫"、"喊"、"唱"、"吹"、"咬"、"咳"、"哑"、"响"等。"吃"的本义为"说话不流畅"，如"口吃"。口字旁大都在字的左侧或下面，在左侧时写得小一点。在下面的，比如"告"、"哲"等字。甲骨文的"告"字是"牛"和"口"的组合"ᄇ"，因为上古时代常常杀牛以祭告，后来引申为"告示"、"报告"等义。

Common Radicals and Indexing Radicals (18)　口

We know that in ancient characters "口(kǒu)" is shaped like the mouth of a person or an animal "ᄇ", so the characters with "口" as radical are all connected with shape, action or the function of mouth. For example, "嘴(zuǐ)"(mouth), "叫(jiào)"(cry), "喊(hǎn)"(shout), "唱(chàng)"(sing), "吹(chuī)"(blow), "咬(yǎo)"(bite), "咳(ké)"(cough), "哑(yǎ)"(mute) and "响(xiǎng)" (loud). "吃" originally means "unable to speak fluently", such as "口吃(kǒuchī)"(stutter). "口" is often on the left or at the bottom. When it is on the left, it should be written relatively smaller. It can also be placed at the bottom as in the character "告(gào)"(inform) and "哲"(zhé)(wise). The oracle inscription form of the character "告" is combined by "牛(niú)" (cattle) and "口(kǒu)"(mouth) written as "ᄇ". This is because in the remote antiquity, people often used cattle as sacred offerings. The character later extended to mean announcement and report.

52. 喝 drink

hē
喝

字源演变　The etymology of Chinese characters

小篆　　　　楷体

1. 释义　Meaning

drink; drink alcoholic liquor (v.)

2. 书写　Writing

3. 相关词语或表达　Related words or expressions

hē shuǐ
喝水 drink water

hē kuàngquánshuǐ
喝 矿泉水 drink mineral water

hē kěkǒukělè
喝 可口可乐 drink coca cola

hē kāfēi
喝 咖啡 have coffee

hē chá
喝 茶 drink tea

五、作动词的汉字 Characters as Verbs

hē nǎi
喝 奶 drink milk

hē guǒzhī
喝 果汁 drink juice

hē yǐnliào
喝 饮料 drink beverage

Nǐ xiǎng hē shénme yǐnliào?
你 想 喝 什么 饮料？What drinks would you like?

hē jiǔ
喝酒 drink alcoholic liquor

hē zhōu
喝 粥 have porridge

Zhōngguó rén chī zǎofàn hěn xǐhuan hē zhōu.
中国 人 吃 早饭 很 喜欢 喝 粥。

The Chinese prefer to have conjee for breakfast.

hē yào
喝 药 drink medicine

4. 练习　Exercises

(1) 你喜欢喝什么饮料？什么酒？什么茶？请在下边写一写，写得越多越好，可以模仿给出的句式来写 What drinks would you like? What kind of alcohol would you like? What kind of tea would you prefer? Write down as much as possible, and you can follow the given sentence pattern

饮料，我喜欢喝……

①

②

③

酒，我喜欢喝……

①

②

③

茶，我喜欢喝……

①

②
③

（2）阅读短文并回答问题 Read the passage and answer questions

中国是酒的故乡，酿酒的历史也非常久远。酒的种类很多，有白酒、米酒、葡萄酒、啤酒等等。人们喜欢喝酒是因为喝酒的时候，大家一边喝酒一边聊天，人很放松，很高兴；人们还常常通过喝酒交朋友，中国人在喝酒的时候很喜欢干杯，感情越好，越高兴，越要多喝几杯。在中国，北方人喜欢喝白酒；南方人喜欢喝米酒；浪漫的年轻人和老年人则喜欢喝葡萄酒。

China is a birthplace for alcoholic drinks and it has a very long history in making them. There are a variety of alcohol in China including liquor, rice wine, wine and beer. People like to drink because they feel relaxed and happy when drinking and chatting together. People often make friends through drinking and they like to make toasts. The amount of drink they have will increase with the level of the friendship and the fun they have in drinking. In China, the northern Chinese prefer liquor while the southern Chinese prefer rice wine. Romantic young people and the seniors prefer wine.

问题：
① 请举例说说中国有什么种类的酒。
② 人们为什么喜欢喝酒？
③ 北方人喜欢喝什么酒？

五、作动词的汉字 Characters as Verbs

④ 南方人喜欢喝什么酒？
⑤ 老年人喜欢喝什么酒？

5. 汉字知识　The knowledge of Chinese characters

"喝"与"饮"

"喝"是一个形声字，左形右声。其本义是指"声音嘶哑"。现在有两个读音，一个是"hē"，另一个是"hè"，意思是"大声喊叫"，如"喝彩"。

在写这个汉字的时候需要注意的是它的右上边是矮胖的"曰"字，而不是瘦高的"日"字。

另外一个与"喝水"的"喝"同义的是"饮"字，其古文字就是一个低着头，张着大口，伸着舌头对着左下角的酒容器喝酒的形状🍶。"饮"原为动词，但在"冷饮"、"饮料"中就是名词了。

"喝" and "饮"

The character "喝" is a pictophonetic character with pictographic radical on the left and phonetic radical on the right. It originally means hoarse and choking voice. It now has two pronunciations: "hē" and "hè". It means shouting aloud, such as "喝彩(hècǎi)" (cheering).

When writing the character, you have to pay attention that the right part is a stocky "曰" instead of slim and tall "日".

The character "饮(yǐn)" shares the same meaning with "喝" in the phrase "喝水" (drink water). Its ancient form looks like a person who is drinking wine from a container placed in the left corner with his mouth wide open and tongue sticking out. "🍶". "饮" is a verb, but it can also be a noun. For example, in the phrases "冷饮(lěngyǐn)" (cold drink) and "饮料(yǐnliào)" (soft drink).

53. 做 do

zuò
做

字源演变　The etymology of Chinese characters

楷体

1. 释义　Meaning

do; make; be; become; cook (v.)

2. 书写　Writing

ノ 亻 个 仁 什 什 估 估 估 做 做 做
做 做

3. 相关词语或表达　Related words or expressions

(1) zuòshì
　　做事　　handle affairs

Tā zuò shì hěn rènzhēn.
他 做 事 很 认真。He works conscientiously.

zuò zuoyè
做 作业　do homework

Wǒ měitiān wǎnshang zuò zuoyè.
我 每天 晚上 做 作业。I do homework every night.

zuò shénme
做 什么　what (are you/is he/she/are they) doing

Nǐ zài zuò shénme?　Wǒ zài kàn diànshì.
你 在 做 什么?——我 在 看 电视。

五、作动词的汉字 Characters as Verbs

What are you doing?—I am watching TV.

Zuò shénme gōngzuò?
做　什么　工作？　What's your job?

Nǐ bàba zuò shénme gōngzuò?　　　Tā shì lǎoshī.
你爸爸　做　什么　工作？——他 是 老师。
What is your father's line of work?—He is a teacher.

zuò fàn
(2) 做 饭　　cooking

Māma zuò fàn zuò de hěn hǎochī.
妈妈　做饭　做得　很　好吃。My mother is very good at cooking.

zuò yīfu
(3) 做 衣服　　make clothes

Wǒ xiǎng qù zuò yī jiàn yīfu.
我　想 去 做一件衣服。I want to have a suit made.

zuò lǎoshī/dàifu/lǎobǎn
(4) 做 老师/大夫/老板……　　to be a teacher

zuò māma/bàba/yéye
做　妈妈/爸爸/爷爷……　to be a mother/father/grandpa

Wǒ juéde zuò lǎoshī tǐng hǎo de.
我 觉得 做 老师　挺 好 的。I think it is good to be a teacher.

Tā jiù yào zuò māma le.
她 就要　做　妈妈了。She is going to be a mother.

4. 练习　**Exercises**

(1) 选择填空 Insert the correct answer in the blanks

　　听　说　看　吃　喝　做

　　　　　　　　　yǐnliào
① 妹妹喜欢_____饮料（soft drinks）。

② 哥哥常_____电视。

③ 我每天_____作业。

　　Hánguórén
④ 韩国人（Korean）喜欢_____米饭。

⑤ 爸爸不喜欢_____话。

　　　　　　　yīnyuè
⑥ 你喜欢_____音乐（music）吗？

（2）仿照下列形式看图说话 Talk about the pictures in the form of the given example

例：
  A：她在做什么呢？
  B：她在做饭呢。

1. A：她在_____呢？
  B：她在_____呢。

2. A：她在_____呢？
  B：她在_____呢。

例：
  A：她做什么工作？
  B：她是老师。

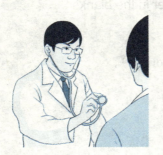

3. A：他_____？
  B：他是_____。

五、作动词的汉字 Characters as Verbs

5. 汉字知识　The knowledge of Chinese characters

常见的偏旁部首(19)　亻

"亻"称为单人旁或单立人。作形旁的字多和人或人的活动有关系，例如："他"、"你"、"们"、"位""做"、"作"、"代"、"保"等等。比如"休"字在甲骨文中写作"㑺"，很像一个人倚靠大树的样子。它是一个会意字，其本义就是歇息的意思。更有意思的是"保"字。在古文字中，"保"字是一个大人背着一个小孩的形象"㑂"，由此便引申出"保护"之意。

Common Radicals and Indexing Radicals (19)　亻

" 亻 " is called single person radical or standing person radical. The characters with it are largely related to people or the activities of people, such as "他(tā)" (he), "你(nǐ)" (you), "们(men)" (plural suffix for people), "位(wèi)"(unit of people), "做(zuò)" (do), "作(zuò)" (do), "代 (dài)"(take the place of; generation) and "保(bǎo)" (protect). Let's take a look at the character "休(xiū)(rest)" in the oracle inscription "㑺". Isn't it look like a person leaning against a big tree? It is an associative compound character which means taking a break. The character "保" is even more interesting. In ancient characters, "保" appears like an adult carrying a child on its back "㑂", so the character developed the meaning of "保护(bǎohù)" (protect).

54. 打 hit

dǎ
打

字源演变　The etymology of Chinese characters

小篆　　　　　楷体

1. 释义　Meaning

dǎ hit　　打 dá　dozen

2. 书写　Writing

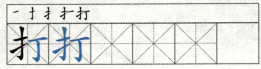

3. 相关词语或表达　Related words or expressions

(1) 打人 dǎ rén beat someone

Dǎ rén de háizi bù shi hǎo háizi.
打 人 的 孩子 不 是 好 孩子。Only bad kids beat other kids.

dǎ jià
打架 fight

Tā xiǎo shíhou chángcháng gēn nánháizi dǎ jià.
她 小 时候 常常 跟 男孩子打架。

She used to fight with boys when she was a child.

dǎ máoyī
打 毛衣 knit a sweater

五、作动词的汉字 Characters as Verbs

Māma gěi wǒ dǎ le yī jiàn báisè de máoyī.
妈妈 给我 打了一件 白色的 毛衣。

My mom knitted a white sweater for me.

dǎ shǒushì
打 手势 make a gesture

Tā gěi wǒ dǎ shǒushì ràng wǒ bié shuōhuà le.
他给我打 手势 让 我别 说话 了。

He gestured me to stop talking.

dǎ jiāodao
打 交道 have dealings with; come into contact with

Yīshēng měitiān hé bìngrén dǎ jiāodao.
医生 每天 和 病人 打 交道。

Doctors deal with patients every day.

dǎ diànhuà
打 电话 make a phone call

Yǒu le shǒujī, rénmen dǎ diànhuà gèng fāngbiàn le.
有 了手机，人们 打 电话 更 方便 了。

It is more convenient for people to make phone calls with cell phones.

dǎsǎo
打扫 clean

Wǒ měi ge zhōumò dōu yào dǎsǎo yīxià fángjiān.
我 每个 周末 都 要 打扫 一下 房间。

I need to clean my room every weekend.

dǎ zhé
打 折 discount

Shāngdiàn de dōngxi dǎ zhé le, yuánlái yī bǎi kuài de dǎ qī zhé, qī shí
商店 的 东西 打 折了，原来 100 块 的 打七折， 70

kuài le.
块 了。

The store is offering a 30% discount. You only have to pay 70 yuan for the thing that was priced at 100 yuan.

dá
(2) **打** dozen

Zuótiān wǒ mǎi le yī dá qiānbǐ. I bought a dozen pencils yesterday.
昨天 我 买了一打 铅笔。

汉语常用100字

4. 练习　Exercises

（1）根据拼音写出词语 Write down the words and expressions according to *pinyin*

dǎ rén　　　　　　（　　　）

dǎsǎo　　　　　　（　　　）

dǎ zhé　　　　　　（　　　）

dǎ shǒushì　　　　（　　　）

dǎ jiāodao　　　　（　　　）

dǎ diànhuà　　　　（　　　）

（2）用所给词语完成句子 Complete the following sentences with words in the parentheses

① 我经常_____。（打扫）

② 我在给_____。（打电话）

③ 最近商店_____。（打折）

④ 售货员跟_____。（打交道）

5. 汉字知识　The knowledge of Chinese characters

常见的偏旁部首（20）　手部

最初刻在青铜器上的"手"字都是一只手的形状，因此作形旁的字都和手或手的动作有关。手字旁在左侧时写成"扌"，俗称提手旁，比如"找"、"扫"、"挂"、"提"、"抓"、"把"、"拉"、"推"等等。表示手的古文字还有"又"字，"又"的甲骨文写作""，也是一只右手的掌形，我们在"取"字当中看到了右手，它朝一只耳朵伸过去想抓住它。

"打"是个形声字，左形右声，其本义是"击"，如"打鼓"。

Common Radicals and Indexing Radicals (20)　手

Originally, the character "手" engraved on bronze wares is the shape of an hand "", thus the characters with "手" as the pictographic radical are largely related to hands or movements of hands. "手" is written as "扌"

五、作动词的汉字 Characters as Verbs

when it is on the left such as "找(zhǎo)" (look for)、"扫(sǎo)" (sweep)、"挂(guà)" (hang)、"提(tí)" (carry)、"抓(zhuā)" (catch)、"把(bǎ)" (hold)、"拉(lā)" (pull)、"推(tuī)" (push). The character "又" in ancient Chinese characters is written as "㕯" which also signifies hands. "又" is in the form of a right hand. We can see a right hand in the character "取(qǔ) (take, get; fetch)", which is holding out to grab an ear.

The character "打" is a pictophonetic character with pictographic radical on the left and phonetic radical on the right. It originally means beat or strike, such as "打鼓(dǎ gǔ)" (beat a drum).

55. 学 study

xué
学

字源演变   The etymology of Chinese characters

小篆   繁体   楷体

1. 释义   Meaning

study; learn (v.)

2. 书写   Writing

3. 相关词语或表达   Related words or expressions

(1) 学(习)   xuéxí   study, learn

Wǒ xǐhuan xuéxí Hànyǔ, gēge xǐhuan xué Yīngyǔ.
我 喜欢 学习 汉语，哥哥 喜欢 学 英语。
I prefer learning Chinese while my brother prefers learning English.

shàng xué
上 学   go to school

Mèimei jīntiān qù shàng xué le.
妹妹 今天 去 上 学 了。 My sister has gone to school today.

xuésheng
学生   student

五、作动词的汉字 Characters as Verbs

Tā shì yī ge xuésheng.
她 是 一个 学生。 She is a student.

xuéxiào
学校　　　　　school

Wǒmen xuéxiào yǒu liǎng wàn ge xuésheng.
我们 学校 有 20000 个 学生。
There're 20000 students in our school.

dàxué
大学　　　　　university

zhōngxué
中学　　　　　middle school

xiǎoxué
小学　　　　　elementary school

(2) xuéwen
学问　　　　　knowledge; learning

Tā hěn yǒu xuéwen.
他 很 有 学问。 He is learned.

shùxué
数学　　　　　mathematics

wénxué
文学　　　　　literature

hànxué
汉学　　　　　sinology

lìshǐxué
历史学　　　　history

4. 练习　Exercises

(1) 根据拼音写出词语 Write down the words and expressions according to *pinyin*

　　shàng xué　　(　　)

　　xuéxí　　　　(　　)

　　xuésheng　　(　　)

　　xuéwen　　　(　　)

　　xuéxiào　　 (　　)

　　dàxué　　　 (　　)

　　zhōngxué　　(　　)

汉语常用100字

xiǎoxué　　　（　　）
wénxué　　　（　　）
shùxué　　　（　　）

（2）用所给词语完成句子 Complete the following sentences with words in the parentheses

① 我每天_____。（学习）
② 你什么时候_____?（上……学）
③ 那个_____。（学校）
④ 你在_____学习?（大学）
⑤ 爸爸_____。（学问）

5. 汉字知识　The knowledge of Chinese characters
常见的偏旁部首（21）　子部

古文字中的"子"字，像一个头大身小的婴孩形象。作形旁的字多和孩子及其动作状态有关。如"好"在古汉字中是一个妇女抱着孩子的形状"🝱"。再比如"孩"、"孙"等。"子"亦作声旁，如"仔"、"字"。

学是一个简化字，繁体写作"學"，是一个会意字，篆书写作"𧺒"，上部左右为双手，中间"爻"为双手所持之物，下部为双膝拥抱一幼儿。整个字的含义是，不好好学就管教（孩子）。

Common Radicals and Indexing Radicals (21)　子

The ancient form of the character "子" appears like a baby with a big head and a small body. When it is used as a pictographic radical, it is mostly related to children and their actions. For example, the character "好(hǎo)" (good) looks like a woman holding a baby in its ancient form "🝱". There are other examples: "孩(hái)" (kid) and "孙(sūn)" (grandchild). "子" can also serves as a phonetic radical such as "仔(zǎi)" (young animal) and "字(zì)"(character).

The character "学" is a simplified character which is written as "學" in

五、作动词的汉字 Characters as Verbs

traditional Chinese. It is an associative compound character which is written as "㪤" in its sealed character form. The left upper and right upper parts look like two hands of an adult. The "爻" in the middle are the things, that are held in hands. The lower part of the character appears like a kid between the legs of the adult. The character thus shows that if the kid does not study hard, the adult will discipline him/her.

56. 买 buy

mǎi
买

字源演变　The etymology of Chinese characters

甲骨文　　　　小篆　　　　繁体　　　　楷体

1. 释义　Meaning

buy (v.)

2. 书写　Writing

3. 相关词语或表达　Related words or expressions

(1) mǎi
买 buy

Zuótiān wǒ qù shūdiàn mǎi le yī běn shū.
昨天　我去　书店　买了一本　书。

I bought a book in the bookstore yesterday.

(2) mài
卖 sell

Zhè jiàn yīfu mài chūqù le.
这　件衣服　卖　出去了。This piece of clothes has been sold.

(3) mǎifāng
买方 buyer

五、作动词的汉字 Characters as Verbs

(4) mǎifāng
　　卖方 seller

　　Mǎifāng yào fù　　qián, mǎifāng yào gěi huò.
　　买方　要　付(pay)钱，卖方　要　给　货(goods)。
　　The buyer has to pay and the seller has to deliver.

(5) mǎimai
　　买卖 business

　　Tā bàba shì zuò mǎimai de.
　　他爸爸 是 做　买卖　的。His dad is a businessman.

4. 练习　Exercises

(1) 仿照例子,用括号里的词语替换带下划线的词语完成句子 Follow the example and complete the sentences by replacing the underlined words with the words in the brackets

　　例子：昨天我买了一本书。I bought a book yesterday.
　　① _____。(他　一个面包)
　　② _____。(妈妈　两件衣服)
　　③ _____。(爸爸　三瓶酒)
　　④ _____。(哥哥　四支笔)
　　⑤ _____。(姐姐　五斤苹果)
　　⑥ _____。(老师　六本书)

(2) 选择填空 Insert the correct answer in the blanks

　　　　　　买　卖　买方　卖方　买卖
　　① 以后我想去中国做____。
　　② 今天早上我____了一杯咖啡喝。
　　③ 那家商店每天____很多东西。
　　④ ____付钱以后____要马上给货。

5. 汉字知识　The knowledge of Chinese characters
"买"与"卖"

"买"是一个简化字,繁体字写作"買"。"買"的上部是由"网"演变而成

汉语常用100字

的，下部是贝壳。用网取得贝，这是一个会意字。跟"买"的含义相反的字是"卖"，上部多了一个"十"字，读音也只是声调不同，要注意分辨。两个字的繁体下部都是"贝"，贝壳在古代曾被当作货币使用，当然跟买卖关系密切了。

"买" and "卖"

买 is a simplified character which is written as "買" in traditional Chinese. The upper part of "買" was developed from the character "网" while the lower part signifies shell. It means capturing seashell by using a net, so the character is an associative compound character. The character which has the opposite meaning to it is "卖". It adds "十" to the character "买". The two characters differ only in tone, so we need to pay attention. The traditional forms of the two characters are both "贝(bèi)"(shell). In the ancient times, seashells were used as currencies, so it was closely connected with buying and selling.

57. 给 give

gěi
给

字源演变 The etymology of Chinese characters

小篆

繁体

楷体

1. 释义　Meaning

give, for, to (prep; v.)

2. 书写　Writing

3. 相关词语或表达　Related words or expressions

(1) 动词 verb

Tā gěi le wǒ yī běn shū.
他给了我一本书。He gave me a book.

Qǐng gěi wǒ yī bēi shuǐ.
请给我一杯水。Please give me a glass of water.

(2) 介词 preposition

Qǐng dàjiā gěi wǒ bāngbāngmáng.
请大家给我帮帮忙。

Everybody, would you please do me a favor.

Gěi wǒ chū ge zhǔyi ba!
给我出个主意吧！Please give me a suggestion.

汉语常用100字

Wǒ gěi māma dǎ le yī ge diànhuà.
我 给 妈妈 打了一个 电话。I just called my mother.

Wǒ gěi lǎoshī fā le yī fēng yóujiàn.
我 给 老师 发了一封 邮件。I sent an email to my teacher.

4. 练习　Exercises

(1) 请把"给"字放在适当的位置 Please put the character "给" in the proper place of the sentences

① A 我 B 他 C 一本书 D 看。

② 请你 A 老师 B 打个 C 电话吧 D！

③ 我 A 常常 B 朋友 C 发 D 短信（duǎnxìn, message）。

④ A 爸爸 B 我 C 100块钱 D 买衣服。

⑤ A 请 B 你们 C 我 D 出个主意，好吗？

⑥ 昨天 A 我 B 朋友寄 C 了 D 一封信。

(2) 连词成句 Arrange the following words in correct order to form a sentence

① 邮件 我 哥哥 发 给

② 姐姐 妹妹 一 件 给 衣服

③ 我 帮忙 给 来 大家

④ 常常 妈妈 给 打 我 电话

五、作动词的汉字 Characters as Verbs

5. 汉字知识　The knowledge of Chinese characters
常见的偏旁部首（22）　糸部

"糸"的古文字像是蚕做的茧或一绺细丝线"🕸"，本义指蚕丝，做左旁时常写作"纟"，俗称绞丝旁。凡是以"糸"为偏旁的字都和纺织、颜色有关，比如"丝"、"绸"、"线"、"绳"、"绣"、"缝"、"红"、"绿"、"紫"、"纸"、"结"、"经"、"纬"、"组"、"细"等等。"给"的本义就是缫丝时将断掉的丝线系在一起；"累（lěi）"的本义是指绳索；"紧"的本义是丝线缠得很结实；"继"和"续"的本义都是把丝连接上。

Common Radicals and Indexing Radicals (22)　糸

"糸" appears like a cocoon of a silkworm or a lock silk thread. "🕸" in its ancient form. It originally means silk and is often written as "纟" when serves as a left radical. It is commonly known as skein radical. The characters with it as a radical are all related to textile and color, such as "丝(sī)"(silk), "绸 (chóu)"(silk), "线(xiàn)"(thread), "绳(shéng)"(rope), "绣(xiù)"(embroider), "缝(féng)"(knit), "红(hóng)"(red), "绿(lǜ)"(green), "紫(zǐ)"(purple), "纸(zhǐ)"(paper), "结(jié)"(knot), "经 (jīng)"(warp), "纬(wěi)"(weft), "组(zǔ)"(set), "细(xì)"(minute). "给" originally means tying the broken silk threads together when making a skein. "累(lěi)" originally refers to rope. "紧(jǐn)" primarily means tying threads firmly together. "继(jì)" and "续(xù)" both means linking threads together in its original sense.

58. 来 come

lái
来

字源演变 The etymology of Chinese characters

甲骨文　　　　小篆　　　　　繁体　　　　　楷体

1. 释义　Meaning

come; bring; can form a directional complement or a complex directional complement with certain verbs. (v.)

2. 书写　Writing

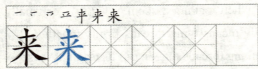

3. 相关词语或表达　Related words or expressions

(1) come

Tā yǐjing lái le.
他已经来了。He has already come.

Chē lái le.
车来了。The car is coming.

Tā míngtiān lái Běijīng.
她明天来北京。She will come to Beijing tomorrow.

(2) (used as a substitute for some other verb)

Lái yī bēi píjiǔ.
来一杯啤酒。A glass of beer, please.

五、作动词的汉字 Characters as Verbs

Chàng de tài hǎo le, zài lái yī ge.
唱 得太 好了,再 来一个。Bravo, sing another song.

(3) (used before a verb, indicating an intended or suggested action)

Nǐ ná nà ge, zhè ge wǒ zìjǐ lái ná.
你拿那个,这 个我 自己来拿。

You take that and I'll take this myself.

(4) verb.+ complement (used after a verb, indicating motion towards the speaker)

Tā cóng nàbiān zǒulái le.
他 从 那边 走来了。There he comes.

Tā gěi wǒ sònglái le yī běn shū.
他给 我 送来了一本 书。He brought a book for me.

Tā pǎojìn jiàoshì lái le.
他 跑进 教室 来了。He ran into the classroom.

4. 练习 Exercises

(1) 把"来"放在合适的位置 Please put the character "来" in the proper place of the sentences

① A 他 B 昨天 C 中国 D 了。

② A 一碗 B 米饭 C。

③ A 我 B 看 C 一下 D。

④ A 妈妈 B 给 C 我寄 D 了一封信。

⑤ A 他 B 走进 C 房间 D 了。

(2) 连词成句 Arrange the following words in correct order to form a sentence

① 了 妹妹 已经 来

②他 来 跑 进 的 我 房间 了

③朋友 我 带给 来 一件 礼物

④这个 太 好吃 菜 了，来 再 一个 吧。

5. 汉字知识　The knowledge of Chinese characters
"来"字的起源与演变

甲骨文的"来"字是麦子的形状"🌾"，有根、叶、茎，麦穗。所以古文中的"来"字指的就是小麦。后来"麦"字出现后，"来"在原有字形中加上表示行动的符号变成"徕"，借用为"来去"的"来"。在之后的演变中又逐渐简化，变成现在的样子。

The Origin and Evolution of "来"

The oracle form of the character "来" is written as "🌾" which appears like the shape of wheat with root, leaf, stalk and wheat head. The ancient form of the character "来" thus refers to wheat. After the appearance of the character "麦(mài)" (wheat), the character "来" was changed into "徕" through adding a symbol which suggests an action. The character was borrowed to mean "来" (come) as in the phrase "来去" (come and leave). The character was changed into its current form after gradual simplification.

59. 去 go

qù
去

字源演变 The etymology of Chinese characters

甲骨文　　　　金文　　　　　小篆　　　　　楷体

1. 释义　Meaning

go, leave, depart (v.)

2. 书写　Writing

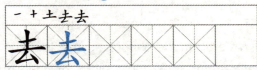

3. 相关词语或表达　Related words or expressions

(1)　Tā zuótiān qù Shànghǎi le.
　　他 昨天 去 上海 了。He went to Shanghai yesterday.

　　Wǒ qù guo Chángchéng.
　　我 去 过 长城。I've been to the Great Wall.

　　Wǒ qù shāngdiàn mǎi dōngxi.
　　我 去 商店 买 东西。I'll go to buy some stuff in the shop.

　　Wǒ qù mǎi dōngxi.
　　我 去 买 东西。I'll go to buy some stuff.

　　Wǒmen kàn diànyǐng qù.
　　我们 看 电影 去。Let's go to the movies.

(2) qùnián
　　去年 last year

　　Tā qùnián lái guò Zhōngguó.
　　他 去年 来 过 中国。He has been to China last year.

　　guòqù
　　过去 go over, in the past, former

　　Shìqing yǐjing guòqù le, bié xiǎng le.
　　事情 已经 过去 了，别 想 了。

　　The thing is past. Don't think about it.

　　Guòqù tā shì ge lǎoshī, xiànzài tuìxiū le.
　　过去 他是个 老师，现在 退休了。

　　He used to be a teacher. Now he has retired.

(3) 用在动词后，表示趋向。

　　used after a verb to suggest the movement away of the speaker in the middle of an action.

　　Háizi xiàng māma pǎoqù.
　　孩子 向 妈妈 跑去。The kid is running toward his mother.

　　Wǒ gěi gēge jìqù le yī fēng xìn.
　　我 给 哥哥 寄去了一 封 信。I sent a letter to my elder brother.

4. 练习　Exercises

(1) 给下列汉字注音并组词 Write down the phonetic symbols of the following Chinese characters and make up a word for each of them

　　来(　)　　　　　去(　)

　　买(　)　　　　　给(　)

　　学(　)　　　　　打(　)

　　做(　)　　　　　看(　)

　　吃(　)　　　　　喝(　)

(2) 选择填空 Insert the correct answer in the blanks

　　　　　　　　来　去

　① 现在我在中国，我是上个月____的。

五、作动词的汉字 Characters as Verbs

② 我给妈妈寄____了一件衣服。
③ 朋友给我带____了很多水果。
④ 我们买东西____吧。

5. 汉字知识　The knowledge of Chinese characters

"去"字释义

"去"的古文字上部是一个正面站立的人,写作"𠫓",看上去像是向前行走的样子。有人说它是一个形声字,上部是一个正在向前行走的人,下部表示这个字的读音。意思是从所在地到别的地方,如"从北京去上海"。引申为"除去;除掉",如"这句话去掉了几个字。"还可以表示"过去的时间",如"去年"。

The Explanation of the Meaning of Character "去"

The ancient form of the character "去" looks like the frontal look of a standing person. It is written as "𠫓", which looks like a forward-walking person. Some people say it is a pictophonetic character with the upper part signifies a person who is walking forward and the lower part suggests the pronunciation of the character. It means go from one place to another, such as "from Beijing to Shanghai". It was extended to mean "除去(chúqù)" and "除掉(chúdiào)" (get rid of). For example, "这句话去掉了几个字" (This sentence was reduced of some characters). It can also indicate passed time, such as "去年(qùnián)" (last year).

60. 出 out

字源演变　The etymology of Chinese characters

　甲骨文　　　　　　金文　　　　　　小篆　　　　　　楷体

1. 释义　Meaning

go out; out (v.)

2. 书写　Writing

3. 相关词语或表达　Related words or expressions

（1）proceed from inside to outside

　　chū guó
　　出　国 go abroad

　　chū mén
　　出　门 go out

　　Chū mén wǎng zuǒ guǎi jiù dào le.
　　出　门　往　左　拐　就　到　了。
　　Go out of the door and turn left, you won't miss it.

（2）出 主意 put forth ideas
　　chū zhǔyi

　　Nǐ gěi wǒmen chū ge zhǔyi ba.
　　你 给 我们　出 个 主意 吧。 Would you please give us an idea?

五、作动词的汉字 Characters as Verbs

chū qián
出 钱 pay money

Mǎi zhè liàng chē, nǐ chū le duōshao qián?
买 这 辆 车, 你 出 了 多少 钱？

How much money did you contribute for this car?

chūbǎn
出版 publish

Zhè shì wǒ xīn chūbǎn de shū.
这 是 我 新 出版 的 书。This is my newly published book.

(3) jìn
进 enter, in

Tā zǒuchū jiàoshì le.　　Tā zǒujìn jiàoshì le.
他 走出 教室 了。——他 走进 教室 了。

He walked out of the classroom.—He walked into the classroom.

chūlái　　　jìnlái
出来 come out　进来 come in

chūqù　　　jìnqù
出去 go out　进去 go in

Tā cóng jiàoshì lǐ chūlái le.
他 从 教室里 出来 了。He is coming out from the classroom.

Tā cóng wàibian jìnlái le.
他 从 外边 进来了。He is coming in from the outside.

Nǐ chūqù ba, wǒ zài fángjiān lǐ xiūxi yīxià.
你 出去 吧, 我 在 房间 里休息一下。

You can leave now. I want to have a rest in the room.

Nǐ jìnqù ba, wǒ zài wàibian děng tā.
你 进去 吧, 我 在 外边 等 他。

Please enter the room. I'll wait outside for him.

汉语常用100字

4. 练习　Exercises

根据图片选择填空 Insert the correct answer in the blanks according to the pictures

出来　　出去　　进来　　进去

五、作动词的汉字 Characters as Verbs

5. 汉字知识　The knowledge of Chinese characters

"出"字的释义

"出"的篆书写作"𡳿"，上部是"足"，下部为象征古人穴居的穴形，合起来表示脚离开洞穴向外出行。"出行"、"出发"、"出走"用的都是它的本义。"出"的反义词最常用的有两个，一个是"人"，另一个是"进"。

The Explanation of the Meaning of Character "出"

The character "出" is written as "𡳿" in its sealed character form. It has "足(zú)" (foot) on the top and a lower part like a cave which indicates the cave the ancients lived in, suggesting a person is walking out of a cave in combination. "出" as in the phrases "出行(chūxíng)" (go out), "出发(chūfā)" (set out) and "出走(chūzǒu)" (run away; leave) all use its original meaning. It has two antonyms of "入(rù)" and "进(jìn)" which both means enter.

61. 上 go up

shàng
上

字源演变　The etymology of Chinese characters

甲骨文　　　　金文　　　　小篆　　　　楷体

1. 释义　Meaning

ascend; go up; get on; on; in; last (v.; prep.; adv.)

2. 书写　Writing

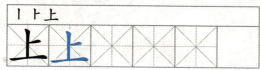

3. 相关词语或表达　Related words or expressions

(1) shàng chē　　　　　　xià chē
　　上　车 get on　　　　下　车 get off

　　shàng shān
　　上　山 go up a hill or mountain

　　xià shān
　　下　山 go down a hill or mountain

　　shàng lóu　　　　　　xià lóu
　　上　楼 go up stairs　　下　楼 go down stairs

(2) shàng bān　　　　　　xià bān
　　上　班 go to work　　下　班 get off work; knock off

　　shàng kè　　　　　　xià kè
　　上　课 attend class　　下　课 get out of class; finish class

(3) shàngbian
上边 above; over; on top of; on the surface of

xiàbian
下边 below, under

Shū zài zhuōzi shàng(biān), shūbāo zài zhuōzi xiàbian.
书 在 桌子 上(边)，书包 在 桌子 下边。
The book is on the table and the bag is under the table.

zhuōzi shàng(biān) yǒu yī běn shū, zhuōzi xiàbiān yǒu yī ge shūbāo.
桌子 上(边) 有一本 书，桌子 下边 有一个 书包。
There is a book on the table and a bag under the table.

(4) shàng yī cì   xià yī cì
    上 一 次 last time   下 一 次 next time

shàng ge yuè   xià ge yuè
上 个 月 last month   下 个 月 next month

shàng ge xīngqī   xià ge xīngqī
上 个 星期 last week   下 个 星期 next week

4. 练习　Exercises

(1) 根据英语翻译写出相应的词组 Write down the phrases according to the English translation

go up a hill　　　(　　)

go down stairs　　(　　)

go to work　　　(　　)

finish class　　　(　　)

above　　　　　(　　)

below　　　　　(　　)

last time　　　　(　　)

next month　　　(　　)

last week　　　　(　　)

(2) 选择填空 Insert the correct answer in the blanks

上班　下课　上楼　下山　上边　下一次

① 我们每天8点____，下午6点下班。

五、作动词的汉字 Characters as Verbs

② 山很高,____的时候要小心。
③ 这一次没有时间,我们____再见面吧。
④ 书没在桌子____。
⑤ 现在正在上课,____以后我想回家。
⑥ 孩子____去睡觉了。

5. 汉字知识　The knowledge of Chinese characters
"上"与"下"

"上"是一个指事字,甲骨文写作"⌒",下边的长横就像是一个标杆,上面的表示所指的是标杆以上的部位。如"桌子上"。跟它相对的字是"下",也是一个指事字,作标杆的长横当然就是在上边了,如"床下"。"上"作为动词,在"上山、上楼"中表示从低到高;"上学、上街"中表示去哪儿。此外,"上"还表示时间或顺序在前的,如"上午、上回",相对的,我们就有"下午、下回"。

"上" and "下"

The character "上" is an indicative character which is written as "⌒" in its oracle inscription. The long bar at the bottom likes an index bar. The top part refers to the part above the bar. For example, "桌子上(zhuōzi shang)" (on the desk). The character opposite to it in meaning is "下", which is an indicative character also. The index bar thus is on the top. For example, "床下(chuángxià)" (under the bed). "上", as a verb, means going from a lower place to a higher place, such as in the phrases "上山(shàng shān)" (climb mountain) and "上楼(shàng lóu)" (go up stairs). "上" as in the phrases "上学(shàng xué)" (go to school) and "上街(shàng jiē)" (go to street;) both indicates going to a certain place. In addition, "上" can also indicates earlier in time or sequence, such as "上午(shàngwǔ)" (morning) and "上回(shànghuí)" (last time). Correspondingly, we also have "下午(xiàwǔ)" (afternoon) and "下回(xiàhuí)" (next time).

62. 走 walk

zǒu
走

字源演变　The etymology of Chinese characters

甲骨文　　　　金文　　　　小篆　　　　楷体

1. 释义　Meaning

walk; move; leave; go away (v.)

2. 书写　Writing

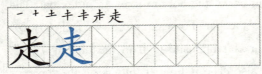

3. 相关词语或表达　Related words or expressions

(1) walk

Wǎnfàn yǐhòu, wǒ cháng yī ge rén zǒu yi zǒu.
晚饭 以后，我 常 一个人 走一走。
I often take a walk alone after dinner.

zǒu lù
走 路 walk

Tā měitiān zǒu lù lái shàng kè.
他 每天 走路来 上 课。He walks to school every day.

(2) leave, go

Tā gāng zǒu.
他 刚 走。He just left.

五、作动词的汉字 Characters as Verbs

zǒukāi
走开 leave; go away; walk away

Wǒ bùxiǎng tīng tāmen shuōhuà, jiù zǒukāi le.
我 不想 听 他们 说话，就 走开了。

I don't want to listen to them so I walked away.

Verb. +走 zǒu

Tā názǒu le wǒ de shū.
他 拿走 了 我 的 书。He took away my books.

(3) through; from

Wǒ měitiān dōu zǒu zhè ge mén.
我 每天 都 走 这 个 门。I use this door every day.

Qù xuéxiào yào zǒu zhè tiáo lù.
去 学校 要 走 这 条 路。I walk this way to school.

4. 练习　Exercises

（1）把下列短语与其相对应的意思连线 Link the following expressions and their meanings

走路　　　　　　　leave

走开　　　　　　　walk

拿走　　　　　　　passing by this door

走这个门　　　　　take sth. away

（2）选词填空 Insert the correct answer in the blanks

　　　　　　走　　走开　　走路　　拿走

① 他____了我的笔。

② ____，别听我们说话。

③ 我每天____那个门进教室。

④ 我喜欢____去学校。

⑤ 他刚____，你就来了。

5. 汉字知识　The knowledge of Chinese characters
常见的偏旁部首(23)　走部

走的篆书写作"𧺆",是一个象形字。上部是一个人两臂摇动、两腿跨步快速前进的样子,下部是一只脚,两者合在一起,"走"的本义就是跑,是快速行走。在现代汉语中一般情况下是步行,要注意分辨。

"走"作形旁的字多和走的动作有关。比如"起"、"赶"、"超"、"越"等。

Common Radicals and Indexing Radicals (23)　走

The character "走" is written as "𧺆" in its sealed character form. It is a pictographic character: the top part looks like a person who is waving his arms and walking forward quickly in large steps; the lower part is a foot. It originally meant walking at a fast pace when combining the two parts together. In modern Chinese, it means walking in most cases. We need to pay attention to it.

The character with "走" as the pictographic radical are all related to walk, such as "起 (qǐ)"(get up), "赶(gǎn)" (chase), "超(chāo)" (surpass) and "越(yuè)" (get over; exceed).

63. 开 open

kāi
开

字源演变   The etymology of Chinese characters

  开

小篆　　　　　繁体　　　　　　楷体

1. 释义　Meaning

open, turn on, run, drive, write out, start, hold (v.)

2. 书写　Writing

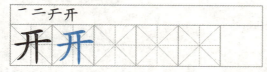

3. 相关词语或表达　Related words or expressions

（1）kāi
　　开 open, turn on

　　kāi mén
　　开　门 open the door

　　kāi chuāng
　　开　窗 open the window

　　kāi dēng
　　开　灯 turn on the light

　　dǎkāi
　　打开 open, turn on

　　dǎkāi diànshì
　　打开　电视 turn on the TV

汉语常用100字

    dǎkāi diànnǎo
    打开 电脑 boot the computer

    dǎkāi shū
    打开 书 open your book

    dǎkāi bāozhuāng
    打开 包装 tear away the package

    kāi
(2) 开 drive, run

    kāi chē
    开 车 drive a car

    kāi fēijī
    开 飞机 fly an airplane

    kāishǐ
(3) 开始 start

    kāishǐ shàng kè
    开始 上 课 start a lesson

    kāishǐ gōngzuò
    开始 工作 start working

    kāi
(4) 开 write out; make a list of

    kāi dānzi
    开 单子 make a list

    kāi yàofāng
    开 药方 give a prescription

    kāi fāpiào
    开 发票 issue an invoice

    kāihuì
(5) 开会 hold or attend a meeting

    kāi yùndònghuì
    开 运动会 hold a sports meeting

    kāi wǎnhuì
    开 晚会 hold an evening party

4. 练习 Exercises

(1) 选择填空 Insert the correct answer in the blanks

        开始   打开   开会   开车

① 你____要小心。

② 今天晚上公司____。

五、作动词的汉字 Characters as Verbs

③ 我们＿＿＿上课吧！
④ 太热了，我们＿＿＿窗户(chuānghu)(window)吧！

(2) 完成句子 Complete the sentences with the words given in the brackets

① 同学们＿＿＿，看第56页(yè)(page)。(打开)
② 今天学校＿＿＿，很多同学准备参加比赛(bǐsài)(match)。(开)
③ 你什么时候＿＿＿？(开始)
④ 买东西以后，我要＿＿＿。(开)
⑤ 他的爸爸是司机(sījī)(driver)，＿＿＿。(开车)

5. 汉字知识　The knowledge of Chinese characters

"开"字介绍

"开"是一个简化字，简化以前写作"開"。"開"在古代曾经写作"開"，是一个会意字。整个字的外形左右是两扇关着的门；门里边的"一"是关门的横棍，叫"门闩"；下面是人的两只手，正要取下门闩，是开门的动作。

The Introduction of the Character "开"

"开" is a simplified character which was written as "開" before being simplified. It is an associative compound character and was written as "開" in ancient times. It looks like two closed doors with "一" indicating the bar ("门闩"ménshuān) for closing the door. The lower part is two hands which are taking off the bar to open the door.

64. 能 can

néng
能

字源演变　The etymology of Chinese characters

金文　　　　　小篆　　　　　楷体

1. 释义　Meaning

can; be able to; good at (v.)

2. 书写　Writing

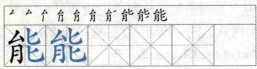

3. 相关词语或表达　Related words or expressions

(1) can (human ability)

Tā de shǒu hǎo le, néng xiě zì le.
他 的 手 好 了，能 写 字 了。

His hands have recovered. He can write now.

Wǒ de sǎngzi　　téng　　, bù néng shuō huà.
我 的 嗓子(throat)疼(ache),不 能 说 话。

My throat is aching. I cannot speak.

(2) can (nature of a substance)

Júzi　　　pí　　hái néng zuò yào.
橘子(orange)皮(skin)还 能 做 药(medicine)。

五、作动词的汉字 Characters as Verbs

Orange skin can be made into medicine.

Zhè zhī bǐ néng huà huàr ma?
这支笔能画画儿吗？Can I draw a picture with this pen?

(3) be capable of

Nà ge rén hěn néng shuō.
那个人很能说。That person is very good at speaking.

Tā hěn nénggàn.
他很能干。He is very capable.

(4) (expressing possibility) can possibly

　　　Zhème wǎn le, tā néng lái ma?
A：这么晚了,他能来吗？It is so late. Is he able to come?

　　　Wǒ kàn tā bù néng lái le.
B：我看他不能来了。I don't think he will come.

(5) (usually used negatively or interrogatively) may, can, have the permission to

　　　Zhèr néng chōu yān　　ma?
A：这儿能抽烟(smoke)吗？Can we smoke here?

　　　Zhèr bù néng chōu yān.
B：这儿不能抽烟。No, it is forbidden here.

4. 练习 Exercises

(1) 把"能"放在合适的位置 Please put the character "能" in the proper place of the sentences

①A我的手B疼，C不D写字。

②你A明天B来上课吗？

③A这个人B很C吃D。

④这个A水果B做C药D。

⑤A上课B不C睡觉D。

(2) 回答问题 Answer the following questions

① 你能跟中国人聊 liáo tiān 天(chat)吗?

Can you chat with Chinese?

② 你的朋友里,谁最能吃?谁最能说?谁最能喝酒?

Among your friends, who can eat most? Who can talk most? And who can drink most?

③ 下个月你能回国吗?

Can you go back to your country next month?

④ 可口可乐能做药吗?

Can Coca Cola be made into medicine?

⑤ 教室 jiàoshì (classroom)里能抽烟吗?

Can we smoke in the classroom?

5. 汉字知识　The knowledge of Chinese characters

"能"的起源与演变

"能"字笔画较多,结构也比较复杂,篆书写作"🐻",它表示的本来是一种与熊比较接近的动物,它的下肢有点儿像鹿。也有人说"能"就是"熊"字的本来的写法。因为熊力大无比,后来"能"被借用为"能力"、"才能"的"能"。时间长了,容易发生混淆,为了把两个意思区别开,干脆把本来表示动物的"能"写成"熊"了。这也是汉字形体演变的规律之一。

The Origin and Evolution of "能"

"能" has a complicated structure with multiple stokes. It is written as "🐻" in sealed character form. It originally meant a bearlike animal with deerlike legs. Some people thought "能" was the primary form of the character "熊 (xióng)" (bear). Since bear has incomparable strength, the character "能" later was used in phrases such as "能力(nénglì)" (ability) and "才能(cáinéng)" (talent). After a while, people easily got confused by the two meanings. To distinguish the two meanings, people replaced "能" with the character "熊" to mean bear. This also reflects one of the laws in the evolution of the morphology of the Chinese characters.

65. 会 be able to

huì
会

字源演变　The etymology of Chinese characters

甲骨文

小篆

繁体

楷体

1. 释义　Meaning

can; be able to; be skillful; be likely to; be sure to; understand; know (v.)
Meeting (n.)

2. 书写　Writing

3. 相关词语或表达　Related words or expressions

(1) can, be able to, be skillful

Wǒ huì shuō Hànyǔ.
我 会 说 汉语。I can speak Chinese.

Wǒ bù huì yóuyǒng, wǒ huì tī zúqiú.
我 不会 游泳，我 会 踢足球。
I can't swim, but I can play football.

(2) be likely or possible

Jīntiān tā huì lái ma?　　Wǒ kàn tā bù huì lái le.
今天 他会 来 吗？——我 看 他不 会 来了。

Is he coming today? ——I don't think he is coming.

Míngtiān huì xià yǔ ma?　　Wǒ juéde míngtiān huì xiàyǔ.
明天 会下雨吗？——我 觉得 明天 会下雨。

Is it going to rain tomorrow? ——I think it is going to rain tomorrow.

huìyì
(3) 会议 conference

kāi huì
开 会 hold or attend a meeting

huìmiàn
(4) 会面 to meet

huìjiàn
会见 meet, pay a visit

yì huìr
(5) 一会儿 a little while; in a moment

Qǐng děng yìhuìr.
请 等 一会儿。Please wait a moment.

Wǒ yìhuìr jiù lái.
我 一会儿就来。I will come soon.

4. 练习　**Exercises**

(1) 根据拼音写汉字，并想想它们的意思 Write down the characters according to *pinyin* and think about their meanings

① Māma huì shuō Yīngyǔ.

② Nǐ huì tī zúqiú ma?

③ Jīntiān bú huì xià yǔ.

④ Míngtiān yǒu huìyì ma?

⑤ Nǐmen shénme shíhou huìmiàn?

⑥ Qǐng děng yíhuì'r.

五、作动词的汉字 Characters as Verbs

(2) 选词填空 Insert the correct answer in the blanks

不会　　一会儿　　开会　　会　　会面

① 天气很好,我看今天_____下雨。
② 他学了三年汉语了,他_____说汉语。
③ 下课了,我们休息_____吧!
④ 昨天我跟朋友_____了。
⑤ 现在我们开始_____吧!

5. 汉字知识　　The knowledge of Chinese characters

"会"的起源与演变

"会"是一个简化字,繁体字写作"會",是一个会意字。它最初的含义是指器物的盖子,盖子盖在器物上,上下相合,也就是相会。简化以后的"会"也可以看作是一个新组合的会意字,众人云集不就是会合吗?

"会"字有两个读音,一个是"huì",常用词较多;另一个是"kuài",常用词只有"会计"一个。

The Origin and Evolution of "会"

The character "会" is a simplified associative compound character which is written as "會" in traditional Chinese. It originally referred to the cover of a container. The cover is put on top of the container, so the top was connected to the bottom. In other words, we call it "相会 (xiānghuì)". After being simplified, it can be treated as a new associative compound character. "会合 (huìhé)" can be used to describe a large crowd of people come together.

"会" has two pronunciations: "huì" and "kuài". The first one can be applied to many common words while the latter one is only used in "会计 (kuàiji)" (accountant).

六、作形容词的汉字
Characters as Adjectives

66. 大 big

字源演变　The etymology of Chinese characters

　甲骨文　　　　金文　　　　小篆　　　　楷体

1. 释义　Meaning

big; large; oldest; major (adj.)

2. 书写　Writing

3. 相关词语或表达　Related words or expressions

(1) 大 dà big, large

Zhè ge píngguǒ hěn dà, nà ge píngguǒ hěn xiǎo.
这个 苹果 很大,那个 苹果 很小。

This apple is pretty big while that one is very small.

六、作形容词的汉字 Characters as Adjectives

(2) dà yǔ
　　大雨 heavy rain

　　xiǎo yǔ
　　小 雨 light rain; drizzle

　　Jīntiān yǒu xiǎoyǔ, míngtiān yǒu dàyǔ.
　　今天 有 小雨，明天 有 大雨。
　　We have drizzle today and heavy rain tomorrow.

(3) dàhào
　　大号 large size

　　xiǎohào
　　小号 small size

　　Tā chuān dàhào de yīfu, wǒ chuān xiǎohào de.
　　她 穿 大号 的衣服，我 穿 小号 的。
　　She wears size L while I wear size S.

(4) dàren
　　大人 adult; grown-up

　　xiǎohái
　　小孩 kids; child

(5) dà shì
　　大 事 great event, important matter; major issue

　　xiǎo shì
　　小 事 trifle; minor matter

　　Jié hūn shì yī jiàn dà shì, mǎi cài, zuò fàn dōu shì xiǎo shì.
　　结 婚 是一 件 大 事，买 菜、做 饭 都 是 小 事。
　　Marriage is a major issue while grocery shopping and cooking meals are small issues.

(6) dàgē
　　大哥 eldest brother

　　Wǒ yǒu liǎng ge gēge, dàgē shì dàifu, èr'gē shì lǎoshī.
　　我 有 两个 哥哥，大哥 是 大夫，二哥 是 老师。
　　I have two brothers. The elder brother is a doctor and the younger brother is a teacher.

　　dàjiě
　　大姐 eldest sister

　　lǎo dà
　　老 大 eldest child

　　Tāmen jiā yǒu sān ge háizi, tā shì lǎo dà, tā yǒu liǎng ge mèimei.
　　他们 家 有 三 个 孩子，他是 老 大，他有 两 个 妹妹。

There are three kids in their family. He is the eldest one and he has two younger sisters.

(7) 小 xiǎo small; little; young; tiny (a.)

4. 练习 Exercises

(1) 把下列词语的拼音及意思连线 Link the *pinyin* and their meanings of the following words

大事	dà hào	large size
大哥	lǎo dà	important matter
大号	dà shì	eldest brother
老大	dàgē	eldest child
小孩	xiǎo hào	light rain
小事	xiǎo yǔ	small size
小雨	xiǎo shì	trifle
小号	xiǎohái	child

(2) 选择填空 Insert the correct answer in the blanks

大雨　　老大　　小号　　小事

① 这可不是一件_____, 很重要(zhòngyào, important)。
② 妹妹的脚(jiǎo, feet)不大, 她穿_____的鞋(xié, shoes)。
③ 天气预报(tiānqì yùbào, weather forecast)说明天有_____。
④ 他有两个弟弟, 他是家里的_____。

5. 汉字知识　The knowledge of Chinese characters

"大"与"太"

"大"的篆书写作"大",像一个正面站立的人。为什么用"人"来表示大呢？有人解释说,天大地大,但都无法象形,天地之间万事万物,人就是老大,所以就用人的正面形象来表示大。这的确有道理。在古代"大"和

六、作形容词的汉字 Characters as Adjectives

"太"是不分的,天空很大,所以叫"太空",江苏省有个"太湖",其实就是大湖。后来为了把两个字区别开,给"太tài"加了一点儿。

"大"有时读"dài",如"大夫"。

"大" and "太"

The character "大" is written as "大" in sealed character form which resembles the frontal look of a standing person. Why do we use "人" to indicate large. Some people explain that we cannot create a pictographic character for heaven and earth although they are enormous. Since humans are of the highest level among multitudes of creatures, so we use the frontal look of a person to express the concept of large. This does stand to reason. In ancient times, there was no distinction between "大" and "太". The sky is enormous, so we call it "太空(tàikōng)" (the space). There is "太湖(Tàihú)" (a lake) in Jiangsu province. In fact, it means "大湖(dàhú)" (a great lake). To distinguish the two characters, we later added a dot to "太".

"大" is sometimes pronounced as "dài" as in the phrase "大夫(dàifu)" (doctor).

67. 多 many

duō
多

字源演变 (The etymology of Chinese characters)

| 甲骨文 | 金文 | 小篆 | 楷体 |

1. 释义　Meaning

many, much; more; (adj.) more than

2. 书写　Writing

′ ク タ タ 多 多

多 多

3. 相关词语或表达　Related words or expressions

(1) 多 duō many, a lot of

Jīntiān lái de rén hěn duō, zuótiān lái de rén hěn shǎo.
今天 来 的 人 很 多，昨天来的 人 很 少。

Many people come today. Few people came yesterday.

(2) ······多 duō more than

Wǒ lái Běijīng yī nián duō le.
我 来 北京 一 年 多 了。I have stayed in Beijing for over a year.

(3) 多 duō more

六、作形容词的汉字 Characters as Adjectives

shǎo
少 lack

Jīntiān hěn lěng, nǐ yào duō chuān diǎn yīfu.
今天 很 冷,你要 多 穿 点衣服。

It is very cold today. You need to wear more clothes.

Fángjiān lǐ shǎo le yī zhāng zhuōzi.
房间 里少了一 张 桌子。

There's still one chair short in the room.

duōshǎo
(4) 多少 how many

Nǐmen bān yǒu duōshao ge xuésheng?
你们 班 有 多少 个 学生?

How many students are there in your class?

Zhè běn shū duōshao qián?
这 本 书 多少 钱? How much is this book?

duō xíng ā/ya
(5) 多+形+(啊/呀) (used in exclamations) to what an extent

Jīntiān de tiānqì duō hǎo a!
今天 的天气 多 好啊! What a nice day it is!

duō xíng
(6) 多+形? (used in questions) to what extent

Nǐ jīn nián duō dà le?
你今年 多 大了? How old are you?

Nǐ duō gāo?
你多 高? How tall are you?

Zhè tiáo lù yǒu duō cháng?
这 条 路有 多 长? How long is this road?

Nǐ xuéxí le duō cháng shíjiān?
你学习了多 长 时间? How long have you been studying?

shǎo
(7) 少 few; little; less; be short; lack

4. 练习 Exercises

(1) 根据翻译写出词语并注音 Write down the words and *pinyin* according to the English translations

many （ ）（ ）

汉语常用100字

few   (   )(   )
how many   (   )(   )
how old   (   )(   )
how long   (   )(   )

(2) 选择填空 Insert the correct answer in the blanks

多大　多长　多少　大　小　多　少

① 他今年25岁,我今年22岁,他比我_____。
② 昨天来了5个人,今天来了7个人,_____了2个人。
③ 那个房间不大,很_____。
④ 今天只来了一个人,来的人很_____。
⑤ 那条路有_____?
⑥ 我今年30岁,你今年_____?
⑦ 你的衣服_____钱?

5. 汉字知识　The knowledge of Chinese characters

"多"字的意思

"多"是一个会意字,篆书写作"多",上下两个月字重叠的样子。"月"字在古代指肉,上下两块肉堆积起来就表示数量多的意思。在古代汉语中,"多"还有贤德、美好等含义,这是阅读古籍时要注意的。

The Meaning of Character "多"

The character "多" is an associative compound character which was written as "多" in sealed character form. It looks like a piled up two "月". The character "月" referred to meat in the old times. The pile of two pieces of meat indicated a large number. In ancient Chinese, "多" also has the meaning of being virtuous and kind. We must pay attention to this when reading ancient books.

68. 早 early

zǎo
早

字源演变　The etymology of Chinese characters

小篆　　　　　楷体

1. 释义　Meaning

(early) morning; long ago; as early as; in advance (adj.)

2. 书写　Writing

3. 相关词语或表达　Related words or expressions

(1) 　zǎo
　　早 early

　　wǎn
　　晚 late

　　Wǒ zǎo jiù lái le.
　　我 早 就 来 了。I came very early.

　　Tā zǎo lái le yī ge xiǎoshí.
　　他 早 来 了 一 个 小时。He came an hour earlier.

　　Duìbuqǐ, wǒ lái wǎn le.
　　对不起,我 来 晚 了。Sorry, I'm late.

(2) 　zǎoshang/zǎochen
　　早上 / 早晨 morning

汉语常用100字

    wǎnshang
    晚上 evening, night

    Zǎoshang hǎo!
    早上　　好！Good morning.

    Wǎnshang hǎo!
    晚上　　好！Good evening.

    Nǐ zǎo!
    你 早！Good morning.

    wǎn'ān!
    晚安！Good night.

    zǎofàn/zǎocān
(3) 早饭/早餐 breakfast

    chī zǎofàn/zǎocān
    吃 早饭/早餐 have breakfast

    wǎnfàn/wǎncān
    晚饭/晚餐 dinner

    chī wǎnfàn/wǎncān
    吃晚饭/晚餐 have dinner

    wǎn
(4) 晚 late

    wǎnshang
    晚上 evening, night

    wǎnhuì
    晚会 party

4. 练习　Exercises

(1) 写一写 Write down the following words and phrases

    早上（　　　）　　早晨（　　　）

    你早（　　　）　　早上好（　　　）

    早饭（　　　）　　早餐（　　　）

    晚上（　　　）　　晚饭（　　　）

    晚餐（　　　）　　晚会（　　　）

(2) 完成句子 Complete the following sentences

    ① A：你早！

       B：_____！

六、作形容词的汉字 Characters as Adjectives

②A：晚上好！
　B：＿＿＿＿＿＿＿＿＿＿＿＿＿＿＿！
③我们八点上课，他十点才来，他＿＿＿＿＿＿＿。（晚）
④＿＿＿＿＿＿＿你做什么？（早上）
⑤你＿＿＿＿＿＿＿了吗？（早饭）

5. 汉字知识　The knowledge of Chinese characters

"早"字的意思

"早"的篆书写作"𠜎"，是一个会意字。上部是"日"，下部是"甲"，是十干（即"甲、乙、丙、丁、戊、己、庚、辛、壬、癸"，它们和十二支共配成六十组，用来表示年、月、日的次序）的开始，合起来表示太阳刚出来的时候。另一种解释是下部像是人头，日在头上，表示太阳刚刚升起。

The Meaning of Character "早"

The character "早" is an associative compound character which was written as "𠜎" in sealed character form. "日" is on the top and "甲" is at the bottom. "甲" is the first one of the ten Heavenly Stems (i.e. 甲, 乙, 丙, 丁, 戊, 己, 庚, 辛, 壬, 癸, which are combined with the twelve Earthly Branches to form 60 groups to designate years, months and days). Combining the two parts indicated the time when the Sun just rises. There is also another explanation: the lower part resembles the head of a person. The Sun is above the head, so the character means the time when the Sun rises.

69. 高 tall

gāo
高

字源演变　The etymology of Chinese characters

甲骨文　　　金文　　　小篆　　　楷体

1. 释义　Meaning

high, tall; of a high level or degree (adj.)

2. 书写　Writing

3. 相关词语或表达　Related words or expressions

(1) gāo
高 high, tall

ǎi
矮 low, short

Nà ge rén hěn gāo, zhè ge rén hěn ǎi.
那个人 很 高，这个人 很 矮。

That person is very tall while this person is very short.

Nà kē shù　　hěn gāo, zhè kē shù hěn ǎi.
那棵 树(tree)很 高，这棵树 很 矮。

That tree is very tall while this tree is very short.

六、作形容词的汉字 Characters as Adjectives

gāoshān
高山 high mountain

shēngāo
身高 height

Gēge shēngāo yī mǐ ba.
哥哥 身高 一米八。My elder brother is 180 centimeters tall.

(2) gāo
高 high

dī
低 low

Tā de Hànyǔ shuǐpíng hěn gāo, wǒ de Hànyǔ shuǐpíng hěn dī.
她 的 汉语 水平(level)很 高，我 的 汉语 水平 很 低。
Her Chinese is very good, but my Chinese is very poor.

Jīntiān de qìwēn gāo, zuótiān de qìwēn dī.
今天 的 气温(air temperature)高，昨天 的 气温 低。
The temperature is very high today, but the temperature was very low yesterday.

gāojí
高级 senior; high-ranking; high-grade; advanced

gāozhōng
高中 high school

gāodàng
高档 top grade; superior quality

dīdàng
低档 low grade

gāojià
高价 high price

dījià
低价 low price

(3) dī
低 low

ǎi
矮 low, short

4. 练习 Exercises

(1) 根据拼音写词语 Write down the words according to *pinyin*

gāo (   )   ǎi (   )   dī (   )

gāoshān (　　　)　　　　shēngāo (　　　)
gāojí (　　　)　　　　　gāozhōng (　　　)
gāodàng (　　　)　　　　dīdàng (　　　)
gāojià (　　　)　　　　　dījià (　　　)

（2）选词填空 Insert the correct answer in the blanks

高　　矮　　低

① 她的汉语很好，水平很_____。
② 昨天很冷（cold），气温很_____。
③ 他的爸爸妈妈都很高，可是他很_____。

5. 汉字知识　The knowledge of Chinese characters

"高"字的有关知识

"高"是一个象形字，甲骨文写作"峞"，像楼台层叠高筑的样子，其本义是高大。"高"还可以作为偏旁，凡是以"高"为偏旁的形声字大都与高大的意思有关。例如"亭"字，"高"为形符，省掉了下面的"口"，"丁"为声符，它的本义是指在高处盖的小建筑物。

"高"现在是一个常用词，用法也有很多，不仅用于高楼大厦，还有许多引申和比喻的用法，如"水平高"、"高科技"、"高速"、"高寿"、"高见"等等。

The Knowledge about the Character "高"

The character "高" is a pictographic character which was written as "峞" in oracle inscription form. It resembles a multi-layer high building, so it originally meant tall and big. "高" can also be used as a radical. The pictophonetic characters with "高" as the radical largely means tall and big. For example, "高", without "口" at the bottom, serves as the pictographic radical in the character "亭 (tíng)". "丁" is the phonetic radical. The character "亭" thus originally referred to a small building at a high place.

Nowadays, "高" is a common character with many usages. In addition

六、作形容词的汉字 Characters as Adjectives

to indicating tall buildings, it also has many extended and metaphorical meanings. For example, "水平高(shuǐpíng gāo)"(high level), "高科技(gāo kējì)" (advanced science and technology), "高速(gāosù)" (high speed), "高寿(gāoshòu)" (long life) and "高见(gāojiàn)" (wise opinion).

70. 胖 fat

pàng

胖

字源演变 The etymology of Chinese characters

小篆　　　　楷体

1. 释义　Meaning

fat; stout; plump (adj.)

2. 书写　Writing

3. 相关词语或表达　Related words or expressions

(1) 胖 pàng fat

Hǎojiǔ bú jiàn, nǐ pàng le.
好久 不见,你 胖 了。
I haven't seen you for a long time. You have gained some weight.

(2) 瘦 shòu thin,; tight

Zuìjìn shēntǐ bù hǎo, shòule.
最近 身体 不 好, 瘦了。
I don't feel very good recently, so I lost some weight.

六、作形容词的汉字 Characters as Adjectives

Zhè jiàn yīfu tài shòu le, wǒ bù néng chuān.
这 件衣服太 瘦 了,我不 能 穿。

This coat is too small for me to fit in.

(3) féi
肥 fat; loose-fitting

jiǎn féi
减 肥 to lose weight

Nà zhī xiǎo zhū hěn féi.
那只 小 猪 很肥。That pig is very fat.

Nà jiàn yīfu yǒudiǎnr féi.
那 件衣服有点儿 肥。That coat is a little big.

(4) pàngzi
胖子 a fat person; fatty

shòuzi
瘦子 a thin person

shòuròu
(5) 瘦肉 lean meat

féiròu
肥肉 fat

Wǒ bù chī féiròu, wǒ chī shòuròu.
我 不 吃 肥肉, 我 吃 瘦肉。I don't like fat. I like lean meat.

féi
肥 fat; loose-fitting

jiǎn féi
减 肥 to lose weight

shòu
瘦 thin, tight

4. 练习　Exercises

(1) 写一写 Write down the following sentences

① 哥哥很瘦,妈妈有点胖。

② 那只小猫很瘦,这只猪很肥。

③ 那件衣服有点瘦,这件衣服有点肥。

④ 你吃瘦肉，我吃肥肉。

⑤ 我正在减肥。

（2）选词填空 Insert the correct answer in the blanks

瘦　　胖　　肥

① 他吃得很多，所以他很_____。
② 她很瘦，她的衣服也很_____。
③ 那是一只小_____猪。

6. 汉字知识　The knowledge of Chinese characters
常见的偏旁部首(24)　月部

"月"是个象形字"⟨图⟩"。以"月"为偏旁的字多与月光、时间有关。比如"望"，其本义指每个月的中间一天；"朔"指的是每个月的第一天。由于"月"与"肉"的小篆是非常相似的，因此"月"字在古代又通"肉"字，人的身体部位，包括各器官内脏的字几乎都用"月"作偏旁部首，如人体从上到下依次为"脸"、"脖"、"胸"、"肚"、"腰""腿"、"脚"等等。

Common Radicals and Indexing Radicals (24)　月

The character "月" is a pictographic radical which was written as "⟨图⟩" in its ancient form. The characters that have it are largely related to moonlight and time. For example, the character "望(wàng)" originally referred to the middle day of every month; the character "朔(shuò)" referred to the first day of every month. Since the sealed character forms of "月" and "肉(ròu)"(meat; flesh) were similar, so the two characters were interchangeable in the old times. The characters for body parts of human, including internal organs, all use "月" as their radical. For example, "脸(liǎn)" (face), "脖(bó)" (neck), "胸(xiōng)" (breast), "肚(dù)" (belly), "腰(yāo)" (waist), "腿(tuǐ)" (leg) and "脚(jiǎo)" (foot).

71. 老 old

lǎo
老

字源演变 The etymology of Chinese characters

甲骨文　　　　　金文　　　　　小篆　　　　　楷体

1. 释义　Meaning

old, aged, outdated (adj.); always (adv.)

2. 书写　Writing

3. 相关词语或表达　Related words or expressions

(1) 老 lǎo old, aged, outdated (a.)

Nǎinai bāshí suì, hěn lǎo, wǒ èrshí suì, hěn niánqīng, tā wǔ suì, hěn xiǎo.
奶奶 80 岁,很 老,我 20 岁,很 年轻,他 5 岁,很 小。

Grandma is 80 years old. She is very old. I am 20 years old. I am pretty young. He is 5 years old. He is very young.

Zhè ge fángzi yībǎi nián le, hěn lǎo le.
这 个 房子 100 年了,很 老了。

The building is 100 years old. It is very old.

Tā shì wǒ de lǎo tóngxué, yě shì wǒ de lǎo péngyou.
他 是 我 的 老 同学,也 是 我 的 老 朋友。

汉语常用100字

He is my former classmate and also my old friend.

Zhè ge lǎoren shì wǒ yéye.
这 个 老人 是 我 爷爷。This old man is my grandpa.

lǎo
(2) 老 always (ad.)

    lǎoshì
    老是 always

    Tā lǎo(shì) chídào.
    他老(是）迟到。 He is always late.

(3) prefix

    Lǎo Wáng
    老 王 Lao Wang (used in terms of address before the surnames of acquaintances or friends to indicate intimacy or informality)

    Lǎo èr
    老 二（the second oldest child）

In kinship terms before numerals to indicate order of seniority

Wǒmen jiā yǒu liǎng ge háizi, wǒ shì lǎo dà, dìdi shì lǎo èr.
我们 家有 两 个 孩子,我 是 老 大,弟弟是 老 二。
Our family has two children. I am the elder one and my brother is the younger one.

        lǎoshī
(4) 老师 teacher

    lǎobǎn
    老板 boss

    lǎogōng
    老公 husband

    lǎopo
    老婆 wife

    lǎohǔ   yī zhī lǎohǔ
    老虎 tiger   一只老虎 a tiger

    lǎoshǔ   yī zhī lǎoshǔ
    老鼠 rat, mouse   一只 老鼠 a rat

    lǎojiā
    老家 hometown; native place; birth place

    Wǒ de lǎojiā zài Běijīng.
    我 的 老家在 北京。Beijing is my hometown.

      niánqīng
(5) 年轻 young

六、作形容词的汉字 Characters as Adjectives

4. 练习　Exercises

（1）请根据英语的意思写出汉字 Write down the Chinese characters according to the English meaning

例如：old (老)

boss (　　　)　　　　teacher (　　　)
hometown (　　　)　　tiger (　　　)
husband (　　　)　　　wife (　　　)
always (　　　)　　　　mouse (　　　)

（2）选词填空 Insert the correct answer in the blanks

老　　老板　　老师　　老是　　老虎　　老婆　　老家

① 他_____去那个商店买东西。
② 他们家是_____做饭。
③ _____在教室里上课。
④ 昨天我看见一只_____。
⑤ 我的奶奶很_____了。
⑥ 他是公司的_____。
⑦ 我的_____在山东。

5. 汉字知识　The knowledge of Chinese characters

"老"字的起源与发展

　　"老"的古文字形是一个驼背挂杖的长发老人的形象"𦒻"，表示"年岁大"。它最初专指老人或长者，"敬老院"指的就是专门为老年人养老服务的社会福利事业组织，又称"养老院"。后来"老"逐渐也用于活的时间比较长的动物和植物，或很久以前就存在的，比如"老马"、"老树"、"老同学"、"老朋友"。再后来，就连一些没有生命力的物体也用"老"来表示年代久远，如"老房子"、"老牌子"。

The Origin and Evolution of "老"

　　The ancient form of the character "老" is written as "𦒻" which looks like a humpbacked old person with long hair and a walking stick, indicating

263

"old age". At first, it referred to old people specifically. "敬老院(jìnglǎoyuàn)"(seniors' home) refers to the social welfare institution for the old people. It is also called "养老院(yǎnglǎoyuàn)". Gradually the character was used for animals and plants that have lived for a long time or that existed long ago. For example, "老马(lǎomǎ)" (old horse), "老树(lǎoshù)" (old tree), "老同学(lǎotóngxué)" (former classmate) and "老朋友(lǎopéngyou)" (old friend). We now use it to describe some lifeless objects that have been existed for a long time, such as "老房子(lǎofángzi)" (old house) and "老牌子(lǎopáizi)" (old brand).

72. 长 long

cháng

字源演变   The etymology of Chinese characters

甲骨文   小篆   繁体   楷体

1. 释义   Meaning
long (adj.)

2. 书写   Writing

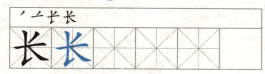

3. 相关词语或表达   Related words or expressions

cháng
长 long

duǎn
短 short

Tā de tóufa hěn cháng, wǒ de toufa hěn duǎn.
她的头发很 长，我的头发很 短。

Her hair is pretty long and my hair is very short.

Wǒ děng le nǐ hěn cháng shíjiān.
我 等了你很 长 时间。

I have been waiting for you for a long time.

chángdù
长度 length

汉语常用100字

duō cháng
多　　长 how long

Zhè tiáo hé yǒu duō cháng?
这 条 河 有 多　　长? How long is this river?

Cóng nǐ jiā dào xuéxiào zǒu lù duō cháng shíjiān?
从　你家 到　学校　走路多　　长　时间?
How long does it take for you to walk to school from your home?

chángqī
长期 long term

duǎnqī
短期 short term

4. 练习　Exercises

(1) 请将下列形容词中意思相反的词语连线 Please link the adjectives of the opposite meanings

大	短
多	小
早	少
高	晚
胖	矮
长	瘦

(2) 选词填空 Insert the correct answer in the blanks

　　　　　长　　短　　长期　　长度　　多长

① 长城有10000里(lǐ, 1/2kilometer),很_____。

② 他要_____住在中国,可能20年。

③ 学完一课要_____时间?

④ 这条路的_____是500米。

⑤ 男孩子的头发一般(yībān, usually)都很_____。

六、作形容词的汉字 Characters as Adjectives

6. 汉字知识　The knowledge of Chinese characters
"长"字的释义

"长"读cháng时与"短"相对；还有一个读音是"zhǎng"。在甲骨文里，它是一个弓腰拄杖、长发被风吹起的老人形象"🗡"。古人认为身体发肤受之父母，是不能毁坏的，所以年龄越大，头发就越长。"长者"表示年纪较大、排行最大或辈分大的人。家里最大的男孩子称为"长子"；"长兄"的意思是"大哥"。"长"还表示"领导人"，如"校长"、"院长"、"市长"、"局长"等。另外，读"zhǎng"时还可以做动词，是"生长"的意思。

The Meaning of Character "长"

When pronounced as cháng, the character "长" is opposite to "短". It also has another pronunciation—zhǎng. It is written as "🗡" in its oracle inscription form. It is the image of a humpbacked old person with his hair floating in the wind and a walking stick. The ancients thought that body and hair are given by parents which is why they would endure, so the hair grew longer with age. "长者(zhǎngzhě)" (seniors) refers to elders, the person who is the oldest of his generation or is ranked highest on the family tree. The oldest boy of a family is called "长子 (zhǎngzǐ)"; "长兄(zhǎngxiōng)" means the eldest brother. "长" can also be used for leaders, such as "校长 (xiàozhǎng)" (school principal), "院长 (yuànzhǎng)" (hospital director), "市长 (shìzhǎng)" (mayor) and "局长 (júzhǎng)" (bureau chief). In addition, it can be a verb when pronounced as "zhǎng", meaning "生长 (shēngzhǎng)" (grow).

73. 白 white

字源演变 The etymology of Chinese characters

甲骨文　　　　金文　　　　小篆　　　　楷体

1. 释义　Meaning

white (adj.)

2. 书写　Writing

3. 相关词语或表达　Related words or expressions

(1) 黑 hēi　black

　　红 hóng　red

　　绿 lǜ　green

　　黄 huáng　yellow

　　蓝 lán　blue

　　紫 zǐ　purple

六、作形容词的汉字 Characters as Adjectives

huī
灰　grey

chéng
橙　orange

　　　　báisè　　　hēisè
(2) 白色 white　黑色 black

Tā de yīfu shì báisè de, wǒ de yīfu shì hēisè de.
他的衣服是 白色 的，我 的衣服是 黑色的。

His jacket is white and mine is black.

báifà
白发 white hair

　　　báitiān
(3) 白天 daytime

Hěn duō rén zài báitiān gōngzuò, wǎnshang shuì jiào.
很 多 人 在 白天　工作，　晚上　睡 觉。

Many people work during the day and sleep during the night.

　　　míngbai
(4) 明白　understand

Nǐ míngbai zhè ge wèntí le ma?
你 明白 这个 问题 了 吗? Did you understand this question?

4. 练习　Exercises

(1) 把与下列词语相对应的意思、拼音进行连线 Link the following words with their correspondent meanings and pronunciations

红	white	bái
白	black	hóng
黑	blue	lán
蓝	green	hēi
绿	purple	zǐ
紫	grey	huī
灰	red	lǜ
黄	orange	chéng
橙	yellow	huáng

汉语常用100字

(2) 选词填空 Insert the correct answer in the blanks

白色　　白天　　明白　　黑色　　白发

① 今天学习的生词(shēngcí)(new words)你都_____了吗？
② 今天_____很热。
③ 妈妈有很多_____了。
④ 黑板(hēibǎn)(blackboard)是_____的。
⑤ 雪(xuě)(snow)是_____的。

5. 汉字知识　The knowledge of Chinese characters
常见的偏旁部首(25)　白部

"白"的古字形写作"𐌏"，像太阳刚刚露出地平面，喷薄欲出的样子。这时天色开始变白，由此演绎出"白色"、"白天"的"白"。"白色"与其他颜色相比在某种意义上似乎成了无色，于是"白"又有了"什么都没有"之类的意义，比如"白费力气"的"白"表示毫无效果；"白吃白拿"的"白"意思是不花一点代价。

凡是以"白"为偏旁的形声字大多与白色、明亮有关。比如"皎"、"皓"都是形容像月光一样洁白明亮；"皙"本义为肤色白；"的"的本义是清楚明白，如"的确"。

Common Radicals and Indexing Radicals (25)　白

The character "白" is written as "𐌏" in its ancient form, appearing like the rising sun that just emerges in the horizon. The sky is turning white at this time, so the character developed that meaning of being white as in the phrase "白色(báisè)" (white color) and "白天(báitiān)" (daytime). In a sense, white seems to be colorless as compared with other colors, so "白" acquired the meaning of "having nothing". For example, "白" in the phrase "白费力气(bái fèi lìqi)" means without any effect; "白" in the phrase "白吃白拿(bái chī bái ná)" means without any cost.

The pictophonetic characters with "白" as the radical are mostly related

六、作形容词的汉字 Characters as Adjectives

to white or bright. Such as "皎(jiǎo)" and "皓(hào)". Both are used to describe something as spotlessly white and bright as moonlight. "晳(xī)" originally means fair skin. "的(dí)" originally means clearly understanding something, such as "的确(díquè)".

74. 甜 sweet

tián
甜

字源演变　The etymology of Chinese characters

小篆　　　　　楷体

1. 释义　Meaning

sweet (adj.)

2. 书写　Writing

3. 相关词语或表达　Related words or expressions

（1）tián
　　甜 sweet

　　　Zhè ge táng zhēn tián!
　　　这 个 糖 真 甜！The candy is really sweet!

　　　tiánpǐn
　　　甜品 dessert

　　　tiánshí
　　　甜食 sweet foods

　　　Wǒ bù xǐhuan tiánshí.
　　　我 不 喜欢 甜食。I don't like sweet stuff.

（2）tián
　　甜 comfortable, pleasant

六、作形容词的汉字 Characters as Adjectives

Háizi shuì de hěn tián.
孩子 睡 得 很 甜。The children are sleeping soundly.

tiánměi
甜美 pleasant, sweet

Tā xiàode hěn tiánměi.
她 笑得 很 甜美。She has sweet smiles.

tián yán mì yǔ
甜 言 蜜 语 sweet words and honeyed phrases

Tā chángcháng duì nǚ péngyou shuō tián yán mì yǔ.
他 常常 对女 朋友 说 甜 言 蜜语。
He often gives his girl friend sweet talks.

suān
(3) 酸 sour, acid

kǔ
(4) 苦 bitter

là
(5) 辣 hot, spicy

xián
(6) 咸 salty

4. 练习　**Exercises**

（1）将下列物品与他们所对应的味道连线 Link the following objects with their corresponding flavors

糖（sugar）　　　　酸（sour）

盐（salt）　　　　　苦（bitter）

醋（vinegar）　　　辣（spicy）

咖啡（coffee）　　　咸（salty）

辣椒（pepper）　　　甜（sweet）

（2）选词填空 Insert the correct answer in the blanks

　　　　甜食　　甜　　甜美　　甜言蜜语

① 她太胖了,不能再吃_____了。

② 别说_____了,我不喜欢。

③ 那儿有我_____的回忆(huíyì, memories)。

④ 糖很_____,别吃太多了。

汉语常用100字

5. 汉字知识　The knowledge of Chinese characters
"甜"与"苦"

"甜"是一个会意字,由"舌"和"甘"左右组合而成。舌是味觉器官,可以感知甘甜。古人认为味甘达到极高的程度就是甜,像糖或蜜的味道。与"苦"相对。由此义可引申为幸福或舒适,如"甜蜜的生活"、"睡得很甜"。"他的嘴很甜"意思就是"他喜欢说好听的话。"

"甜" and "苦"

The character "甜" is an associative compound character which is formed by "舌" and "甘". "舌(shé)" (tongue) is a taste organ that can feel sweetness. Ancient people believed the highest level of sweetness is "甜" like the taste of sugar or honey. It is opposite to "苦(kǔ)" (bitterness). The character "甜" thus can have an extended use to mean happiness or comfort as in the phrases "甜蜜的生活(tiánmì de shēnghuó)" (happy life) and "睡得很甜(shuì de hěn tián)" (sound sleep). "他的嘴很甜(tā de zuǐ hěn tián)" means he talks sweetly.

75. 饿 hungry

字源演变　The etymology of Chinese characters

　小篆　　　　　繁体　　　　　楷体

1. 释义　Meaning

hungry (adj.)

2. 书写　Writing

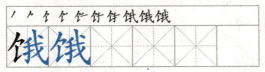

3. 相关词语或表达　Related words or expressions

(1) 饿 è hungry

Jīntiān méi chī zǎofàn, xiànzài wǒ hěn è.
今天 没 吃 早饭，现在 我 很 饿。
I didn't have breakfast this morning, so I am hungry right now.

(2) 饱 bǎo full

Chī le hěn duō, wǒ chībǎo le.
吃 了 很 多，我 吃饱 了。 I've had a lot of food. I am pretty full.

(3) 渴 kě thirsty

汉语常用100字

Yī tiān méi hē shuǐ, xiànzài hěn kě.
一天 没喝 水，现在 很渴。

I haven't drunk all day long. I am very thirsty now.

kǒu kě
口 渴 thirsty

Nǐ kǒu kě ma? hē diǎn shuǐ ba.
你口渴吗？喝点 水 吧。Are you thirsty? Drink some water.

4. 练习 Exercises

(1) 将下列词语与他们所对应的意思连线 Link the following words and their meanings

胖	thin
瘦	long
长	short
短	fat
白	sweet
黑	white
甜	hungry
饿	full
饱	thirsty
渴	black

(2) 选词填空 Insert the correct answer in the blanks

　　　　　饿　渴　饱　喝　吃

① 我_____了一杯水。
② 今天没吃早饭，现在很_____。
③ 你想_____米饭吗？
④ 你吃_____了吗？
⑤ 我有点儿_____，你有水吗？

276

六、作形容词的汉字 Characters as Adjectives

5. 汉字知识　The knowledge of Chinese characters

"饿"与"饱"

　　"饿"是一个形声字。左边是表意的形旁"食"部,"食"作形旁的字多和饮食有关。右边是声旁。没有吃的感觉很饿,相反就是"饱"。表示"饿"的还有一个形声字"饥",两个字还可组合成词语"饥饿"。

"饿" and "饱"

　　The character "饿" is a pictophonetic character. "食" used as the pictographic radical is on the left. The characters with pictographic radical "食" are mostly related to food. The phonetic radical is the right part. Having nothing to eat makes people feel hungry. To the contrary, people feel full ("饱", bǎo). The pictophonetic character "饥" (jī) also means hungry. The two characters can combine to form a phrase "饥饿(jī'è)"(hungry).

76. 热 hot

rè
热

字源演变 The etymology of Chinese characters

小篆　　　　　　繁体　　　　　　楷体

1. 释义　Meaning

hot; popular (adj.); heat up (v.)

2. 书写　Writing

3. 相关词语或表达　Related words or expressions

(1) 热　hot
rè

Zhèr xiàtiān hěn rè, dōngtiān hěn lěng.
这儿 夏天 很 热，冬天 很 冷。

It's hot in summer and cold in winter here.

Wǒ yào yī bēi rè kāfēi.
我 要一杯 热 咖啡。I want to have a cup of hot coffee.

Qiūtiān lái le, tiānqì liáng le.
秋天 来了，天气 凉 了。

The autumn has come and the weather is getting colder.

六、作形容词的汉字 Characters as Adjectives

(2) rè
　　热 heat up

　　　Fàn liáng le, rè yíxià ba.
　　　饭 凉了,热 一下吧。The food is cold. You'd better heat it up.

(3) rèqíng
　　热情 warm, warm-hearted

　　　Zhōngguó rén hěn rèqíng.
　　　中国 人 很 热情。The Chinese people are very warmhearted.

(4) rènao
　　热闹 lively

　　　Wǎnhuì hěn rènao.
　　　晚会 很 热闹。The evening party is very exciting.

(5) popular; hot

　　　Xiànzài xué Hànyǔ hěn rè.
　　　现在 学 汉语 很 热。Learning Chinese is very popular now.

　　　rèmén
　　　热门 popular, in great demand

　　　rèmén shāngpǐn
　　　热门 商品（merchandise in great demand）

　　　rèmén huàtí
　　　热门 话题（hot topics）

(6) lěng
　　冷 cold

(7) liáng
　　凉 cool

4. 练习　Exercises

(1) 请给下列词语注音并翻译成英语 Write down the *pinyin* of the following words and translate them into English

　　热（　　）（　　　　）

　　冷（　　）（　　　　）

　　凉（　　）（　　　　）

　　热门（　　）（　　　　）

　　热闹（　　）（　　　　）

　　热情（　　）（　　　　）

(2) 连词成句 Arrange the following words in correct order to form a sentence

① 水　　热　　很
② 冬天　　冷　　很
③ 饭　　凉　　不
④ 很　　那儿　　热闹
⑤ 是　　音乐（music）　　这　　热门
⑥ 很　　他们　　热情

5. 汉字知识　The knowledge of Chinese characters
常见的偏旁部首(26)　火部

"火"作形旁的字大多和火有关。火字旁一般在左侧，比如"烧"、"烤"、"灯"。"灬"是"火"字的变体，作偏旁在字的下部。

"热"是一个简化字，繁体字写作"熱"，本来是一个形声字，简化之后成为一个新组合的会意字。上部的"执"就是用手拿着，如"执笔"。下面的火字底"灬"表示火苗。用手拿着火，当然就热了。

Common Radicals and Indexing Radicals (26)　火

The characters with "火" as the pictographic radicals are largely connected with fire. It is generally on the left as in the characters "烧 (shāo)" (burn), "烤 (kǎo)" (bake), "灯 (dēng)" (light). "灬" is a variant of "火". As a radical, it is placed at the bottom of a character.

"热" is a simplified character which was written as "熱" in traditional Chinese. It is used to be a pictophonetic character. After being simplified, it became a newly associative compound character. "执 (zhí)" on the top means holding something in your hand, as in "执笔(zhíbǐ)" (holding a pen). "灬" signifies flames. It is clearly very hot if you hold flames in your hand.

77. 好 good

hǎo
好

字源演变 The etymology of Chinese characters

甲骨文　　　金文　　　小篆　　　楷体

1. 释义　Meaning

good, nice, well, fine (adj.)

2. 书写　Writing

3. 相关词语或表达　Related words or expressions

(1) hǎo
好 good, nice, well, fine

Wǒ de Hànyǔ bù hǎo, tā de Hànyǔ hěn hǎo.
我 的 汉语 不 好，他 的 汉语 很 好。
My Chinese is poor. His Chinese is very good.

　　Nǐ shēntǐ hǎo ma?
A: 你 身体 好 吗？How is your health?

　　Wǒ shēntǐ hěn hǎo.
B: 我 身体 很 好。I am fine.

(2) huài
坏 bad, ruin, spoiled

汉语常用100字

Zhè zhī bǐ shì huài de.
这 支笔是 坏 的。This pen is broken.

Niúnǎi huài le, bié hē le.
牛奶 坏 了,别 喝 了。The milk has gone bad. Don't drink it.

(3) hàochī
好吃 delicious

hǎohē
好喝 tasty

hǎotīng
好听 pleasant to hear

hǎowán
好玩 amusing; interesting

(4) Nǐ hǎo!
你好！Hello!

Zǎoshang hǎo!
早上 好！Good morning!

Xiàwǔ hǎo!
下午 好！ Good afternoon!

Wǎnshang hǎo!
晚上 好！ Good evening!

4. 练习　Exercises

(1) 写一写 Write down the following words and expressions

好事(　　　)　　　坏事(　　　)

好玩(　　　)　　　你好(　　　)

好喝(　　　)　　　好吃(　　　)

好听(　　　)　　　早上好(　　　)

下午好(　　　)　　　晚上好(　　　)

(2) 连词成句 Arrange the following words in correct order to form a sentence

① 身体　吗　你　好 ？

② 是　他　一个　不　坏人 。

六、作形容词的汉字 Characters as Adjectives

③ 菜　这个　　了　坏,吃　别　了。

④ 晚上　大家　好　！

5. 汉字知识　The knowledge of Chinese characters
常见的偏旁部首(27)　女部

　　以"女"为偏旁组成的字有数百个,大都和女性有关系,比如一些称谓词:"妈妈"、"奶奶"、"姥姥"、"姐姐"、"妹妹"、"姑姑"、"姨"等等。"妻"与"夫"相对。"姓"是远古氏族的标志,同一氏族的人不能互相通婚,男人一定要娶不同姓的女人。这样,姓对女人来说就很重要。因此"姓、婚、姻"等字也用"女"作表意偏旁。

　　"好"是一个会意字。因为"女人"又可称为"女子",古人认为女人貌美,所以就用"女"和"子"合起来表示美好的意思。还有一种解释说,"好"在古汉字中是一个妇女抱着孩子"㜽",一个女人有了孩子就是一件好事。发展到后来,一切美善的东西,不管是具体的还是抽象的,都可以用"好"来形容了。

Common Radicals and Indexing Radicals (27)　女

　　There are hundreds of characters that take "女" as their radical and most of them are related to the female, including "妈妈(māma)"(mother), "奶奶(nǎinai)"(grandmother, father's mother), "姥姥 (lǎolao)"(grandmother, mother's mother), "姐姐(jiějie)"(elder sister), "姑姑(gūgu)"(aunt, father's sister), "姨(yí)"(aunt, mother's sister) and some other address terms. "妻(qī)" (wife) corresponds to "夫(fū)" (husband). "姓(xìng)" (family name) is the symbol of remote clans. People of the same clan were forbidden to marry. Men must marry women of different family names, therefore the family name was very important to women. As a result, "姓(xìng)" (family name), "婚(hūn)" (marriage) and "姻(yīn)" (marriage) all use "女" as the pictographic radical.

　　"好" is an associative compound character. Since "女人(nǚrén)" can be called "女子(nǚzǐ)". Ancient people believed women were beautiful, so they combined "女" and "子" to express the meaning of beauty. There is also another explanation: in ancient character, "㚩" depicted a woman holding a baby, and it was a nice thing for a woman to have a child. In later development, all the nice and beautiful things, no matter concrete or abstract one, people can use "好" to describe it.

78. 新 new

xīn
新

字源演变　The etymology of Chinese characters

　甲骨文　　　　　金文　　　　　小篆　　　　　楷体

1. 释义　Meaning

good, nice, well, fine (adj.)

2. 书写　Writing

3. 相关词语或表达　Related words or expressions

(1) 新 xīn new(a.); newly (adv.)

Zhè běn shū hěn xīn, nà běn shū hěn jiù.
这 本 书 很 新，那 本 书 很 旧。
This book is pretty new. That one is very old.

Tā shì wǒ de xīn péngyou, tā shì wǒ de lǎo péngyou.
他 是 我 的 新 朋友，她 是 我 的 老 朋友。
He is my new friend and she is my old friend.

Nà shì wǒ xīn mǎi de yīfu.
那 是 我 新 买 的衣服。That's my new clothes.

汉语常用100字

(2)   xīnnián
    新年 new year

    Xīnnián kuàilè!
    新年 快乐！Happy new year!

(3)   xīnshēng
    新生 new students

    lǎoshēng
    老生 old students

    Tāmen shì yī niánjí xīnshēng, wǒmen shì sì niánjí lǎoshēng.
    他们 是一年级 新生，我们 是四 年级 老生。
    They are freshmen. We are seniors.

(4)   xīnxiān
    新鲜 fresh (a.)

    Xiàyǔ yǐhòu de kōngqì hěn xīnxiān.
    下雨 以后 的 空气 很 新鲜。The air is very fresh after the rain.

(5)   xīnwén
    新闻 news (n.)

(6)   jiù
    旧 used

(7)   lǎo
    老 old

4. 练习 Exercises

(1) 请写一写下列意思相反的词组并记住用法 Please write the following words with opposite meanings and remember their usages

    新书——旧书（   ）（   ）

    新手表——旧手表（   ）（   ）

    新手机——旧手机（   ）（   ）

    新生——老生（   ）（   ）

    新朋友——老朋友（   ）（   ）

    新同学——老同学（   ）（   ）

六、作形容词的汉字 Characters as Adjectives

(2) 选词填空 Insert the correct answer in the blanks

新　旧　老　新鲜　新闻

① 他是_____来的老师。
② 妈妈的这件衣服穿了10年,很_____了。
③ 你看今天的_____了吗?
④ 我们认识5年了,是_____朋友。
⑤ 今天的蔬菜(shūcài, vegetables)很_____。

5. 汉字知识　The knowledge of Chinese characters

"新"字的起源与演变

"新"是"薪"的本字。甲骨文左边是一棵树的形状,右边是"斤"。"斤"本来是一种跟斧相似的工具。"新"的本义是用斧头砍伐木材,用来做柴火。后来,借用它来记录新鲜、新旧的"新"。用得多了,为了避免混淆,干脆给本来表示柴火的"新"字加上一个草字头,于是就有了"薪"字。成语"釜底抽薪"的"薪"就是这样来的。

"新"还表示刚开始,如"新年"(公历的一月一号,又称元旦)。新婚夫妇又叫"新郎"、"新娘"。

The Origin and Evolution of "新"

"新" is the original form of the character "薪(xīn)" (firewood). In its oracle inscription form, the left side depicts a tree, and the right side is "斤". "斤" used to be an axe-like tool. So the character "新" originally means chopping wood by axe to get firewood. Later, the character "新" was also used to describe something that is fresh and new. To distinguish the two characters, we added a cover to the character "新" to indicate firewood. This is the origin of "薪"(xīn). For example, "薪" in the idiom "釜底抽薪 (fǔ dǐ chōu xīn)" (withdraw the firewood from a boiling cauldron).

"新" also means the beginning, such as "新年(xīnnián)" (new year). (Please notice that the New Year refers to January 1 on the Gregorian calendar. Spring Festival is called "春节 chūnjié" or "年 nián"). Newlywed couple is called "新郎(xīnláng)" (groom) and "新娘(xīnniáng)" (bride).

79. 对 correct

duì
对

字源演变　The etymology of Chinese characters

甲骨文　　　　小篆　　　　　繁体　　　　　楷体

1. 释义　Meaning
right, yes (adj.)

2. 书写　Writing

3. 相关词语或表达　Related words or expressions

(1) 对 right
    duì

Tā huídá duì le.
他 回答 对了。He got the right answer.

Nǐ shuō de bú duì.
你 说 得不对。What you say is not right.

(2) 错 wrong, fault
    cuò

Nǐ huídá cuò le.
你 回答 错了。You got the wrong answer.

Zhè shì wǒ de cuò, bú shi tā de cuò.
这 是我 的 错,不 是他 的 错。It's my fault, not his.

六、作形容词的汉字 Characters as Adjectives

búcuò
不错 pretty good

Nǐ de Hànyǔ zhēn búcuò.
你的 汉语 真 不错。Your Chinese is really good.

duì
(3) 对 yes

    Nǐ shì Zhōngguó rén ma?
A：你 是 中国 人 吗？Are you Chinese?

    Duì, wǒ shì Zhōngguó rén.
B：对，我 是 中国 人。Yes, I am Chinese.

duì
(4) 对, pair, couple (classifier)

yí duì ěrhuán
一对 耳环 a pair of earrings

yí duì fūqī
一对 夫妻 a couple

4. 练习 **Exercises**

(1) 写一写 Write down the following sentences

Zhè ge Hànzì nǐ xiěduì le.
这 个 汉字你 写对 了。

You write the character in the right way.

Duìbuqǐ, wǒ shuōcuò le.
对不起，我 说错 了。

Sorry, I said something wrong.

Nǐ shì lǎoshī, duì bu duì?
你是 老师，对 不 对？

 You are a teacher, aren't you?

Tā méiyǒu cuò.
他 没有 错。

He didn't do anything wrong。

Nà jiàn yīfu zhēn búcuò.
那 件 衣服 真 不错。

That coat looks really nice.

(2) 选择填空 Insert the correct answer in the blanks

对　　错　　对不对　　不错

① 那儿的菜_____,很好吃。
② 对不起,我做_____了。
③ 你是中国人,_____?
④ 很好,你回答_____了。

5. 汉字知识　The knowledge of Chinese characters

常见的偏旁部首(28)　又部

"又"的甲骨文和"右"都是人的右手形状 ，因此以"又"组合的字很多都与手或手的动作有关。比如,古代打仗时的胜利者往往用割取对方阵亡者的左耳来统计战果,而"取"字的甲骨文 就表现为战胜者手拿一只被割下的耳朵的形象。

Common Radicals and Indexing Radicals (28)　又

In oracle inscription forms, both of the character "又" and the "右" had the shape of a right hand " ". As a result, the characters with "又" as the radical are mostly related to hands or the actions of hands. For example, in ancient times, the victors of a war usually cut off the left ears of their dead enemies to count the number and claim their victory. So the character "取 (qǔ)" (take) was written as " " in its oracle inscription form, depicts the victor holding an ear in his hand.

80. 美 beautiful

měi
美

字源演变　The etymology of Chinese characters

甲骨文　　　　金文　　　　小篆　　　　楷体

1. 释义　Meaning

beautiful, good, pretty; happy (adj.); short for the United States or America (n.)

2. 书写　Writing

3. 相关词语或表达　Related words or expressions

(1) 美 měi beautiful, good, pretty

Zhè ge dìfang zhēn měi.
这 个 地方 真 美。This place is beautiful.

měilì
美丽 beautiful

Tā shì ge měilì de gūniang.
她 是 个 美丽 的 姑娘。She is a pretty girl.

měishí
美食 good food

měijiǔ
美酒 good wine

汉语常用100字

měiwèi
美味 delicacy

měijǐng
美景 beautiful scenery

měi
(2) 美 happy

Kǎoshì tōngguò le, tā xīnli hěn měi.
考试 通过(pass)了,她心里 很 美。

She has passed the test. She feels very happy.

měihǎo
美好 happy, glorious

měihǎo de shēnghuó
美好 的 生活 happy life

Měizhōu
(3) 美洲 America

Měiguó
美国 United States

Měiyuán
美元 U.S. dollar

chǒu
(4) 丑 ugly

Tā zhǎng de hěn chǒu.
她 长 得 很 丑。She looks very ugly.

4. 练习 Exercises

(1) 请把下列词语的拼音和意思连线 Please link the *pinyin* and meanings of the following words

美丽	měihǎo	good wine
美好	měishí	beautiful
美食	měiwèi	happy
美味	měijiǔ	good food
美酒	měilì	delicacy
美景	Měizhōu	Americas
美洲	Měiguó	U.S. dollar
美国	Měiyuán	beautiful scene
美元	měijǐng	U.S.

六、作形容词的汉字 Characters as Adjectives

(2) 选择填空 Insert the correct answer in the blanks

      美   丑   美酒   美元   美洲   美丽

① 她不漂亮,有点_____。
② 我在那儿喝了很多_____。
③ 美国是一个_____的国家。
④ 我去过很多_____的地方。
⑤ 大家都赞美(zànměi, praise)他,他的心里_____极了。
⑥ 我有500_____。

5. 汉字知识　The knowledge of Chinese characters

"美"字的意思

"美",小篆写作"羑",是一个会意字。有人解释说,上部是一只羊,下部是一个"大"字,羊长大了,它的肉味道甘美,很好吃,所以人们把好吃的东西叫做美味。也有人解释说,人以羊状饰而舞。不管哪一种解释,从造字方法来看,都属于会意。

The Meaning of Character "美"

"美" written as "羑" in sealed character form is an associative compound character. Some people explain that the upper part is a sheep and the lower part is a character "大 (dà)" (big). The sheep will taste very delicious after it grows big, so people call delicious food "美味(měiwèi)". Some people have another explanation: the person is dancing with a sheep-shaped ornament. In terms of character formation, both explanations concur that the character is an associative compound character.

七、作虚词的汉字
Characters as Function Words

81. 不 no

bù
不

字源演变 The etymology of Chinese characters

甲骨文　　　　金文　　　　小篆　　　　楷体

1. 释义　Meaning

used to form a negative; used as a negative answer (adv.)

2. 书写　Writing

3. 相关词语或表达　Related words or expressions

（1）(used before verbs, adjectives and some adverbs; never before "有") not

Míngtiān wǒ bù qù shàng kè.
明天 我 不 去 上课。I will not go to school tomorrow.

Tā bù xǐhuan xuéxí.
他 不 喜欢 学习。He doesn't like study.

七、作虚词的汉字 Characters as Function Words

Tā jīntiān bù lái le.
他 今天 不 来了。He is not coming today.

Jīntiān de tiānqì bù hǎo.
今天 的 天气 不 好。The weather is bad today.

Zhèlǐ de rén bù duō.
这里的 人 不 多。There're not many people here.

Attention: Used as "A不A" to form a question.(A is a verb or adj.)

Míngtiān nǐ qù bu qù?　Míngtiān nǐ qù ma?
明天　你去不去？（=明天 你去 吗？）Will you go tomorrow?

Nǐ è bu è?　　Nǐ è ma?
你饿不饿？(=你饿吗？) Are you hungry?

(2) (used by itself in responses) not; no

　　　Tā zhīdào ma?
A：他 知道 吗？ Did he know it?

　　　Bù, tā bù zhīdào.
B：不, 他不 知道。No, he didn't.

　　　Tā bù zhīdào ba?
A：他不 知道 吧？ He doesn't know it, does he?

　　　Bù　tā zhīdào.
B：不, 他 知道。yes, he does.

4. 练习　**Exercises**

(1) 请用"不"写出下列词语的否定形式 Please write the negative form of the following words using "不"

是(　　)看(　　)做(　　)

喝(　　)给(　　)买(　　)

来(　　)会(　　)能(　　)

大(　　)多(　　)甜(　　)

好(　　)对(　　)饿(　　)

(2) 请写出下列句子的否定形式 Please write down the negative form of the following sentences

① 明天我去学校。

　　I will go to school tomorrow.

② 我喜欢打球。

　　I like playing balls.

③ 他会唱歌。

　　He can sing.

④ 这里的人很多。

　　There are a lot of people here.

⑤ 他是美国人。

　　He is American.

5. 汉字知识　The knowledge of Chinese characters

"不"的起源与演变

甲骨文的"不"字写作"不",上面的一横表示地面,下面的须状曲线表示植物初生时向地下生长的根系。所以,"不"字的本义是植物的胚种。后来其本义消失,假借为否定副词。所以它还有一个读音是"fǒu",作助词使用,同"否"。和肯定词对用时,表示否定的意思,一般是在古文中出现。

需要注意的是"不"字在读"bù"的时候,读音常常要发生变化,在第四声的字前面时,"不"字要读第二声,如"不是、不会"、"不要"。

The Origin and Evolution of Character "不"

The character "不" is written as "不" in its oracle inscription form. The bar on the top signifies the land while the curves at the bottom depict the roots of the plant that grow into the earth. Therefore, it originally means the germ of the plant. It later gradually lost its original meaning and was changed into a negative adverb. It thus has another pronunciation: "fǒu". As an auxiliary word, it equals "否". It is the opposite of a positive adverb, indicating a negative meaning. It often appears in ancient literature.

We need to pay attention that the character often changes its tone of pronunciation. When it is placed before a character of the fourth tone, it should pronounced in the second tone, such as in the phrase "不是", "不会" and "不要".

82. 没 not have

méi
没

字源演变 The etymology of Chinese characters

小篆　　　　楷体

1. 释义 Meaning

[used to negate "有"] not have, be without(v.); [used to form the negation of a completed action];[used to form the negation of a past experience] (adj.)

2. 书写 Writing

3. 相关词语或表达 Related words or expressions

(1) used to form the negation of a completed action

Wǒ zuótiān méi qù Chángchéng.
我 昨天 没 去 长城。I didn't go to the Great Wall yesterday.

Shāngdiàn hái méi guān mén.
商店 还 没 关 门。The store is not closed yet.

(2) used to form the negation of a past experience

Tā méi qù guo Shànghǎi.
他 没 去 过 上海。He has never been to Shanghai.

注意：

*"没"做否定词时否定的是过去的动作，"不"做否定词否定的常常是将来和习惯性动作。

*动词"是"的否定形式是"不是"，"有"的否定形式是"没有"。形容词的否定也要用"不"，如：

Note: as a negative, "没" negates past actions. "不" often negates habitual actions and actions in the future.

As a verb, the negative form of "是" is "不是" and the negative form of "有" is "没有". We add "不" to adjectives to form their negative forms. For example,

Zuótiān tā bìng le, tā méi lái shàng kè.
昨天 他 病 了,他 没 来 上 课。
He got sick yesterday, so he was absent from school

Wǒ míngtiān bú qù túshūguǎn.
我 明天 不 去 图书馆。I'm not going to the library tomorrow.

Tā búshi Zhōngguó rén.
她 不是 中国 人。She is not Chinese.

Jīntiān bù rè.
今天 不 热。It's not hot today.

Tā méi yǒu qián.
她 没 有 钱。She doesn't have money.

  Nǐ chōu yān ma?
A：你 抽 烟 吗？Do you smoke?

  Wǒ bù chōu yān.
B：我 不 抽 烟。I don't smoke.

méiyǒu
(3) 没有　　have not

méi guānxi
(4) 没 关系　　never mind

méi yòng
(5) 没 用　　useless

4. 练习　Exercises

（1）看拼音写出句子 Write down the sentences according to *pinyin*

① Mèimei méiyǒu qián.

七、作虚词的汉字 Characters as Function Words

② Méi guānxi.

③ Wǒ méi qù guo Běijīng.

④ Zuótiān māma méi gōngzuò.

(2) 选词填空 Insert the correct answer in the blanks

不　　没

① 下个月我＿＿＿＿＿＿＿去美国。

② 去年他＿＿＿＿＿＿＿工作，今天他找到了。

③ 她＿＿＿＿＿＿＿是日本人。

④ 我＿＿＿＿＿＿＿有这本书。

⑤ 她＿＿＿＿＿＿＿高。

⑥ 我＿＿＿＿＿＿＿常常喝酒。

5. 汉字知识　The knowledge of Chinese characters

"没"的起源与演变

"没"字有两个读音，一个是"mò"，古代汉字写作"🦩"，左边是一个"水"旁。其实，更早的"没"字只有右边的部分，是一个会意字。上部是"回"的古写，是一个象形字，表示很深的水，下部是人的一只手，是指一个人下到水中去取东西。所以，它最初的含义是"沉没、淹没"。后来又给这个字加了一个"水"旁。

"没"字的另一个读音是"méi"，它的使用频率很高，如"没有"、"没来"、"没看见"、"没听说"等等。仔细想想，这两个字读音表示的含义是有联系的，后者是由前者引申演变而来的。为了区别这两个含义，读音也发生了变化。

The Origin and Evolution of "没"

The characters "没" has two pronunciations, one of which is "mò". It is written as "🦩" with radical "水" on the left. In fact, the character "没" only had the right part in an earlier times and was an associative compound characters. The upper part is the ancient form of "回". It is a pictographic character which means very deep water. The lower part is a hand of a person. The character thus depicts a person going into the water to get something. Therefore, it originally means "sunken and submerge". We later added "水" to the character.

　　The other pronunciation of the character is "méi", which is used more frequently. For example, "没有(méiyǒu)"(not have), "没来(méi lái)"(didn't come), "没看见(méi kànjiàn)"(didn't see) and "没听说(méi tīngshuō)" (never heard of). Think about it carefully. These two pronunciations are connected. The latter one was evolved from the first one. To distinguish its two meanings, we gave them each a pronunciation.

83. 很 very

hěn
很

字源演变 The etymology of Chinese characters

小篆　　　　　楷体

1. 释义　Meaning

very, quite, awfully (adv.)

2. 书写　Writing

3. 相关词语或表达　Related words or expressions

（1）very (used before adj.)

Tā hěn piàoliang.
她 很 漂亮。She is very pretty.

Xiànzài wǒ hěn'è.
现在 我 很饿。I'm very hungry now.

Zhèr hěn měi.
这儿 很 美。It's very beautiful here.

Tā Hànyǔ shuō de hěn hǎo.
他 汉语 说 得 很 好。He speaks Chinese very well.

汉语常用100字

(2) used before some auxiliary verb or verb

Míngtiān hěn kěnéng xià yǔ.
明天 很 可能 下 雨。It is probably going to rain tomorrow.

Tā hěn huì chàng gē.
他 很 会 唱 歌。He sings very well.

Wǒ hěn xǐhuan Hànyǔ.
我 很 喜欢 汉语。I like Chinese very much.

Tā hěn yuànyì qù Běijīng.
他 很 愿意 去 北京。He would love to go to Beijing.

4. 练习　Exercises

(1) 写一写 Write down the following words and phrases

很大（　　　　）　　很少（　　　　）

很晚（　　　　）　　很高（　　　　）

很瘦（　　　　）　　很白（　　　　）

很甜（　　　　）　　很渴（　　　　）

很好（　　　　）　　很美（　　　　）

很想（　　　　）　　很喜欢（　　　　）

(2) 连词成句 Arrange the following words in correct order to form a sentence

① 很　这个　甜　菜

② 喜欢　我　不　很　汉字　写

③ 的　我　很　哥哥　高

④ 吃　日本　很　想　我　菜

⑤ 今天　的　人　来　多　很

七、作虚词的汉字 Characters as Function Words

5. 汉字知识　The knowledge of Chinese characters
常见的偏旁部首(29)　彳部

彳部俗称双立人,"彳"作形旁的字大多和道路、行走、行动有关。"彳"总在字的左侧。比如"行"、"往"、"得"等。"很"是个形声字,左形右声,其本义是不听从。

容易跟彳部混淆的是单立人"亻",带单立人的汉字有很多:比如:"住"、"位"、"他"、"你"、"们"、"做"、"休"、"信"等等。

Common Radicals and Indexing Radicals (29)　彳

Radical "彳" is commonly known as two standing people. The characters with "彳" are mostly related to roads, walking and action. It is always on the left side of a character, such as "行(xíng)" (walking), "往(zhù)" (living) and "得(dé)" (get). "很" is a pictophonetic character with the pictographic radical on the left and the phonetic radical on the right. It originally means do not obey.

People tend to confuse it with singly standing person "亻". There are a large amount of characters with this radical, such as "住(zhù)" (live), "位(wèi)" (position), "他(tā)" (he), "你(nǐ)" (you), "们(men)" (plural suffix), "做(zuò)" (do), "休(xiū)" (rest) and "信(xìn)" (believe), etc.

84. 也 also

字源演变　The etymology of Chinese characters

小篆　　　　楷体

1. 释义　Meaning

also, too, either, used in both affirmative and negative sentences.

2. 书写　Writing

3. 相关词语或表达　Related words or expressions

（1）也　also, too, as well, either

Nǐ qù, wǒ yě qù.
你去，我也去。If you go, I'll go too.

Nǐ bù qù, wǒ yě bù qù.
你不去，我也不去。If you do not go, I shall not go either.

Tā huì chàng gē, yě huì tiàowǔ.
她会唱歌，也会跳舞。She can both sing and dance.

Rènshi nǐ hěn gāoxìng.
A：认识你很高兴。Nice to meet you.

Wǒ yě hěn gāoxìng.
B：我也很高兴。Nice to meet you too.

七、作虚词的汉字 Characters as Function Words

Gēge hěn gāo, dìdi yě hěn gāo.
哥哥 很 高,弟弟也 很 高。
The elder brother is very tall and the younger brother is also very tall.

(2) 一点儿+(名词 n)+也+没/不…… not at all

Zhè jiàn yīfu wǒ yīdiǎnr yě bù xǐhuan.
这 件衣服 我 一点儿也不 喜欢。I don't like this dress at all.

Wǒ yīdiǎnr zǎofàn yě méi chī.
我 一点儿 早饭 也 没 吃。I had nothing for breakfast.

Jīntiān yīdiǎnr yě bù lěng.
今天 一点儿也不 冷(cold)。It's not cold at all.

注意:"也"只能用在动词或形容词前边。不能用于名词之前。

Note: "也" can only be used before verbs and adjectives and cannot be used before nouns.

4. 练习 Exercises

(1) 根据拼音写出句子 Write down the sentences according to *pinyin*

① Tā shì Zhōngguó rēn, wǒ yě shì Zhōngguó rén.

② Wǒ yě xǐhuan hē píjiǔ.

③ Māma yě huì shuō Hànyǔ.

④ Běijīng yě hěn lěng.

⑤ Zhè ge cài yě hěn hǎochī.

(2) 根据提示,用"也"造句 Make sentences with "也" according to the clues

① 他是学生,我是学生。

② 姐姐很漂亮,妹妹很漂亮。

③ 弟弟学习汉语,哥哥学习汉语。

④ 他想去商店,我想去商店。

⑤ 我没吃早饭。(一点儿……也……)

⑥ 今天不热。(一点儿……也……)

5. 汉字知识　The knowledge of Chinese characters
"也"字的起源

"也"的古文字写作"也",好像一种盛水的器皿。它的本义就是古代的一种器皿,即"匜"的本字。"匜"是古代人盥洗时舀水用的器具,形状像瓢。随着时间的推移,"也"的本义逐渐停止使用,后来就借用作虚词。

The Origin of "也"

"也" is written as "也" in its ancient character form which resembles a container for holding water. It referred to a container in the old times. It is the original form of "匜 (yí)". It also referred to a utensil in toilet which looked like a ladle and was used for scooping water by ancients. With the progress of time, "也" gradually lost its original meaning and became a functional word.

85. 都 all

dōu
都

字源演变 The etymology of Chinese characters

金文

小篆

楷体

1. 释义　Meaning

all, both; even; already (adv.)

2. 书写　Writing

3. 相关词语或表达　Related words or expressions

（1）all, both

Míngtiān wǒmen dōu qù Shànghǎi.
明天　我们　都 去　上海。
Both of us are going to Shanghai tomorrow.

Wǒ hé māma dōu huì shuō Yīngyǔ.
我 和 妈妈 都 会 说 英语。
My mom and I both can speak English.

Nǐ bié gěi wǒ lǐwù, wǒ shénme dōu bú yào.
你别 给 我 礼物，我 什么 都 不 要。
Don't give me any gift. I want nothing at all.

Rúguǒ nǐ yǒu wèntí, nǐ shénme shíhou dōu kěyǐ lái wèn wǒ.
如果你有问题,你什么时候都可以来问我。

You can come to ask me whenever you have a problem.

Wǒ gāng dào zhèlǐ de shíhou shéi dōu bù rènshi.
我刚到这里的时候谁都不认识。

I didn't know anyone when I first came here.

(2) even, often used in special structures in conjunction with "连" and interrogative words.

lián   dōu
连……都……

Zhè ge wèntí tài róngyì le, lián xiǎoháizi dōu huì.
这个问题太容易了,连小孩子都会。

This problem is too easy. Even kids can solve it.

Gāng lái Zhōngguó, wǒ lián yī jù Hànyǔ dōu bù huì shuō.
刚来中国,我连一句汉语都不会说。

I could not speak even a single sentence in Chinese when I first came to China.

(3) already

Dōu shí'èr diǎn le, Nǐ hái bù shuì jiào.
都 12 点了,你还不睡觉。

It is already 12' o clock. Why don't you go to bed?

4. 练习 Exercises

(1) 用"都"改写句子 Rewrite the sentences using "都"

例:我去,妈妈也去。→我和妈妈都去。

① 我是中国人,他也是中国人。

② 我喜欢汉语,爸爸也喜欢汉语。

③ 我很好,他也很好。

④ 姐姐很漂亮,妹妹也很漂亮。

七、作虚词的汉字 Characters as Function Words

⑤ 哥哥学习英语，弟弟也学习英语。

（2）请把"都"放在合适的位置 Please put "都" in the proper position of the sentences

① A 我们 B 是 C 中国人 D。(都)

② A 他病了(bīng le be sick)，B 什么 C 不想 D 吃。(都)

③ A 他 B 连一个字 C 不会 D 写。(都)

④ A 10 点了 B，你 C 快点儿起床吧 D！(都)

5. 汉字知识　The knowledge of Chinese characters
常见的偏旁部首(30)　阝部

"阝"是由表示城邦的"邑"字演变而来的，因为这个部首通常出现在合体字的右边，又酷似人的耳朵的形状，所以称为"右耳旁"。"邑"原是都城之意，它作偏旁组成的字多用于地方泛称、地名专名或姓氏，如"都"、"邦"、"那"、"邮"、"郑"等字。

"都"字有两个读音，一个是"dū"，这个音义出现的时间较早，"首都"、"通都大邑"、"大都会"等词语中的"都"采用的就是这一音义。另一个是用作副词时的读音"dōu"，这一用法虽然出现得比较晚，但在现代汉语中，不论是口语还是书面语，使用率都非常高。

Common Radicals and Indexing Radicals (30)　阝

"阝" is developed from the character "邑(yì)" which means city-state. Since this radical often appears on the right side of a compound character and it resembles an ear of a person, so we call it right ear radical. "邑" used to mean capital and the characters with it are largely used as general or special names of places or family names, such as "都(dū)" (capital), "邦 (bāng)" (nation), "那 (nà) (that)", "邮 (yóu) (post)" and "郑 (zhèng) (a surname)".

  The character "都" has two pronunciations. One is "dū", which appeared earlier as in the phrases "首都(shǒudū)" (capital), "通都大邑 (tōng dū dà yì)" (a large city), and "大都会 (dà dūhuì)" (cosmopolis). As an adverb, it is pronounced as "dōu". Although appeared later, it is frequently used in modern colloquial and written language.

86. 就 just

jiù
就

字源演变　The etymology of Chinese characters

小篆

楷体

1. 释义　Meaning

adv.

(1) at once, right away

(2) as early as, already,

(3) as soon as, right after

(4) exactly, precisely

(5) only, merely, just

2. 书写　Writing

3. 相关词语或表达　Related words or expressions

（1）at once, right away

Tā mǎshàng jiù huílái.
他 马上 就 回来。He will come back soon.

Tiān hěn kuài jiù hēi le.
天 很 快 就 黑了。The sky will get dark soon.

（2）as early as, already

Māma zǎoshang wǔ diǎn jiù qǐchuáng le.
妈妈　早上　5 点　就　起床　了。

My mother got up as early as 5 in the morning.

Zhè jiàn shì wǒ zǎo jiù zhīdào le.
这　件　事我　早 就　知道 了。I've heard of it long ago.

（3）as soon as, right after

Wǒ shuō wán jiù zǒu.
我　说　完　就走。I'll leave when I finish talking.

Zhè ge wèntí tā yī kàn jiù huì.
这　个　问题他一看　就 会。

He only took a look at the problem and knew immediately how to solve it.

Wǒ xià le kè jiù qù chīfàn.
我　下了课就去　吃饭。I'll go to eat as soon as I finish class.

（4）exactly, precisely

Zhèr jiù shì wǒ de jiā.
这儿就　是 我 的 家。This is my home.

（5）only, merely, just

Tāmen jiù yǒu yī ge érzi.
他们　就　有　一个儿子。They have just one son.

4. 练习　Exercises

（1）解释下列句子中"就"的意思 Explain the different meaning of "就" in the following sentences

① 他很快就回来。

He will come back soon.

② 他们早就结婚了。

They got married long time ago.

③ 我一吃完早饭就去上课。

I will go to school when I finish my breakfast.

④ 那儿就是我们学校。

That is our school.

七、作虚词的汉字 Characters as Function Words

⑤ 我就一个朋友。

I have just one friend.

(2) 请把"就"放到合适的位置 Please put "就" in the proper position of the sentences

① A 爸爸 B 马上 C 回来 D。

② A 今天我们 B 7点 C 上课 D。

③ A 昨天我 B 看完 C 电视 D 睡觉了。

④ A 他 B 是 C 我的 D 男朋友。

⑤ 我 A 有 B 一个 C 弟弟 D。

5. 汉字知识   The knowledge of Chinese characters

"就"字的起源与演变

"就"是一个会意字，篆书写作"就"。左偏旁是筑起的高丘，右偏旁的"尤"字表示特异、突出。全字的意思是向高处趋就，择高而居。这个含义至今还在使用，如"就高不就低"、"就职"、"就餐"等等。后来，它又演变出副词、连词等虚词的用法，使用率越来越频繁。

The Origin and Evolution of "就"

"就" is an associative compound character which is written as "就" in sealed character form. The left side is a pile-up hillock and the right side is the character "尤" which means outstanding and prominent. The character thus means moving to a higher place to live. The character still retains this meaning as in the phrases "就高不就低(jiù gāo bù jiù dī)" (stay at a higher place rather than a lower place), "就职(jiù zhí)" (inauguration) and "就餐(jiù cān)" (have a meal). It later developed the usage of being a functional word such an adverb and a conjunction, and this usage is more frequently adopted.

87. 才 only

cái

字源演变 The etymology of Chinese characters

甲骨文　　　　金文　　　　小篆　　　　楷体

1. 释义　Meaning

adv.

(1) used before a verb to indicate that sth. has just happened

(2) used before a verb to indicate that sth. is rather late by general standards

(3) (followed by a numerical expression) only

(4) (preceded by an expression of reason or condition) not unless; not until

(5) (used in an assertion or contradiction, emphasizing what comes before "才", usu. with "呢" at the end of the sentence) actually; really

2. 书写　Writing

3. 相关词语或表达　Related words or expressions

（1）Used before a verb to indicate that sth. has just happened.

Tā cái zǒu.
他才走。He just left.

七、作虚词的汉字 Characters as Function Words

Wǒ cái cóng Běijīng huílái bùjiǔ.
我 才 从 北京 回来不久。 I just came back from Beijing.

(2) Used before a verb to indicate that sth. is rather late by general standards.

Wǒ shí diǎn cái qǐchuáng, māma liù diǎn jiù qǐchuáng le.
我 10点 才 起床， 妈妈 6 点 就 起床 了。
I did not get up until 10 in the morning while my mother got up at 6.

Tā sān ge xiǎoshí cái xiěwán zuòyè, wǒ yī ge xiǎoshí jiù xiěwán le.
他 3 个 小时 才 写完 作业，我 1 个 小时 就 写完 了。
He spent three hours on his homework while I finished it in just one hour.

Nǐ zěnme cái lái?
你 怎么 才 来？ Why do you come so late?

(3) (followed by a numerical expression) only

Jīntiān cái lái le sān ge rén.
今天 才 来了 三 个 人。 Only three people came today.

Tā cái shì ge hái zi, bié yāoqiú　　　　　　　tài gāo.
他 才 是 个 孩子，别 要求(require, request)太 高。
He is only a kid. Don't be too harsh on him.

(4) (Preceded by an expression of reason or condition) not unless; not until

Zhǐyǒu nǔlì xuéxí, cái néng xuéhǎo Hànyǔ.
只有 努力 学习，才 能 学好 汉语。
You can only master Chinese language if you work hard on it.

Nǐ yào duō xiūxi, nǐ de bìng cái néng hǎo.
你要 多 休息，你的 病 才 能 好。
You can only get better if you take more rest.

(5) (Used in an assertion or contradiction, emphasizing what comes before "才", usu. with "呢" at the end of the sentence) actually; really

　　　cái　　　ne
a) 才+adj +呢。

Xīngqīwǔ rén bù duō, xīngqīliù rén cái duō ne.
星期五 人不 多，星期六 人 才 多 呢。
There weren't many people on Friday. It was on Saturday that

315

people swarmed the place.

    cái shì
b）才+是……

  Lǐ Dànián bù shi wǒ de nán péngyou, tā cái shì wǒ de nán péngyou ne.
  李大年 不 是 我 的 男 朋友，他才是 我 的 男 朋友 呢。

  Li Dalian is not my boyfriend, he is.

   cái bù ne
c）才+不+verb+呢。

  Nà yàng de dìfang wǒ cái bú qù ne.
  那 样 的 地方 我 才 不 去 呢。

  I will not go to a place like that.

4. 练习 Exercises

（1）选词填空 Insert the correct answer in the blanks

       才 就

① 昨天晚上弟弟12点＿＿＿回来，哥哥8点＿＿＿回来了。

② 我6岁＿＿＿上学了，他8岁＿＿＿上学。

③ 我骑自行车10分钟＿＿＿到了，他走路半个小时＿＿＿到。

（2）连词成句 Arrange the following words in correct order to form a sentence

① 9点 他们 上课 才

② 怎么 你 这么 才 晚 来

③ 我 不 要 才 他 呢 的 礼物

④ 才 弟弟 5岁 今年

七、作虚词的汉字 Characters as Function Words

5. 汉字知识 The knowledge of Chinese characters

"才"字的起源与演变

"才"是一个象形字,篆书写作"才","一"画表示土地,"丨"画露出地面的一少部分,表示刚刚生长出的植物的幼芽,地面以下的部分是植物的根部。幼芽破土而出是新近发生的事,所以"才"有刚才的意思。幼苗可以长大,可以成才,所以又引申出"人才"、"英才"等的词义来。

The Origin and Evolution of "才"

"才" is a pictographic character which is written as "才" in sealed character form. "一" indicates the earth, and the tip of the stroke "丨" comes out the earth, signifying the sprout of a plant. The part below the land is the root of the plant. The green shoots just speared out the earth, so the character "才" has the meaning of just now. The sprout will grow big, so the character developed the meaning of talent, such as "人才 (réncái)" (a talented person) and "英才(yīngcái)" (a gifted person).

88. 和 and

hé
和

字源演变   The etymology of Chinese characters

金文   小篆   楷体

1. 释义 Meaning

(1) (prep.) used to indicate relationship, comparison, ect.

(2) (conj.) and

2. 书写 Writing

3. 相关词语或表达 Related words or expressions

（1）介词(prep.)：

① indicate the object of a verb.

Wǒ hé nǐ shuō shuō huà, hǎo ma?
我 和你 说 说 话，好 吗?

May I have a talk with you please?

② denoting relations.

Zhè shì hé nǐ méi guānxi.
这 事 和你 没 关系。This is none of your business.

七、作虚词的汉字 Characters as Function Words

③ denoting comparison.

Tā hé wǒ dìdi yíyàng dà.
他和 我弟弟 一样 大。He is as old as my younger brother.

(2) 连词(conj.)：

and

Lǎoshī hé tóngxuémen dōu hěn xǐhuan tā.
老师 和 同学们 都 很 喜欢 她。

Teachers and students all like her very much.

Wǒ qù guo Běijīng, Shànghǎi hé Guǎngzhōu.
我 去 过 北京、 上海 和 广州。

I have been to Beijing, Shanghai and Guangzhou.

注意：在多数情况下，"跟"可以替换成"和"，而意思不会改变。

Note: In most cases, we can replace "跟" with "和" without changing the meaning.

4. 练习　Exercises

(1) 看拼音写出句子，并想一想它们的意思 Write down the sentences according to *pinyin* and think about their meanings

① Zuótiān wǒ hé péngyou qù mǎi dōngxi le.

② Nǐ hé shuí shuō huà ne?

③ Wǒ hé tā bú shì tóngxué.

④ Zhè jiàn yīfu hé nà jiàn yíyàng piàoliang.

⑤ Wǒ xǐhuan chī jiǎozi, miàntiáo, mǐfàn hé bāozi.

汉语常用100字

（2）选词填空 Insert the correct answer in the blanks

和　　也

① 妈妈_____爸爸一起去美国了。
② 我去商店，妹妹_____去。
③ 我想买水果_____面包。
④ 我不喜欢吃米饭，他_____不喜欢。
⑤ 弟弟_____我一样高了。

5. 汉字知识　The knowledge of Chinese characters

"和"字的起源与演变

"和"是一个形声字，篆书写作"龢"，"口"在左旁，表意；"禾"表音，在右。正好跟现行汉字的写法相反。它最初的含义是"应和"的意思，读"hè"，成语"一唱一和"中的"和"用的就是它的本义。现代汉语中有五个读音，用法都不一样，要注意分辨。另外四种分别是：①hé（老师和学生）②huó（和面）③huò（和稀泥）④hú（打麻将用语）。

The Origin and Evolution of "和"

"和" is a pictophonetic character, which is written as "龢" in sealed character form. "口" as the pictographic radical is on the left while the phonetic radical "禾" is on the right. It is written just in the opposite way of the modern Chinese. It originally means echo, pronounced as "hè", as in the idiom "一唱一和 (yī chàng yī hè)" (a person sings and another person echoes him). It has five pronunciations in modern Chinese with different usages. We have to pay attention to this. The other four pronunciations are: ①hé (老师和学生 lǎoshī hé xuésheng, teachers and students) ②huó (和面 huó miàn, mix flour and water) ③huò (和稀泥 huò xīní, blur the distinction between right and wrong) ④hú (used in majong, indicating winning).

89. 在 indicating the position of a person or thing

zài
在

字源演变　The etymology of Chinese characters

甲骨文　　　金文　　　小篆　　　楷体

1. 释义　Meaning

(1) (v.) ① exsit

② indicating the position of a person or thing.

(2) (prep.) indicating time, place, condition, scope, etc.

(3) (adv.) indicating an action in progress.

2. 书写　Writing

3. 相关词语或表达　Related words or expressions

（1）动词 (v.)

① exist

Nà běn shū xiànzài hái zài.
那 本 书 现在 还 在。The book is still there.

② indicating the position of a person or something.

汉语常用100字

Fàn zài zhuōzi shàng.
饭 在 桌子 上。The meal is on the table.

Xiǎo Wáng bù zài jiā.
小 王 不在家。Xiaowang is not at home.

（2）介词(prep.)

① indicating time.

Huǒchē zài xiàwǔ sān diǎn dào.
火车 在 下午 3 点 到。

The train will arrive at 3 o'clock this afternoon.

② indicating place.

Wǒ zài túshūguǎn kàn shū.
我 在 图书馆 看 书。I am reading books in the library.

Tā zhù zài Běijīng.
他 住 在 北京。He lives in Beijing.

③ indicating condition, scope, etc.

Tā zài xuéxí shàng hěn nǔlì.
他 在 学习 上 很 努力。He works very hard in study.

（3）副词（adv.）

indicating an action in progress.

Wàibian zài xià yǔ.
外边 在 下 雨。It is raining outside.

4. 练习 Exercises

（1）根据拼音提示写出句子 Write out the sentences according to the phonetic symbols

① Tāmen zài fànguǎn chī fàn.

② Tā zuò zài yǐzi shang.

③ Tā zài tīng yīnyuè.

④ Wǒmen zài shàngwǔ bā diǎn kāi huì.

七、作虚词的汉字 Characters as Function Words

⑤ Tāmen bān de xuésheng zài èrshí rén yǐxià.

⑥ Nǐ de shū zài zhuōzi shang.

（2）**请把"在"放在合适的位置** Please put "在" in the proper position of the sentences
① A 妈妈 B 不 C 家 D。
② A 我 B 教室 C 学习 D 汉语。
③ A 我们 B 吃 C 晚饭 D。
④ A 朋友 B 住 C 中国 D。
⑤ A 出发时间 B 明天 C 上午 D 10 点。

5. 汉字知识　The knowledge of Chinese characters
"在"字的有关知识

　　"在"是一个形声字。金文和小篆右下边的"土"是表意的形符，意思是有土地才可以存在。左上边是声符，在现行汉字中它已经失去了表音的功能，其实它是由"才"演变而来的。"在"的小篆写作"𡉒"，声符的形体还比较容易看出来。不过，它的读音与"在"也有了比较大的差异，表音的功能有限。

Knowledge about the Character "在"

　　" 在 " is a pictophonetic character. " 土 " at the right bottom is a pictographic radical, indicating the earth is the basis for living. The left upper part is the phonetic radical which has lost its function for indicating the pronunciation in modern Chinese. In fact, it was evolved from the character "才". The character "在" is written as "𡉒" in sealed character form. We can easily tell its phonetic radical. But its pronunciation differs greatly from " 在 ", so it has function in indicating the pronunciation is limited.

90. 向 toward

xiàng

字源演变 The etymology of Chinese characters

甲骨文　　　　　金文　　　　　小篆　　　　　楷体

1. 释义　Meaning

(v.) face

(prep.) to; toward, from

2. 书写　Writing

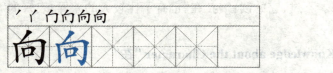

3. 相关词语或表达　Related words or expressions

（1）动词(v.) face

　　Zhè ge fángjiān xiàng dōng.
　　这 个 房间　向 东。This room fronts east.

（2）介词(prep.)

　　① toward(to indicate the direction of actions)

　　　Xiàng qián kàn.
　　　向　前　看。Look forward/ look straight ahead

　　　Xiàng zuǒ guǎi.
　　　向　左　拐。Turn left.

七、作虚词的汉字 Characters as Function Words

② from, to (to denote the object of the action)

Wǒ xiàng lǎoshī jiè　　　　le yī běn shū.
我　向　老师　借（borrow）了一本　书。
I borrowed a book from my teacher.

Xiàng nǐ de māma wèn hǎo.
向　你的　妈妈　问　好。Please say hello to your mother.

Xiàng lǎoshī qǐng jià.
向　老师　请　假。Ask teacher for leave.

Wǒ yào xiàng nǐ xuéxí.
我　要　向　你 学习。I have to learn from you.

4. 练习　Exercises

（1）写一写 Write down the following expressions

向前看（　　　）　　向后看（　　　）

向左拐（　　　）　　向右拐（　　　）

向东走（　　　）　　向西走（　　　）

向南跑（　　　）　　向北跑（　　　）

（2）选词填空 Insert the correct answer in the blanks

在　向　和　也

① 今天我_____家休息。

② 妈妈_____会说汉语。

③ 我_____朋友一起去吃饭。

④ 他_____爸爸问好。

⑤ 我_____哥哥借了10块钱。

5. 汉字知识　The knowledge of Chinese characters

"向"字的起源与演变

"向"的篆书写作"𠱾"，是一个象形字，指的是房屋墙壁上朝向北方的窗户，是一个名词。后来，逐渐引申出动词、介词的用法来，如"面向讲台"、"向前走"等等。在现代汉语中，"向"已经不再作为名词来用了。

汉语常用100字

The Origin and Evolution of "向"

"向" is written as "𠖉" in sealed character form and it is a pictographic noun which refers to the north-facing window on the wall of a house. It later developed the usages of verb and preposition, such as "面向讲台(miànxiàng jiǎngtái)" (facing the platform) and "向前走 (xiàng qián zǒu)" (walk forward). In modern Chinese, it is no longer used as a noun.

91. 从 from

cóng
从

字源演变　The etymology of Chinese characters

小篆　　　　　繁体　　　　　楷体

1. 释义　Meaning

(1) prep. [used to indicate the starting point] from

(2) pass by

2. 书写　Writing

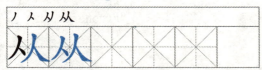

3. 相关词语或表达　Related words or expressions

（1）from (often used with "到、往、向" as "从……到/往/向……")

① used to indicate the starting point of the place.

Cóng dōng dào xī.
从　东　到　西。From east to west.

Cóng wǒ de jiā dào xuéxiào zǒu lù shí fēnzhōng.
从　我　的家　到　学校　走路10　分钟。
It takes 10 minutes to walk from my home to school.

Cóng zhèr wǎng nán zǒu jiù shì yóujú.
从　这儿　往　南　走就　是 邮局。

汉语常用100字

Go south from here, you'll find the post office.

Wǒ cóng Měiguó lái.
我 从 美国 来。I come from America.

② used to indicate the starting point of the time.

Měitiān cóng bā diǎn dào shí'èr diǎn, wǒ xuéxí Hànyǔ.
每天 从 8 点 到 12 点，我 学习 汉语。

I study Chinese from 8 am to 12 am every day.

Wǒ cóng míngtiān kāishǐ gěi nǐ fǔdǎo.
我 从 明天 开始 给 你 辅导(coach)。

I will tutor you from tomorrow.

③ used to indicate the starting point of the scope

Cóng dì yī kè dào dì wǔ kè, wǒmen dōu yào kǎoshì.
从 第一课 到 第五课，我们 都 要 考试。

The exam covers the first lesson to the fifth lesson.

Cóng xiǎohái dào lǎorén dōu xǐhuan tā.
从 小孩 到 老人 都 喜欢 他。

Kids and old people all adore him.

④ used to indicate the development or variation.

Cóng wú dào yǒu.
从 无(nothing) 到 有。grow out of nothing

Cóng chūn dào xià, cóng qiū dào dōng, sìjì búduàn de
从 春 到 夏，从 秋 到 冬，四季 不断(continuously) 地

biànhuà.
变化。

From spring to summer and from autumn to winter, the seasons are changing constantly.

(2) pass by

Wǒmen cóng zhè tiáo lù zǒu ba.
我们 从 这 条 路 走 吧。Let's take this road.

4. 练习 Exercises

(1) 替换练习 substitution drill

从____到____

上午　　　下午

10点	12点
今天	明天
北京	上海
教室	图书馆
上课	下课
老人	孩子
学生 、	老师
第一课	第三课
没有	有
坏	好

（2）选词填空 Insert the correct answer in the blanks

从　　在　　向

① 我____教室学习。

② ____你的妈妈问好。

③ ____这儿____左拐(turn left)就到了。

④ 你____哪儿出发？

⑤ 他____那儿等你。

5. 汉字知识　The knowledge of Chinese characters

"从"字的起源

"从"是会意字，甲骨文是"[illegible]"，像一前一后、二人相随的样子；后来篆书写作"[illegible]"，加上了行动符号，强调了行走的意义。现在的简化字又恢复了它的古字。因此，"从"除了做介词以外，还表示"跟随、顺从、参加"等意思，比如"从军"、"听从"、"力不从心"等。

The Origin of "从"

"从" is an associative compound character which is written as "[illegible]" in oracle inscription form. It looks like two people in tandem. In sealed character form, it is written as "[illegible]", adding an action symbol to stress the meaning of walking. The simplified character resumed the ancient form. The character in addition to being a preposition also has the meanings of following, obeying and joining. For example, "从军(cóngjūn)" (join the army), "听从(tīngcóng)" (follow) and "力不从心(lì bù cóng xīn)" (the soul is willing but the flesh is weak).

92. 比 indicating difference in manner, degree or quantity by comparison

bǐ

字源演变　The etymology of Chinese characters

甲骨文　　　　金文　　　　　小篆　　　　　楷体

1. 释义　Meaning

(v.) (1) compare

(2) for example; such as

(prep.) indicating difference in manner, degree or quantity by comparison.

2. 书写　Writing

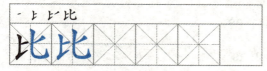

3. 相关词语或表达　Related words or expressions

（1）介词(prep.)：indicating difference in manner, degree or quantity by comparison.

Wǒ bǐ nǐ gāo.
我 比你 高。I'm taller than you.

Wǒ bǐ nǐ pǎo de kuài.
我 比你跑 得 快。I can run faster than you.

Wǒ bù bǐ nǐ gāo.
我 不比你 高。I am no taller than you.

Wǒ méiyǒu nǐ gāo.
我 没有 你 高。I am shorter than you.

注意:"不比"和"没有"意思不同。"我不比你高。"意思是我跟你差不多高。"我没有你高。"意思是我比你矮。

Note: "不比" is different from "没有"。"我不比你高" means I am nearly as tall as you. "我没有你高" means I am shorter than you.

(2) 动词(v.)

bǐ
比　　match

Wǒmen bǐ yi bǐ shéi pǎo de kuài.
我们 比一比 谁 跑 得 快。Let's have a race.

Wǒ gēn tā bǐ dǎ lánqiú.
我 跟 她比打 篮球。I am having a basketball match with her.

bǐjiào
(3) 比较　　compare

Qǐng bǐjiào yīxiàr zhè liǎng ge hànzì.
请 比较 一下儿 这 两 个 汉字。
Please compare these two Chinese characters.

bǐ sài
(4) 比赛　　match

Míngtiān yǒu lánqiú bǐsài.
明天 有 篮球 比赛。We have a basketball match tomorrow.

bǐfang
比方　　for example, such as

bǐrú
比如　　for example, such as

4. 练习　Exercises

根据给出的资料写"比"字句 Make sentences with "比" with given information

(1) 哥哥今年20岁。弟弟今年19岁。

(2) 姐姐唱歌唱得很好。妹妹唱得不太好。

七、作虚词的汉字 Characters as Function Words

（3）今天35°C。昨天28°C。

（4）我喜欢汉语。他不太喜欢汉语。

（5）哥哥有很多钱。弟弟没有很多钱。

5. 汉字知识　The knowledge of Chinese characters
"比"与"从"

"比"的篆书写作"𠤎𠤎"，跟"从"字一样，也是两个人字并列，只是和"从"的方向相反。这就是人们分析这两个字的结构时说的：二人相随为"从"，二人并列为"比"。显然，"比"也是一个会意字。

"比" and "从"

"比" is written as "𠤎𠤎" in sealed character form. As the character "从", it is also two persons who stand side by side but in opposition direction. People analyze the structures of the two characters: two people following each other forms the character "从" and "比" is the opposite of it. Apparently, "比" is an associative compound character.

93. 为 for

wèi
为

字源演变   The etymology of Chinese characters

甲骨文　　　　小篆　　　　繁体　　　　楷体

1. 释义　Meaning

(prep.) (1) indicating the object of one's act of service.

(2) indicating an objective.

2. 书写　Writing

3. 相关词语或表达　Related words or expressions

(1) indicating the object of one's act of service.

① wèi
为+n

Wèi rénmín fúwù.
为 人民 服务。serve the people

Bú yòng wèi wǒ dānxīn.
不 用 为 我 担心(worry)。Don't worry about me.

七、作虚词的汉字 Characters as Function Words

② 为+v/clause
wèi

Xuéxiào wèi wǒmen xuéxí Hànyǔ tígōng le hěn hǎo de tiáojiàn.
学校 为 我们 学习 汉语 提供(offer,provide)了 很 好 的 条件(condition)。

The school provides us with very good conditions for learning Chinese.

(2) indicating an objective.(it can be used as "为了"、"为着")

① 为+n
wèi

Dàjiā dōu wèi zhè jiàn shì gāoxìng.
大家 都 为 这 件 事 高兴。We are all happy about this.

Wèi wǒmen de yǒuyì gān bēi.
为 我们 的 友谊 干 杯。For our friendship, cheers!

② 为+v/clause
wèi

Tā wèi cānjiā kǎoshì zuò zhǔnbèi ne.
他 为 参加 考试 做 准备(preparation)呢。

He is preparing for the exam.

Wèi le xuéhǎo Hànyǔ, wǒ lái dào Zhōngguó.
为 了 学好 汉语，我 来 到 中国。

I came to China to improve my Chinese.

Wèile jiārén shēnghuó de gèng hǎo, tā nǔlì de gōngzuò.
为了 家人 生活 得 更 好，他 努力地 工作。

He works very hard to make her family live better.

4. 练习 Exercises

(1) 把"为"放在正确的位置上 Put "为" in the proper position of the sentences

① A 我们 B 他 C 毕业而 D 高兴。

② A 让 B 我们 C 健康(jiànkāng health)D 干杯。

③ A 我 B 可以 C 你 D 做什么吗？

④ A 参加 B 比赛(bǐsài match)，C 他们每天练习 D。

(2) 选词填空 Insert the correct answer in the blanks

    为 给 从 在

① 昨天我_____妈妈电话了。
② _____找到一个好工作,他努力学习汉语。
③ _____我的家到学校,走路10分钟。
④ 我下午_____图书馆看书。
⑤ _____我们的友谊干杯。
⑥ 请再_____我一杯咖啡,好吗?

5. 汉字知识　The knowledge of Chinese characters

"为"字的意思

  "为"是一个简化字,繁体写作"爲"或"為"。它是一个会意字。甲骨文写作"🖼",篆书写作"🖼",上部是"爪",是人的一只手;下部是一头大象,是以手牵着大象的样子。大象的身体比人大很多,这种举动当然被看作是很有作为的了。表示这种意义时读作"wéi"。后来,它的用法越来越多,有的用法声调发生了变化,读作"wèi"。

The Meaning of Character "为"

  "为" is simplified character which is written as "爲" or "為" in traditional Chinese. It is an associative compound character. In oracle inscription form, it is written as "🖼". In sealed character form, it is written as "🖼" with "爪" on the top, signifying a hand, and an elephant at the bottom. The character means pulling an elephant by hand. Since the elephant is much larger than people, this action is regarded as an accomplishment. When expressing this meaning, the character is pronounced as "wéi". Its usages gradually increased with time, and the character sometimes is pronounced as "wèi" with some usages.

94. 的 auxiliary word

de
的

字源演变　The etymology of Chinese characters

小篆

楷体

1. 释义　Meaning

(aux.)

(1) used after an attribute

(2) attached to a verb, a noun, a pronoun or an adjective as a nominalizer.

(3) used in the structure "是……的" to emphasize the affirmative tone.

2. 书写　Writing

3. 相关词语或表达　Related words or expressions

（1）Used after an attribute

① pron./n.+的+n.

nǐ de bǐ/lǎoshī de shū
你的笔/老师 的 书 your pencil/teacher's book

② v.+的+n.

lái de rén
来的 人 people who come

③ adj.+的+n.

    cōngmíng de rén
    聪明　的 人 a smart person

④ prep.+的+n.

    Duì wèntí de kànfǎ
    对　问题 的　看法 attitude on some issues

⑤ clause+的+n.

    nǐ　jìlái　de xìn
    你寄来 的 信 the letter from you

    Tā de yīfu duō, wǒ de　yīfu　hěn shǎo.
    他的衣服 多，我 的(衣服)很　少。

    He has plenty of clothes while I have few.

    Liǎng ge xiǎohái, dà de xiǎohái bā suì, xiǎo de xiǎohái sān suì.
    两　个　小孩，大 的(小孩)八　岁，小　的(小孩)三　岁。

    He has two children: the elder one is eight years old and the younger one is three years old.

    Yóu yǒng de rén hěn duō.
    游　泳 的(人)很　多。Many people are swimming.

(2) used in the structure "是……的" to emphasize the affirmative tone.

    Wǒ shì zuótiān lái de.
    我　是　昨天　来的。I came here yesterday.

4. 练习　**Exercises**

(1) 抄写句子 Write down the following sentences

    我的书（　　　　　　　　　　　　　　　　　　　　　）

    你的家（　　　　　　　　　　　　　　　　　　　　　）

    来的人（　　　　　　　　　　　　　　　　　　　　　）

    去的地方（　　　　　　　　　　　　　　　　　　　　）

    聪明的人（　　　　　　　　　　　　　　　　　　　　）

    漂亮的衣服（　　　　　　　　　　　　　　　　　　　）

    我买的东西（　　　　　　　　　　　　　　　　　　　）

    对问题的看法（　　　　　　　　　　　　　　　　　　）

    他是坐飞机来的。（　　　　　　　　　　　　　　　　）

七、作虚词的汉字 Characters as Function Words

(2) 阅读并回答问题 Read the assay and answers the questions

　　　我是北京大学的留学生,我是从英国来的。我们的老师都很好,有三位老师,一位是男的,两位是女的。我们班的同学也都很可爱。我的好朋友玛丽(Mǎ lì, Mary)是个漂亮的女孩,她是从美国来的。她喜欢买东西,你看,这些东西都是她买的,好看吗?

问题:
① "我"是哪个学校的留学生?

② "我"是从哪儿来的?

③ "我"有几位女老师?

④ "我"的好朋友是哪国人?

⑤ "这些东西"是谁买的?

5. 汉字知识　The knowledge of Chinese characters
查字典的方法

　　查字典最简单的方法是音序检字法,只要知道这个字的读音,再根据拼音排列的顺序,很快就能在字典中找到它。可我们要查找的汉字并不一定都是认识的,要是不知道汉字的读音,我们可以用部首检字法。
　　首先,找到这个汉字的部首,看看它有几画;
　　其次,在字典的"部首目录"中,根据部首的笔画数找到这个部首的页码或号码,把字典翻到"检字表",找到这个部首;
　　再次,看看除了部首以外,这个汉字还剩几画;
　　最后,在这个部首的相应笔画数下,你就可以找到你需要的字了。

汉语常用100字

Method of Consulting a Dictionary

The simplest way of consulting a dictionary is pinyin sequence indexing system. After knowing the pronunciation of the character, we can find the character in the dictionary quickly according to the pinyin sequence. But we have to know the pronunciations of the characters before we find them in the dictionary. If we don't know the pronunciation, we can use the indexing radical system.

First, we should identify the indexing radical of the character to find out how many strokes it has;

Then, based on the number of strokes, we should find out the page or number of the radical in the "indexing radical list" of the dictionary. After that, we have to find the radical in the "index of Chinese characters" section;

Third, we have to find out how many strokes the character still has except the radical;

Finally, we can find the character under the corresponding number of strokes of the radical.

95. 得 auxiliary word

de
得

字源演变 The etymology of Chinese characters

甲骨文　　　　金文　　　　小篆　　　　楷体

1. 释义　Meaning

(aux.) (1) used between a verb or an adjective and its complement to indicate result or degree.

(2) used after certain verbs to indicate possibility.

2. 书写　Writing

3. 相关词语或表达　Related words or expressions

(1) used between a verb or an adjective and its complement to indicate result or degree.

① v./adj.+得+complement

　Tā shuō de hěn kuài.
　他 说 得 很 快。He speaks very fast.

② S+v.+O+v.+得+adj.

　Tā chàng gē chàng de hěn hǎotīng.
　她 唱 歌 唱 得 很 好听。She is very good at singing.

S+O+v.+的得+adj.

Tā gē chàng de hěn hǎotīng.
她 歌 唱 得 很 好听。 She is very good at singing.

③ adj.+得+很

Gēge de Hànyǔ hǎo de hěn.
哥哥 的 汉语 好 得 很。 My brother is good at Chinese.

(2) used after certain verbs to indicate possibility or permission

① v.+得/不得

Niúnǎi huài le, chī bu de.   Niúnǎi huài le, bù néng chī.
牛奶 坏 了, 吃 不 得。(=牛奶 坏 了, 不 能 吃。)

The milk has gone bad. We can't drink it.

② v.+得/不+complement

chī de wán chī bu wán
吃 得 完 : 吃 不 完

can eat all the food: cannot eat all the food

注意:区别"的、地、得"

Notes: pay attention to the difference between "的、地 and 得"

a) "的" usually used before a noun. "……+的+n."

wǒ de shū
我 的 书 my book

piàoliang de huā
漂亮 的 花 beautiful flowers

tā mǎi de yīfu
他 买 的 衣服 clothes he bought

b) "地" usually used before a verb. "……+地+v."

qīngqīng de guānshàng mén
轻轻 地 关上 门 gently closed the door

kāixīn de xiào le
开心 地 笑 了 smiled happily

c) "得" usually used before an adjective or an adjective clause.

"……+得+adj."

pǎo de hěn kuài
跑 得 很 快 run very fast

七、作虚词的汉字 Characters as Function Words

(3) 地 ^(de)

used after an adjective, a noun or a phrase to form an adverbial adjunct before the verb

Wǒ mànman de xíguàn le zhèr de shēnghuó.
我 慢慢 地 习惯 了这儿的 生活。

I gradually got used to life here.

4. 练习　Exercises

(1) 选词填空 Insert the correct answer in the blanks

　　　　　　　　　的　　地　　得

① 他是我____哥哥。

② 妹妹写汉字写____很漂亮。

③ 我买____衣服很便宜。

④ 我慢慢____习惯(be accustomed to)了这儿的生活(life)。 ^(xíguàn　　　　　　　　　　shēnghuó)

⑤ 老师说____太快了。

⑥ 明天我要早早____起床(get up)。 ^(qǐchuáng)

(2) 选择正确的答案 Choose the correct answer

① 美国太远了，一天____。

　A 回得来　　　　　B 回不来

② 你要了这么多菜，我们____。

　A 吃得完　　　　　B 吃不完

③ 你写的字很大，我____。

　A 看得清楚(clear)　　B 看不清楚

④ 老师说话的声音(voice)很大，我____。 ^(shēngyīn)

　A 听得见　　　　　B 听不见

汉语常用100字

5. 汉字知识　The knowledge of Chinese characters
"得"字的有关知识

"得"是一个多音多义字，其中最初的一个含义是"得到"，读作"dé"，是一个动词，至今还在使用。甲骨文写作"𢔶"，篆书写作"得"，样子都像是一只手拿着贝壳，是一个会意字，意思是得到了东西。贝壳很美，古时候还曾经被制成货币使用。后来又演变出助词的用法，读轻声。

Knowledge about the Character "得"

"得" has multiple pronunciations and meanings. Originally, it meant procuring something and was pronounced as "dé". It is a verb and is still used today. It is written as "𢔶" in oracle inscription form and "得" in sealed character form. Both of them resemble a hand holding a shell. It is an associative compound character which means getting something. Shells are beautiful and were used as currency in the ancient times. The character is later used as an auxiliary word and is pronounced in a neutral tone.

96. 了 auxiliary word

字源演变 The etymology of Chinese characters

小篆　　　　楷体

1. 释义　Meaning

(aux.)

(1) used after a verb or adjective to indicate completion of work or change.

(2) used after a adjective to indicate completion of change.

(3) modal particle placed at the end of a sentence to indicate a change.

2. 书写　Writing

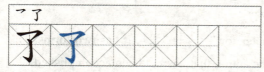

3. 相关词语或表达　Related words or expressions

(1) used after a verb to indicate completion of work.

Zuótiān wǒ mǎi le yī běn cídiǎn.
昨天　我　买　了一本　词典。I bought a dictionary yesterday.

Wǒ chī wǎnfàn le.
我　吃　晚饭　了。I already had the dinner.

<pre>
  Wǒ kànwán le diànyǐng jiù huí jiā le.
  我 看完 了 电影   就 回 家了。I went home after the movie.
</pre>

注意:宾语有数量词或是别的修饰语时,"了"通常用于动词后边。"了"和"就"可以构成"……了……就……"的结构,表示两个动作接连完成。

Note: When the object has a quantifier or other modifiers, "了" is often placed after the verb. "了" and "就" form "……了……就……" structure, indicating the two verbs are accomplished in tandem.

(2) used after a adjective to indicate completion of change.

<pre>
  Háizi dà le.
  孩子 大了。The kids grew up.

  Tiānqì lěng le.
  天气 冷 了。The weather is getting colder.
</pre>

(3) modal particle placed at the end of a sentence to indicate a change.

<pre>
  Guā fēng le.
  刮 风 了。The wind is blowing.

  Tā yǒu qián le.   yǐqián méiyǒu qián
  他 有 钱 了。(以前   没有   钱)
  He got rich. (It means that he was poor)
</pre>

注意:*"了"的否定用"没",有两种形式,表示动作完成的"了"否定形式是"没+动词",不要"了";表示事态变化的"了",否定形式可以有"了"。

*"形容词+了"的否定用"不"。

Note: * The negative character for "了" is "没". It has two forms. The structure "没+verb" is used for the action that has not been accomplished. We don't need "了" in this case. When describing some situation that has been changed, we can add "了" in the negative form.

* "不" is used in the negative form of the structure "adjective+了".

例如(Example):

<pre>
  Zuótiān tā méi lái.
  昨天   他 没 来。He didn't come yesterday.

  Xiànzài wǒ méiyǒu qián le.   yǐqián yǒu qián
  现在   我 没有   钱 了。(以前   有   钱)
</pre>

七、作虚词的汉字 Characters as Function Words

I have no money. (It means that I was rich.)

Wǒ bù xǐhuan tā le.　yǐqián xǐhuan tā.
我 不 喜欢 他 了。(以前 喜欢 他）

I don't like him any longer. (It means that I liked him.)

Jīntiān bù lěng le.　zuótiān hěn lěng
今天 不 冷 了。(昨天 很 冷）

It is not cold today. (It means that it's cold yesterday.)

4. 练习　Exercises

(1) 根据拼音写句子 Write down the sentences according to *pinyin*

① Jīntiān wǒ mǎi dōngxi le.

② Wǒ mǎi le yì běn shū.

③ Tā chī le fàn jiù qù shàng kè.

④ Tiānqì lěng le.

⑤ Zuótiān wǒ méi mǎi dōngxi.

⑥ Tā bú shì lǎoshī le .

⑦ Tā bú piàoliang le .

(2) 请把下列句子中的时间换为"昨天"并改写句子 Change the words indicating the time in the following sentences into "昨天" and rewrite the sentences

如：今天我要去商店。→昨天我去商店了。

① 明天我要去买东西。

② 明天他会来。

③今天我要买一件衣服。
④今天我下了课要去图书馆。

5. 汉字知识　The knowledge of Chinese characters

多音多义字

一个字的字音不同,字义也不同,这叫多音多义字。如"了",作助词用时要读"le";另一个读音是liǎo,比如"了解"、"吃不了"、"了不起";其他前面学过的多音多义字还有:"好"、"都"、"得"、"和"、"长"、"为"等。

有的多音多义字除通常读音外,还有作姓氏、地名、外来语等用途时的特殊读音。记住这些特殊读音,有利于掌握多音多义字。如"单"①dān,"单独"②shàn,姓单、单县(地名)③chán"单于"(古代匈奴族的君主)

Characters with Multiple Pronunciations and Meanings

There are some characters with multiple pronunciations and meanings in Chinese. For example, the character "了" is pronounced as "le" as an auxiliary word. It is also pronounced as "liǎo" as in the phrases "了解(liǎojiě)" (understand), "吃不了(chī bu liǎo)" (inedible) and "了不起(liǎobuqǐ)" (superb). We have learned many characters with multiple pronunciations and meanings such as "好(hǎo)", "都(dōu)", "得(de)", "和(hé)", "长(cháng)" and "为(wèi)".

In addition to its usual pronunciation, many characters with multiple pronunciations and meanings also have special pronunciations for family names, place names and imported words. We can better master these characters with multiple pronunciations and meanings if we can remember their special pronunciations. For example, the character "单": ①dān, "单独"(dāndú,alone) ②shàn, family name or name of a place called "单县" (Shàn Xiàn) ③chán 单于 (Chányú, king of the ancient Huns).

97. 着 auxiliary word

字源演变　The etymology of Chinese characters

楷体

1. 释义　Meaning

(aux.) indicating an action in progress or a continued state

2. 书写　Writing

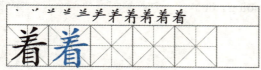

3. 相关词语或表达　Related words or expressions

(1) indicating an action in progress.

"正/在/正在+v+着+呢"

Rénmen chàng zhe, tiào zhe.
人们　唱 着，跳 着。People are singing and dancing.

Wàibian zhèng xià zhe yǔ ne.
外边　正　下 着雨呢。It's raining outside.

(2) indicating a continued state.

Mén kāi zhe.
门　开 着。The door is open.

Tā chuān zhe yī jiàn lánsè de yīfu.
他 穿　着一件 蓝色的衣服。He is wearing blue clothes.

（3）用于存在句，表示以某种姿态存在。"着" is used in sentences for existence, indicating the existence of something in some way.

    Ménkǒu zhànzhe yī ge lǎoren.
    门口　　站着一个　老人。

There is an old man standing at the door.

（4）v_1+着+v_2，构成连动句。

  ①动1表示动2的方式。

    Action 1 suggests the way of action 2.

    Wǒ qí zhe zìxíngchē lái xuéxiào.
    我　骑着　自行车　来　学校。I come to school by bike.

  ②动1和动2之间有一种手段和目的的关系。

    Action 1 and action 2 has the relation of means and purpose.

    Wǒ jí zhe shàng bān.
    我 急着　上　班。I am hurry for work.

  ③动1正在进行中出现动2的动作。(动$_1$+着+动$_1$+着+动$_2$)

    Action 2 begins when action 1 is underway.

    Tā kàn zhe kàn zhe shuìzháo　　　le.
    他 看　着　看　着　睡着(fall asleep)了。

    He fell asleep while reading a book.

4. 练习　Exercises

（1）熟读并写一写下列句子 Read and write the following sentences

    Wǒmen zhèng shàng zhe kè ne, bú yào dǎ diànhuà.
①我们　　正　上　着课呢，不　要 打　电话。

    We are having a lesson now. Don't make phone calls.

    Diànshì kāi zhe, dēng　　　yě kāi zhe.
②电视　开　着，灯(lamp)也 开　着。

    The TV is on, so is the lamp.

    Tā shǒu lǐ ná zhe yī běn shū.
③他　手　里拿着一本　书。

    He holds a book in his hand.

    Māma xiào zhe shuō.
④妈妈　笑　着　说。

    Mom said with a smile.

七、作虚词的汉字 Characters as Function Words

⑤ Bàba kāi zhe chē qù shàng bān.
爸爸 开 着 车 去 上 班。

My father drives to work.

⑥ Tā xiǎng zhe xiǎng zhe xiào le qǐlái.
他 想 着 想 着 笑 了 起来。

He burst into laughter when he was thinking.

(2) 看图用"着"造句 Make sentences with "着" according to the pictures

① 图1：门_____。(开) 　② 外边_____。(下雨)

③ 图3：他们_____去上课。(骑自行车)

④ 图4：他_____睡着了。(看)

5. 汉字知识　The knowledge of Chinese characters
"着"字的有关知识

"着"字出现的时间比较晚，在古代著作里，"着"都写作"著"，明清小说中还都这样写。后来，逐渐出现了"着"这个字。在现行汉字中，"著"和"着"有了明确的分工，"著"只用在"著作"、"土著"等词中。

"着"是一个多音多义字，有动词、助词等多种用法。作动词用时根据不同的组合分别有"zhāo"、"zháo"、"zhuó"三种不同的读音，作助词用时读轻声"zhe"，要注意分辨。

Knowledge about Character "着"

"着" appears relatively late. As late as the Ming Dynasty and Qing Dynasty, it was still written as "著" in ancient literatures. The character "着" gradually appeared later. And the character "著" and "着" are now clearly divided in modern Chinese characters. "著"(zhù) is used only in phrases like "著作(zhùzuò)" (writings) and "土著(tǔzhù)" (native).

"着" has multiple pronunciations and meanings and can be used as a verb and auxiliary word. As a verb, it has three different pronunciations when combined with different characters: "zhāo", "zháo" and "zhuó". As an auxiliary word, it has a neutral tone and is pronounced as "zhe". We need to notice this.

98. 过 auxiliary word

字源演变　The etymology of Chinese characters

小篆　　　　　　繁体　　　　　　楷体

1. 释义　Meaning

(aux.) (1) expressing the completion of action or indicating completion of action as an experience.

(v.) (2) pass; cross; spend.

(v.) (3) used after a verb as a directional complement.

2. 书写　Writing

3. 相关词语或表达　Related words or expressions

（1）Expressing the completion of action or indicating completion of action as an experience.

　① Expressing the completion of action.

　　Chī guo fàn zài qù.
　　吃 过 饭 再 去。I will go there after having a meal.

　② Indicating completion of action as an experience.

Qiánnián wǒ qù guo Chángchéng.
前年 我去过 长城。

I have been to the Great Wall the year before last.

negative form is "没(有)+v.+过"

Wǒ méi kàn guo zhè běn shū.
我 没 看 过 这 本 书。I haven't read this book.

(2) go through; pass; cross; spend.

guò hé
过 河 cross the river

guò qiáo
过 桥 cross the bridge

jīngguò
经过 pass

Cóng wǒ jiā dào xuéxiào yào jīngguò yī ge shāngdiàn.
从 我家到 学校 要 经过一个 商店。

I pass a store on my way from home to school.

Shíjiān guò de zhēn kuài a!
时间 过 得 真 快啊！Time is flying.

(3) Used after a verb as a directional complement.

Tā yóu guo le nà tiáo hé.
他 游 过了那 条 河(river)。He swam across the river.

4. 练习　Exercises

(1) 写一写下列句子，并想一想它们的意思 Write down the following sentences and think about their meanings

① 我去过北京。

② 昨天他去北京了。

③ 我没看过这本书。

④ 昨天我没看这本书。

⑤ 时间过得很快。

⑥ 从我家到学校要经过一个商店。

⑦ 他跑过来了。

七、作虚词的汉字 Characters as Function Words

(2) 选词填空 Insert the correct answer in the blanks

过　　了

① 你去_____长城吗？
② 昨天我买_____一本书。
③ 我没看_____那个电影(diànyǐng, movie)。
④ 听说他病_____。
⑤ 我下_____课就去吃饭。

5. 汉字知识　The knowledge of Chinese characters
常见的偏旁部首(31)　辶旁

"辶"从"辵"部而来，"辵"音"chuò"，是会意字，本义是忽走忽停，在现代汉语中已经绝少使用。作偏旁时多写作"辶"，俗称为"走之儿"。凡从"辵"取义的字多与行走等脚的动作或道路有关。例如"远"、"近"、"这"、"进"、"连"、"迎"、"通"、"追"等等。

"过"的本义是经过，它是一个形声字，作声旁的"咼"读作guō，在现代汉语中只是一个姓氏用字。"咼"单用或作偏旁时都简化为"呙"，只有在"过"字中简化为"寸"了。

Common Radicals and Indexing Radicals (31)　辵

Pronounced as "chuò", "辵" is an associative compound character which originally meant sudden pause in walking and is seldom used in modern Chinese. As a radical, it is often written as "辶" and is commonly known as "走之儿(zǒuzhīr)". The characters that derive their meanings from it are largely connected with walking and other actions of feet or with roads. For example, the characters "远(yuǎn)" (far), "近(jìn)" (near), "这(zhè)" (this), "进(jìn)" (enter), "连(lián)" (link), "迎(yíng)" (meet), "通(tōng)" (connect) and "追(zhuī)" (chase).

"过" originally means going through. It is a pictophonetic character and the phonetic radical "咼" is pronounced as "guō". "咼" is used only for family name in modern Chinese and it is written as "呙" when used singly or as a radical. It is only in the character "过" that it is simplified to be "寸".

99. 呢 auxiliary word

ne
呢

字源演变 The etymology of Chinese characters

小篆

楷体

1. 释义　Meaning

(aux.) (1) used at the end of an interrogative sentence.

(2) used at the end of a statement to give emphasis.

(3) used at the end of a sentence to indicate an action in progress.

(4) used to make a pause within a sentence.

2. 书写　Writing

3. 相关词语或表达　Related words or expressions

(1) used at the end of an interrogative sentence.

Nǐ gàn shénme ne?
你干 什么 呢？ What are you doing?

Wǒ de shū ne?　Wǒ de shū zài nǎr?
我 的 书 呢？(=我 的 书 在 哪儿？) Where is my book?

Wǒ míngtiān qù Shànghǎi, nǐ ne?　Wǒ míngtiān qù Shànghǎi, nǐ qù ma?/
我 明天 去 上海，你呢？(=我 明天 去 上海，你去 吗？/

七、作虚词的汉字 Characters as Function Words

  Nǐ qù nǎr?
  你去哪儿?

I am going to Shanghai. What about you?

(2) used at the end of a statement to give emphasis.

 ① 可+adj+呢。

  Zhèlǐ de yú kě dà ne.
  这里的鱼可大呢。 The fish is so big here.

 ② 才+v+呢。

  Lǎoshī, Běijīng cái hǎo ne.
  老师，北京才好呢。 Professor, Beijing is wonderful.

 ③ 还+v+呢。

  Tā hái huì shuō Hànyǔ ne.
  他还会说汉语呢。 He can also speak Chinese.

(3) used at the end of a sentence to indicate an action in progress.

  zhèng/zhèngzài/zài ne
  正/正在/在+v+呢。

  Tā zhèngzài kàn shū ne.
  他正在看书呢。 He is reading.

(4) used to make a pause within a sentence.

  Jīnnián ne, bǐ qùnián lěng duō le.
  今年呢，比去年冷多了。

This year is much colder than last year.

4. 练习 Exercises

(1) 将问句和正确的答句连线 Link the questions with the correct answers

A:
你写什么呢?
你在哪儿买的这本书呢?
她喜欢谁呢?
王老师呢?
他在哪个房间呢?

B:
他去办公室了。
她喜欢我。
他在211号房间。
我写信呢。
我在学校的书店买的这本书。

汉语常用100字

（2）看图说一说"……正在/正/在+动……呢" look at the pictures and make sentences with "……正在/正/在+动……呢"

① 图1

② 图2

③ 图3

④ 图4

5. 汉字知识　The knowledge of Chinese characters

"呢"字的起源与演变

"呢"字有两个读音。它本来读"ní"，左形右声，其本义是形容小声地不停地说话。比如似声词"呢喃"，它形容燕子的叫声，也形容小声说话。另外，在"呢绒"、"毛呢"等表示衣料的词语中也读"ní"。白话文兴起之后，它被用来作助词，表示疑问的语气。这时读轻声"ne"。

The Origin and Evolution of "呢"

"呢" has two pronunciations. It is originally pronounced as "ní" with pictographic radical on the left and phonetic radical on the right. It primarily described continuously murmuring sound. For example, the onomatopoeia "呢喃(nínán)" describes the chirps of swallows or people speaking in a low

七、作虚词的汉字 Characters as Function Words

voice. In addition, it is also pronounced as "ní" in phrases that describe the materials of clothes such as "呢绒(níróng)" and "毛呢(máoní)" (woolen fabric). After the popularization of the vernacular Chinese, it is used as an auxiliary word to express the interrogative mood and it is pronounced as "ne" in this case.

100. 吗 auxiliary word

ma
吗

字源演变　The etymology of Chinese characters

小篆　　　　　繁体　　　　　楷体

1. 释义　Meaning

(aux.) (1) used at the end of a declarative sentence to transform it into a question.

(2) used at the end of a sentence to ask (a question) in reply.

2. 书写　Writing

3. 相关词语或表达　Related words or expressions

(1) used at the end of a declarative sentence to transform it into a question.

　　Nǐ míngtiān lái ma?
　　你 明天 来吗? Will you come tomorrow?

　　Nǐ bú qù shāngdiàn ma?
　　你不去 商店 吗? Won't you go to the store?

(2) used at the end of a sentence to ask (a question) in reply.(to show the tone of interrogation or blame)

七、作虚词的汉字 Characters as Function Words

Nǐ zhèyàng zuò duì ma?　Yìsi shì "nǐ zhèyàng zuò bú duì".
你 这样 做 对 吗?(意思是"你 这样 做 不 对"。)

Is it right for you to do so? (rhetorical question, means that it is wrong for you to do so.)

Nǐ bú shì Měiguó rén ma?　Yìsi shì "nǐ jiù shì Měiguó rén".
你不 是 美国 人 吗?(意思是"你就 是 美国 人。")

Aren't you American? (means that you are American.)

nándào　　　ma
"难道+……+吗"

Nándào nǐ xǐhuan tā ma?
难道 你 喜欢 他吗?

You like him, don't you? (rhetorical question)

4. 练习　Exercises

(1) 选词填空 Insert the correct answer in the blanks

　　　　　　　　　　吗　呢

① 昨天你去商店了＿＿＿?
② 我喜欢看电影,你＿＿＿?
③ 你不是很喜欢他＿＿＿?
④ A：王老师＿＿＿? B：我也没看见他。
⑤ 他今天来了＿＿＿?

(2) 把下列句子改为用"吗"的疑问句 Change the following sentence into questions with the character "吗"

例：我吃饭了。→你吃饭了吗?

① 昨天我写作业了。

② 我来过中国。

③ 他是我的弟弟。

④ 我很喜欢吃中国菜。

⑤ 他想去上海旅行(lǚxíng, travel)。

⑥ 我不喜欢听音乐(yīnyuè, music)。

5. 汉字知识　The knowledge of Chinese characters
"吗"字的有关知识

"吗"最初是"骂"字的俗体写法。白话文兴起以后，被用来作语气助词，读"ma"轻声。另外，它还是一个方言用字，这时读"má"，如"干吗？"即"干什么"；再如"要吗有吗"，即"要什么有什么"。在音译词中读"mǎ"，如"吗啡"。

Knowledge about the Character "吗"

"吗" is used to be the vulgar form of the character "骂(mà)" (curse). After the popularization of the vernacular Chinese, it is used as a modal particle and is pronounced as "ma". In addition, it is also used in some dialects and is pronounced as "má" in this case. For example, "要吗有吗 (yào má yǒu má)", meaning that we can get what we want. In transliteration words, it is pronounced as "mǎ", such as in the phrase "吗啡 (mǎfēi)" (morphine).

答案 Key to Exercises

1. 一 one

4. 练习 Exercises

(1) 连线 Link the corresponding pronunciations and meanings of words

(2) 略

2. 十 ten

4. 练习 Exercises

(1) 写出汉字并朗读 Write down the Chinese characters and reading them aloud

    10   十
    17   十七
    28   二十八
    59   五十九
    43   四十三
    66   六十六

80　八十
91　九十一

(2) 在空格处填写相应的汉语数字 Fill the blanks with the correct numbers in Chinese

如：十一　十二　十三　<u>十四</u>　十五　十六

① 三十二　三十四　三十六　<u>三十八</u>
② 五十　六十　<u>七十</u>　八十　九十
③ 九十九　八十八　七十七　六十六　<u>五十五</u>
④ 二十一　二十三　二十五　<u>二十七</u>　二十九

3. 百 hundred

4. 练习　Exercises

(1) 写出汉字并朗读 Write down the Chinese characters and reading them aloud

103　　　一百零三
270　　　二百七十
286　　　二百八十六
591　　　五百九十一
405　　　四百零五
974　　　九百七十四
3214　　三千二百一十四（三千两百一十四）
56789　　五万六千七百八十九
104937　十万零四千九百三十七

(2) 用汉字写出下列数字 Write down the following numbers in Chinese

100　　　一百
4210　　四千二百一十（四千两百一十）
67893　　六万七千八百九十三
100054　十万零五十四
603609992　六亿零三百六十万九千九百九十二

答案 Key to Exercises

4. 你 you

4. 练习　Exercises

（1）略

（2）把下列词和短语的拼音及意思连线 Link the corresponding pronunciations and meanings of words and expressions

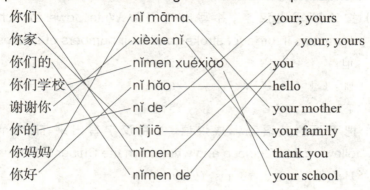

5. 我 I

4. 练习　Exercises

（1）把下列词和短语的拼音及意思连线 Link the corresponding pronunciations and meanings of words and expressions

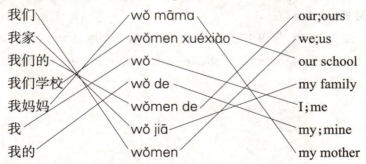

（2）选词填空 Fill in the blanks with correct words

　　　　　　　你　　我　　我的　　我们

你好！

你等我？

汉语常用100字

我们是好朋友。
这是我的书包。

6. 他 he

4. 练习 Exercises

(1) 按笔顺写出汉字，并写出笔画数 Write down the Chinese characters in order of strokes and their numbers of strokes

他：丿 亻 亻 仲 他　　　　5画
她：く 女 女 女 如 她　　　6画
它：丶 宀 宀 它　　　　　　5画

(2) 把下面的英语翻译成汉语，并用汉字写出来 Translate the following into Chinese and write down the Chinese characters

He (他)　　　　　his (他的)
She (她)　　　　her (她的)
It (它)　　　　　its (它的)
They(他们)　　　their (他们的)

7. 这 this

4. 练习 Exercises

(1) 按笔顺写出汉字，并写出笔画数 Write down the Chinese characters in order of strokes and their numbers of strokes

这：丶 亠 亍 文 文 诶 这　　7画
那：丁 丑 丑 用 那 那　　　　6画
些：丨 卜 忄 止 此 此 些 些　 8画
里：丨 冂 日 日 甲 甲 里　　　7画
么：丿 么 么　　　　　　　　3画

(2) 根据图片用所学的汉字完成句子，并写出汉字 Complete the sentences with the Chinese characters you have learned according to the pictures and write down the Chinese characters

图片1：(这)是学校,(那)是医院。
图片2：(这里)有很多老人,(那里)有很多孩子。
图片3：(这些)楼很高,(那些)楼很矮。
图片4：(这么)多水果我吃不完。

8. 谁 who

4. 练习 Exercises

(1) 用拼音写出下列笔画的名称,并将含有下列笔画的汉字写在相应的括号里 Write down the names of the following strokes and write down the Chinese characters with the following strokes in the corresponding brackets

例：丿 tí （我）
㇆ （百）
乙 （谁）
㇇ （你）
亅 （东）

(2) 用"谁"来提问下列句子中表示人称的词 Make a question with the character "谁" for the following words which indicate people in the following sentences

例：我是学生。 谁是学生？

① 小王是谁的朋友？
② 你喜欢谁？
③ 谁是中国人？
④ 这是谁的书？
⑤ 谁是你的同学？
⑥ 你家有三口人,他们是谁？

9. 几 how many

4. 练习　Exercises

（2）用"几"来完成会话 Complete the following conversations with "几"

① A：桌子上有几本书？

　B：桌子　上　有　四本　书。
　　 Zhuōzi shàng yǒu sì běn shū.

　There are four books on the table.

② A：苹果几块钱一斤？

　B：苹果　两　块　钱　一斤。
　　 Píngguǒ liǎng kuài qián yī jīn.

　The apple is two yuan per Jin (0.5 kg).

③ A：你去过北京几次？

　B：我　去　过　北京　三　次。
　　 Wǒ qù guo Běijīng sān cì.

　I've been to Beijing three times.

④ A：北京　的　名胜古迹　都　去　过　了吗？
　　 Běijīng de míngshènggǔjī dōu qù guo le ma?

　Have you been to all the places of interests in Beijing?

　B：我都去过了。

⑤ A：你的女儿几岁了？

　B：我　的　女儿　三　岁了。
　　 Wǒ de nǚer sān suì le.

　My daughter is three years old.

⑥ A：你们班有几名同学？

　B：我们　班　有　八　名　同学。
　　 Wǒmen bān yǒu bā míng tóngxué.

　There're eight students in our class.

答案 Key to Exercises

10. 天 sky

4. 练习 Exercises

(1) 根据拼音写出汉字,并想想他们的意思 Write down the Chinese characters according to *pinyin* and think about their meanings

zuótiān　（昨天）　　xiàtiān　　（夏天）
měitiān　（每天）　　tiānqì　　（天气）
dōngtiān（冬天）　　jīntiān　　（今天）
chūntiān（春天）　　xīngqītiān（星期天）

(2) 请写出带"天"字的词语,写得越多越好 Write down as many words with the character "天" as possible

每天　今天　昨天　明天　后天　春天
夏天　秋天　冬天　天气

11. 年 year

4. 练习 Exercises

(1) 完成句子 Complete the sentences

今年是__2013__年,去年是__2012__年,前年是__2011__年,明年是__2014__年,后年是__2015__年。

(2) 请用汉语介绍一下你最近几年做些什么;写一写你人生的几个时期都做些什么,或准备做些什么,希望能用上我们学过的表示年份和表示时期的词语 Please introduce in Chinese what you have done for the past few years. Write down the things you have done or prepared to do at each stage of your life. You are expected to use the words and phrases we have learned about years and periods

比如:

我的童年是在北京度过的,我的童年非常快乐;我的少年是在北京第五中学度过的,我的少年很有意思;我现在是青年,我想在青年的时候实现自己的理想;中年以后,我打算到世界各地去旅行;老年的时候,我希望把有意思的事记下来写成书。

12. 月 month

4. 练习 Exercises

（1）请把下列词语与它们相对应的意思连线 Link the corresponding meanings of words and expressions

五月 —————— moon
月亮 —————— the present month
上个月 ————— every month
每个月 ————— May
五个月 ————— next month
这个月 ————— last month
下个月 ————— five months

（2）请用汉字写出下列日期 Please write down the following date in Chinese

例：September/ 2009　　（二〇〇九年九月）
　　March/1998　　　　（一九九八年三月）
　　January/2005　　　（二零零五年一月）
　　November/1978　　（一九七八年十一月）
　　August/1996　　　　（一九九六年八月）
　　July/2010　　　　　（二零一零年七月）
　　April/1989　　　　　（一九八九年四月）
　　February/1993　　　（一九九三年二月）
　　October/2008　　　（二零零八年十月）
　　December/2014　　（二零一四年十二月）

13. 日 day

4. 练习 Exercises

（1）根据英文意思写出汉字，并加注拼音 Write down the Chinese characters and *pinyin* according to the English meaning

英文	中文	拼音
diary	日记	rìjì

答案 Key to Exercises

calendar　　　日历　　　rìlì
date　　　　　日期　　　rìqī
day　　　　　 天　　　　tiān
birthday　　　 生日　　　shēngrì
festivals　　　 节日　　　jiérì
japan　　　　 日本　　　Rìběn

（2）请用汉字写出下列日期 Write down the following date in Chinese

例：Sep. 10, 2009　　　（二〇〇九年九月十日）
　　Jan. 1, 2010　　　　（二零一零年一月一日）
　　Jul. 4, 1776　　　　 （一七七六年七月四日）
　　Nov. 27, 2007　　　（二零零七年十一月二七日）
　　Aug. 8, 2008　　　 （二零零八年八月八日）
　　Mar. 31, 1985　　　（一九八五年三月三十一日）
　　Apr. 1, 2003　　　　（二零零三年四月一日）
　　Dec. 25, 2017　　　（二零一七年十二月二十五日）
　　Feb. 14, 1968　　　（一九六八年二月十四日）

14. 星 star

4. 练习　Exercises

（1）填空 Fill in the blanks

歌星　　球星　　影星

Tā hěn huì chànggē, shì yī ge gēxīng; tā shì yī ge hǎo yǎnyuán, tā
她 很 会 唱歌，是 一个 歌星；他是 一个 好 演员，他

shì yī ge yǐngxīng; Yáo Míng lánqiú dǎ de hěn hǎo, shì yī ge qiúxīng.
是一个 影星；姚 明 篮球打得很 好，是 一个 球星。

371

汉语常用100字

（2）请用汉字写出日历中标有下划线的日期（年、月、日、星期 Write down the underlined dates (year, month, day and week) on the calendar in Chinese

10 October 2013						
Sunday	Monday	Tuesday	Wednesday	Thursday	Friday	Saturday
		1	2	<u>3</u>	4	5
6	7	8	9	10	11	12
13	14	15	16	17	18	<u>19</u>
20	21	<u>22</u>	23	24	25	26
27	28	29	<u>30</u>	31		

① 2013年10月3日　星期四
② 2013年10月19日　星期六
③ 2013年10月22日　星期二
④ 2013年10月30日　星期三

15. 东 east

4. 练习　Exercises

（1）据图示写出他们汉语的方位名称 Write down the name of the directions in Chinese according to the illustrations

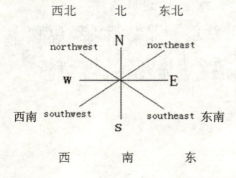

（2）略

372

答案 Key to Exercises

16. 中 middle

4. 练习 Exercises

(1) 请把下列词语与它们相对应的意思连线 Link the corresponding meanings of words and expressions

中文 —————— Chinese food
中药 —————— Chinese medicine
中心 —————— Chinese language
中号 —————— middle school
中餐 —————— center
中学 —————— medium size
手中 —————— in the hand
心中 —————— in the heart

(2) 请根据提示语标出各组的程度 Mark out the level of each group according to the clues

① A 书很难(nán)　B 书很容易(róngyi)　C 书不太难也不太容易
　 A 书(高)级　　　B 书(初)级　　　　C 书(中)级

② 考试(kǎoshì)成绩(chéngjì)：A：58分　　B：100分　　C：80分
　 他们的汉语水平(shuǐpíng)：
　 A(低)等　　　B(高)等　　　　　C(中)等

③ 小王穿L号的衣服，小李穿M号的衣服，小张穿S号的衣服。
　 他们穿的衣服号码：
　 小王(大)号　　小李(中)号　　　小张(小)号

17. 前 front

4. 练习 Exercises

(1) 看图片写出对应的汉语方位词汇并注音 Look at the pictures and write down their corresponding directions in Chinese and their phonetic notations

前门在天安门的 <u>南边</u>，天安门在前门的 <u>北边</u>。

373

北京医院(hospital)有一个前门和一个后门，医院的前门是车站(bus station)，医院的中央是一个操场(playground)。医院的前门在南面，后门在北面。

(2) 将下列对应的词语用线连接起来 Link the corresponding meanings of words and expressions with their pronunciations

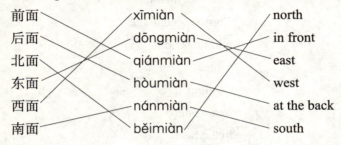

18. 左 left

4. 练习 Exercises

(1) 根据英文意思写出对应的汉语方位词汇并注音 Write down their corresponding directions in Chinese and their phonetic notations

East　　　（东）　　　（dōng）

left　　　（左）　　　（zuǒ）

West　　　（西）　　　（xī）

South　　　（南）　　　（nán）

North　　　（北）　　　（běi)）

right　　　（右）　　　（yòu）

in front　　　（前）　　　（qián）

(2) 请根据下列图示选择填空 Please insert the correct answer in the blanks according to the pictures

妻子(wife)在 丈夫(husband)左边，小狗(dog)在他们中间。

老师 在 黑板(blackboard)右边。

答案 Key to Exercises

A 在<u>左边</u>(zài), B 在<u>中间</u>(zài), C 在<u>右边</u>(zài)。

19. 王 king

4. 练习 Exercises

（1）略

（2）略

20. 男 man

5. 练习 Exercises

（1）略。

（2）选择填空 Insert the correct answer in the blanks

① 他　她

<u>他</u>是男人,<u>她</u>是女人。

② 男　女

妻子(qīzi, wife)是<u>女</u>的,丈夫(zhàngfu, husband)是<u>男</u>的

③ 男厕所　女厕所

他要去<u>男厕所</u>,她要去<u>女厕所</u>。

④ 男　女

爷爷(yéye, grandpa)不喜欢(xǐhuan, like)<u>女</u>孩儿,他喜欢<u>男</u>孩儿。

21. 岁 age

4. 练习 Exercises

完成下列对话 Complete the following dialogue

A：小朋友,你今年<u>几岁了</u>?

B：阿姨,我三岁半了。

A：老先生,您今年<u>多大年纪</u>?

B：我都八十多岁了。

汉语常用100字

A：同学，你今年<u>多大</u>了？

B：我二十一岁。

A：小张，你<u>多大岁数</u>？有女(nǚ) 朋友(péngyou)(girlfriend)了吗？

B：三十岁了，还没有呢。

A：老奶奶，您身体(shēntǐ)(health)真好呀，您高寿？

B：我的孙子(sūnzi)都有儿子(érzi)了，我明年就一百岁了。

(My grandson already has a son. I will be 100-year old next year.)

22. 国 county

4. 练习　Exercises

(1) 请根据英语写出下列国家的汉语名字 Please insert the Chinese names of the following nations

France	法国
Germany	德国
United Kingdom	英国
Thailand	泰国
Japan	日本
India	印度
Brazil	巴西
Switzerland	瑞士
Egypt	埃及
Canada	加拿大
Italy	意大利
Spain	西班牙
Portugal	葡萄牙
Russia	俄罗斯
Australia	澳大利亚
Malaysia	马来西亚
Indonesia	印度尼西亚

答案 Key to Exercises

（2）看国旗写国家名字 Please insert each nation's Chinese name beside its national flag

中国　　韩国　　美国　　加拿大　　澳大利亚　　瑞士

23. 市 city

4. 练习 Exercises

（1）选词填空 Insert the correct answer in the blanks

城市　　夜市　　市场　　黑市

① 大<u>城市</u>的汽车（car）越来越（more and more）多。
② 别去<u>黑市</u>买东西，不安全（safe）。
③ 下班后我喜欢去<u>夜市</u>吃点东西。
④ 我家附近（nearby）有个服装（clothing）<u>市场</u>。

（2）略

24. 家 family

4. 练习 Exercises

（1）把下列词语和它们相对应的意思连线 Link the corresponding meanings of words and expressions

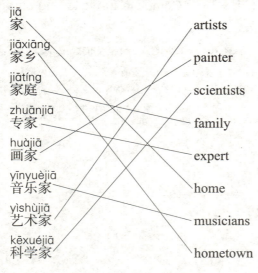

377

（2）填空 Please fill in the blanks

这是一<u>家</u>银行。

这是我的<u>家</u>。

她钢琴弹得很好，她是一个<u>音乐家</u>。

毕加索（Pablo Picasso）是一位<u>画家</u>，他的画很有名。

鲁迅（Lǔ Xùn）写了很多书，是一个<u>作家</u>。

25. 人 person

4. 练习　Exercises

（1）将下列词语和词组与对应的拼音及意思连线 Link the corresponding pronunciations and meanings of words and expressions

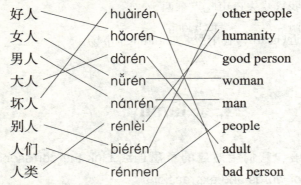

（2）用所给词语完成下列一段话 Complete the following paragraph with the given words

女人　　年轻人　　外国人　　人们　　人类

Wǒmen xuéxiào yǒu hěn duō rén, nánrén, lǎorén
我们　学校　有　很　多　人，男人、<u>女人</u>、老人、<u>年轻人</u>、

Zhōngguó rén　　　　　měitiān dōu hěn máng, dàjiā wèi　　de
中国　　人、<u>外国人</u>。<u>人们</u>每天　都　很　忙，大家　为<u>人类</u>的

wèilái ér nǔlì.
未来　而努力。

答案 Key to Exercises

26. 口 mouth

4. 练习 Exercises

(1) 请写出带"口"字旁的汉字，写得越多越好 Write down as many characters with the radical "口" as possible

吃 喝 可 右 只 句 号 另 台 叹 兄 同 各 后
和 各 吗 呀 员 吹

(2) 选词填空 Insert the correct answer in the blanks

口　口红　口味　口语　口音　口试

① Tāmen jiā yǒu wǔ rén.
　他们家有五口人。

② Nǐ xǐhuan zhè zhǒng　de cài ma?
　你喜欢这种口味的菜吗？

③ Míngtiān yǒu　kè.
　明天有口语课。

④ Tā yǒu Guǎngdōng　.
　他有广东口音。

⑤ Zuótiān de　nán ma?
　昨天的口试难吗？

⑥ Wǒ mǎi le yī zhī　.
　我买了一支口红。

27. 手 hand

4. 练习 Exercises

(1) 根据英文翻译写出相应的词语 Write down the corresponding Chinese words according to the translations

Mobile	(手机)	watch	(手表)
Hand	(手)	sailor	(水手)
Handbag	(手提包)	singer	(歌手)
Skilled hand	(能手)	finger	(手指)

(2) 略

28. 爸 father

4. 练习　Exercises

（1）根据英文意思写出相应的汉字及拼音。(Write down the Chinese characters and *pinyin* according to the English)

father	（爸爸）	(bàba)
mother	（妈妈）	(māma)
elder brother	（哥哥）	(gēge)
elder sister	（姐姐）	(jiějie)
younger brother	（弟弟）	(dìdi)
younger sister	（妹妹）	(mèimei)
(paternal) grandfather	（爷爷）	(yéye)
(paternal) grandmother	（奶奶）	(nǎinai)

（2）请根据图片描述一下这个家庭 Describe the family according to the picture

这是一个大家庭，有爷爷、奶奶、爸爸、妈妈、姐姐和弟弟。

29. 水 water

4. 练习　Exercises

（1）将下列词语和词组与对应的拼音及意思连线 Link the corresponding pronunciations and meanings of words and expressions

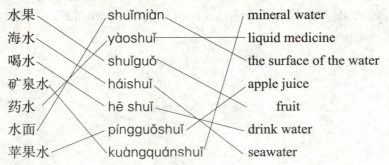

(2) 写出带有水或偏旁氵的字 Write down as many characters with "水" or "氵"as possible

海、江、河、湖、洋、汗

30. 饭 meal

4. 练习　Exercises

(1) 选择填空 Insert the correct answer in the blanks

米饭　　吃饭　　晚饭　　饭馆　　面条

Měitiān wǒ chī sān dùn fàn, zǎofàn, wǔfàn, wǎnfàn. Zǎoshang wǒ
每天 我 吃 三 顿 饭，早饭，午饭、晚饭。 早上 我
chángcháng zài jiā　　zǎofàn wǒ chī bāozi.　Kěshì xiàbān yǐ hòu, wǒ
常常　　　在家吃饭，早饭 我 吃 包子。可是下班 以 后，我
yǒu shíhòu qù　　chī,　　nà jiā fànguǎn de　　hé　　dōu hěn hǎochī.
有 时候 去饭馆吃晚饭，那家 饭馆 的米饭和面条都 很 好吃。

(2) 看图片认一认这些都是什么饭 Please insert the Chinese name beside its picture

米饭　　面条　　馒头　　包子　　饺子

31. 菜 vegetable

4. 练习　Exercises

(1) 看图片，说出下列蔬菜的名字。(Say the names of the following vegetables in the pictures.)

图片1：白菜　　　图片2：油菜　　　图片3：芹菜

图片4：卷心菜　　图片5：菜花　　　图片6：菠菜

(2) 略。

32. 酒 liquor

4. 练习　Exercises

(1) 把下列汉字写在相应的结构后 Write the following Chinese characters next to their corresponding structures

酒　　你　　这　　男　　岁　　国　　左

zuǒyòu jiégòu
左右　结构(你,酒)(left-right structure)

shàngxià jiégòu
上下　结构(男,岁)(top-bottom structure)

zuǒ xià bāowéi jiégòu
左 下　包围　结构(这)(left-bottom-encircled structure)

zuǒ shàng bāowéi jiégòu
左　上　包围　结构(左)(left-top-encircled structure)

sìmiàn bāowéi jiégòu
四面　包围　结构(国)(all-side-encircled structure)

(2) 看图片认一认这些都是什么酒 What are these alcohols in the picture

红酒　　白酒　　果汁　　啤酒

33. 钱 money

4. 练习　Exercises

(1) 略。

(2) 跟朋友互相询问并说出身边物品的价格 Practice with your friends and ask each other about the prices of the things around you

例如:书

A:你的书多少钱?

　　How much is your book?

B:25块。

① 笔̌　　pen; pencil

你的笔多少钱?

3块。

② 手机̌ǔjī　　mobile, cellphone

你的手机多少钱?

5000块。

答案 Key to Exercises

③ 手表(shǒubiǎo)　watch

你的手表多少钱？

4000块。

④ 矿泉水(kuàngquánshuǐ)　mineral water

你的矿泉水多少钱？

5块。

34. 元 ￥ yuan

4. 练习　Exercises

（1）请读出下列钱数并写出汉字 Say the following amount of money and write them down in Chinese

74.56元　　　七十四块五毛六

8324.8元　　八千三百二十四块八毛

207.09元　　二百零七块九分

43.06元　　　四十三块六分

100.8元　　　一百块零八角

50.07元　　　五十块零七分

99.16元　　　九十九块一角六分

（2）看图片识别钱币 Identify the currency in the pictures

1. 一百元　　　2. 二十美元
3. 一万日元　　4. 十欧元
5. 一澳元　　　6. 五加元
7. 十新元　　　8. 一千韩元

35. 衣 clothes

4. 练习　Exercises

（1）将下列词语和词组与对应的拼音及意思连线 Link the corresponding pronunciations and meanings of words and expressions

汉语常用100字

(2) 看图片识别各种衣服并写在图片下边　Identify different kinds of clothes in the pictures and write down their names below the pictures

上衣　　外套　　裤子　　毛衣　　裙子　　衬衣

36. 楼 a storied building

4. 练习　Exercises

选择填空(Insert the correct answer in the blanks)

三楼　　楼道　　三层　　楼房　　高楼大厦　　楼梯

Wǒ de dàxué lǐ dōu shì lóufáng, bàngōnglóu yǒu liù céng, lǎoshī de bàn
我 的 大学 里 都 是 <u>楼房</u>，办公楼 有 六层，老师 的 办

gōngshì zài sāncéng, yǒu lóutī yě yǒu diàntī, lóudào hěn kuānchang.
公 室 在 <u>三层</u>，有 楼梯 也 有 电梯(elevator)，<u>楼道</u> 很 宽敞。

jiàoxuélóu yǒu sì zuò, měi zuò lóu dōu shì sān lóu, zài zhōuwéi de gāolóu dàshà
教学楼 有 4 座，每 座 楼 都 是 <u>三楼</u>，在 周围 的 <u>高楼 大厦</u>

zhīzhōng, xiǎnde yǒuxiē dī'ǎi.
之 中，　显得 有些 低矮。

答案 Key to Exercises

37. 室 room

4. 练习 Exercises

(1) 把下列词语及其相对应的拼音和意思连线 Link the corresponding pronunciations and meanings of words and expressions

(2) 选词填空 Insert the correct answer in the blanks

   室内 室外 办公室 教室 卧室

① 学生去<u>教室</u>上 课(attend class)。（shàng kè）

② 经理在<u>办公室</u>工作(gōngzuò)(to work)。

③ 我在<u>卧室</u>睡觉(sleep)。（shuìjiào）

④ 哥哥在<u>室内</u>看 电视(watch TV)。（kàn diànshì）

⑤ 弟弟在<u>室外</u>踢球 。(play football)。（dìdi zài ... tī zúqiú）

38. 路 road

4. 练习 Exercises

(1) 根据拼音写出相应的词或短语 Write down the corresponding words and expressions according to Pinyin

yì tiáo lù (一条路)

lùkǒu (路口)

guò mǎlù (过马路)

zǒu lù (走路)

(2) 看图写句子 Complete the sentences according to the pictures

① 小明家前边有<u>一条路</u>。

② 前边有<u>一个路口</u>。
③ <u>过马路</u>要小心。
④ 我<u>走路</u>去教室。

39. 店 shop

4. 练习　Exercises

（1）回答问题(Answer the following questions)

　　① 你去哪儿买东西？　　　　　　　　商店
　　　Where do you go shopping?
　　② 你去哪儿吃饭？　　　　　　　　　饭店
　　　Where do you have your meals?
　　③ 你去哪儿买书？　　　　　　　　　书店
　　　Where do you buy books?
　　④ 旅行(lǚxíng, travel)的时候，你住在哪儿？　旅店
　　　Where do you live when you go on a trip?
　　⑤ 你在哪儿买药？　　　　　　　　　药店
　　　Where do you get medicine?
　　⑥ 你常去哪儿买花？　　　　　　　　花店
　　　Where do you usually go to buy flowers?

（2）请写出下列各种商店的名称 Please write the names of the following stores

　花店　　书店　　旅店　　商店　　饭店　　眼镜店

40. 车 vehicle

4. 练习　Exercises

（1）看图写出汉语，并加注拼音 Write down the corresponding Chinese expressions and their phonetic notations according to the pictures

　　　　chūzū qìchē　　　　　　　jiàochē
　图片1 出租 汽车　　　　　图片2 轿车

图片 3 公共汽车 (gōnggòng qìchē)　　图片 4 电车 (diànchē)
图片 5 卡车 (kǎchē)　　图片 6 自行车 (kèchē)

41. 个 a measure word

4. 练习 Exercises

（1）看图片说出东西的数量 Say the numbers of the things in the pictures

这是<u>六个</u>包子。　　　　这儿有<u>六个</u>人。
图上有<u>两个</u>人。　　　　一<u>个</u>月有<u>四个</u>星期。

（2）读短文并回答问题 Read the following passage and answer questions

① 她家有五口人。
② 她有一个哥哥,一个妹妹。
③ 她家有一个小狗,小狗每天吃三个包子。
④ 今天她的好朋友吃了两个苹果。
⑤ 她们两个家庭很友好。

42. 件 piece

4. 练习 Exercises

看图片认识和熟悉下列证件 Look at the pictures and get familiar with the following certificates

图片 1 护照 (hùzhào) passport
图片 2 中国的身份证 (Zhōngguó de shēnfènzhèng) Chinese Identity card
图片 3 学生证 (xuéshēngzhèng) student ID
图片 4 工作证 (gōngzuòzhèng) employec's card

图片5 交通卡 jiāotōngkǎ traffic card

图片6 驾驶证 jiàshǐzhèng driving license

43. 斤 jīn

4. 练习　Exercises

（1）请按笔画顺序写出下面的汉字，并写出笔画数 Write down the Chinese characters in order of strokes and write down their numbers of strokes

斤（4画）　　　个（3画）
件（6画）　　　元（4画）
衣（6画）　　　家（10画）
水（4画）　　　年（6画）
男（7画）　　　几（2画）

（2）当你在市场买下列东西时，试试自己问价钱 Try to ask about the prices of the following things when you go shopping in a market

包子多少钱一斤？　　　一斤苹果多少钱？
鸡蛋多少钱一斤？　　　一斤肉多少钱？

44. 米 meter

4. 练习　Exercises

（1）读出下列一家人的身高 Read out the height of the family members

爷爷 yéye 1.74米 mǐ　　　爷爷一米七四
奶奶 nǎinai 1.58米 mǐ　　　奶奶一米五八
爸爸 bàba 1.80米　　　爸爸一米八零
妈妈 māma 1.65米　　　妈妈一米六五
儿子 érzi 1.87米　　　儿子一米八七

女儿1.73米（nǚér）　　女儿一米七三

(2) 看图片写出汉字和拼音 Write down the corresponding names in Chinese and *pinyin* according to the pictures

1. 大米(dàmǐ)　2. 米饭(mǐfàn)　3. 米醋(mǐcù)　4. 米粉(mǐfěn)

45. 次 time

4. 练习　Exercises

(1) 略

(2) 选择填空 Insert the correct answer in the blanks

件　米　个　斤　次

① 我去过三<u>次</u>西安。
② 妈妈买了两<u>斤</u>肉。
③ 他的身高是一<u>米</u>八。
④ 我喜欢这<u>个</u>国家。
⑤ 这<u>件</u>毛衣真漂亮(piàoliang)(beautiful)。

46. 有 have

4. 练习　Exercises

（略）

47. 是 be

4. 练习　Exercises

(1) 略

(2) 选择填空 Insert the correct answer in the blanks

有　是

① 我<u>有</u>两个哥哥。
② 他<u>是</u>中国人。

③这是我的衣服。
④我没有很多朋友。
⑤他不是老师。

48. 听 listen

4. 练习　Exercises

（1）用"听"完成句子 Complete the sentences with "听"

① 他的 汉语 说 得太 快了,我 听<u>不清楚</u>。
   Tā de Hànyǔ shuō de tài kuài le, wǒ tīng

② 电话 的 声音 太 小了,我 听<u>不见</u>。
   Diànhuà de shēngyīn tài xiǎo le, wǒ tīng

③ 唱 中国歌 也可以 学 中文, 所以 我 常常 在
   Chàng Zhōngguógē yě kěyǐ xué zhōngwén, suǒyǐ wǒ chángcháng zài
   家里听<u>中国歌</u>。
   jiā lǐ tīng

④ 老师 讲 的 话你都 听<u>懂了</u>吗?
   Lǎoshī jiǎng de huà nǐ dōu tīng   ma?

⑤ 在<u>听力</u>课 上, 我们 老师 会 让 我们 练习 发音。
   Zài   kè shàng, wǒmen lǎoshī huì ràng wǒmen liànxí fāyīn.

（2）略

49. 说 say

4. 练习　Exercises

（1）看拼音写出下列词和短语并记住它们的意思 Write down the words and expressions in Chinese according to *pinyin* and remember their meanings

shuō huà　　　（说话）　　shuō yi shuō （说一说）

shuō Yīngyǔ　　（说英语）　shuō Fǎyǔ　　（说法语）

shuō Hànyǔ　　（说汉语）　shuō Rìyǔ　　（说日语）

shuō yíxiàr　　（说一下儿）

答案 Key to Exercises

（2）用上边学习过的词和短语完成句子 Complete the sentences with the words and expressions learned in this lesson

① 去年我去日本了，可是我不会说日语。

② 请说一下儿你的名字，好吗？

③ 我要多练习说汉语，因为我要在中国工作。

④ 我想休息一下儿，请你们别说话了，好吗？

⑤ 请你们说一说你们的家庭。

50. 看 look

4. 练习 Exercises

（1）看拼音写出下列词语并记住它们的意思 Write down the words and expressions in Chinese according to *pinyin* and remember their meanings

kān jiā 看家　　　　　kàn shū 看书

kàn bu jiàn 看不见　　kànwàng 看望

kàn zhe 看着　　　　 kànjiàn 看见

kàn shang 看上　　　 kàn bìng 看病

（2）解释下列句子中"看"的意思 Explain the meaning of "看" in the following sentences

① Wǒ māma bù zài jiā, tā qù kàn wǒ lǎolao qù le.
　我 妈妈 不 在 家，她 去 看 我 姥姥 去 了。

　看望（visit）

② Nǐ kànshàng nà tái diànnǎo le, nà shì xiànzài zuì hǎo de.
　你 看 上 那台 电脑 了，那是 现在 最好 的。

　看上（take a fancy to）

③ Kàn yi kàn zhè dào tí, nǐ kàn de dǒng ma?
　看 一 看 这 道 题，你 看 得 懂 吗？

　看一看（have a quick look）看懂（understand）

④ Tā de yǎnjing bù hǎo, tā qù yīyuàn kàn yǎnjing qù le.
　他的 眼睛 不 好，他 去 医院 看 眼睛 去 了。

　看病（to see a doctor）

391

Nǐ kān zhe háizi, wǒ qù mǎi cài.
⑥ 你 看 着 孩子，我 去 买 菜。

看着（look after）

51. 吃 eat

4. 练习　Exercises

（1）把下列短语与其相对应的拼音连线 Link the corresponding pronunciations and meanings of words and expressions

（2）你喜欢吃什么饭？什么水果？什么菜？请在下边写一写，写得越多越好，可以模仿给出的句式来写 What would you like for dinner? What fruit would you like? What dishes would you prefer? Write down as much as possible, and you can follow the given sentence pattern

Fàn, wǒ xǐhuan chī
饭，我 喜欢 吃……

① 我喜欢吃米饭。

② 我喜欢吃饺子。

③ 我喜欢吃面条。

Shuǐguǒ, wǒ xǐhuan chī
水果， 我 喜欢 吃……

① 我喜欢吃苹果。

② 我喜欢吃香蕉。

③ 我喜欢吃葡萄。

Cài, wǒ xǐhuan chī
菜，我 喜欢 吃……

① 我喜欢吃青菜。

② 我喜欢吃凉拌菜。

③ 我喜欢吃娃娃菜。

(3) 读短文并回答问题 Read the passage and answer questions

问题：

中国人一般一天吃三顿饭。

早饭年轻人吃面包或包子。

晚饭常常在家吃。

水果一般晚饭以后吃。

52. 喝 drink

4. 练习　Exercises

（1）你喜欢喝什么饮料？什么酒？什么茶？请在下边写一写，写得越多越好，可以模仿给出的句式来写 What drinks would you like? What kind of alcohol would you like? What kind of tea would you prefer? Write down as much as possible, and you can follow the given sentence pattern

饮料，我喜欢喝……

① 我喜欢喝果汁。

② 我喜欢喝咖啡。

③ 我喜欢喝可口可乐。

酒，我喜欢喝……

① 我喜欢喝啤酒。

② 我喜欢喝红酒。

③ 我喜欢喝鸡尾酒。

茶，我喜欢喝……

① 我喜欢喝红茶。

② 我喜欢喝花茶。

③我喜欢喝绿茶。

(2) 阅读短文并回答问题 Reading passage and answer question

问题：

① 请举例说说中国有什么种类的酒。

　　白酒、米酒、葡萄酒、啤酒等等

② 人们为什么喜欢喝酒？

　　人们一边喝酒一边聊天,很放松也很高兴,而且,人们还常常通过喝酒交朋友。

③ 北方人喜欢喝什么酒？

　　白酒。

④ 南方人喜欢喝什么酒？

　　米酒。

⑤ 老年人喜欢喝什么酒？

　　葡萄酒。

53. 做 do

4. 练习　Exercises

(1) 选择填空 Insert the correct answer in the blanks

　　　　听　说　看　吃　喝　做

① 妹妹喜欢喝饮料(yǐnliào)(soft drinks)。

② 哥哥常看电视。

③ 我每天做作业。

④ 韩国人(Hánguó rén)(Korean)喜欢吃米饭。

⑤ 爸爸不喜欢说话。

⑥ 你喜欢听音乐(music)吗？

(2) 仿照下列形式看图说话 Talk about the pictures in the form of the given example

1. A：她在做什么呢？ B：她在做作业呢。

2. A：她在做什么呢？ B：她在做衣服呢。

B：他是<u>老师</u>吗？
B：他是<u>医生</u>。

54. 打 hit

4. 练习　Exercises

（1）根据拼音写出词语 Write down the words and expressions according to *pinyin*

dǎ rén (打人)　　　　dǎsǎo (打扫)
dǎ zhé (打折)　　　　dǎ shǒushì (打手势)
dǎ jiāodào (打交道)　dǎ diànhuà (打电话)

（2）用所给词语完成句子 Complete the following sentences with words in the parentheses

① 我经常<u>打扫房间</u>。(打扫房间)
② 我在给妈妈<u>打电话</u>。(打电话)
③ 最近商店<u>总是打折</u>。(打折)
④ 售货员跟<u>顾客打交道</u>。(打交道)

55. 学 study

4. 练习　Exercises

（1）根据拼音写出词语 Write down the words and expressions according to *pinyin*

shàng xué (上学)　　xuéxí (学习)
xuésheng (学生)　　xuéwen (学问)
xuéxiào (学校)　　　dàxué (大学)
zhōngxué (中学)　　xiǎoxué (小学)
wénxué (文学)　　　shùxué (数学)

（2）用所给词语完成句子 Complete the following sentences with words in the parentheses

① 我每天<u>学习汉语</u>。(学习)

② 你什么时候<u>去上学</u>?(上……学)
③ 那个<u>是我的学校</u>。(学校)
④ 你在哪个<u>大学</u>学习?(大学)
⑤ 爸爸很有<u>学问</u>。(学问)

56. 买 buy

4. 练习　Exercises

（1）仿照例子,用括号里的词语替换带下划线的词语完成句子 Follow the example and complete the sentences by replacing the underlined words with the words in the brackets

例子：昨天<u>我</u>买了<u>一本书</u>。

　　　　I bought a book yesterday.

① <u>今天他买了一个面包</u>。(他　一个面包)
② <u>星期天妈妈买了两件衣服</u>。(妈妈　两件衣服)
③ <u>昨天爸爸买了三瓶酒</u>。(爸爸　三瓶酒)
④ <u>下午哥哥买了四支笔</u>。(哥哥　四支笔)
⑤ <u>晚上姐姐买了五斤苹果</u>。(姐姐　五斤苹果)
⑥ <u>星期一老师买了六本书</u>。(老师　六本书)

（2）选词填空 Insert the correct answer in the blanks

　　　　买　　卖　　买方　　卖方　　买卖

① 以后我想去中国做<u>买卖</u>。
② 今天早上我<u>买</u>了一杯咖啡喝。
③ 那家商店每天<u>卖</u>很多东西。
④ <u>买家</u>付钱以后<u>卖家</u>要马上给货。

答案 Key to Exercises

57. 给 give

4. 练习 Exercises

（1）请把"给"字放在适当的位置 Please put the character "给" in the proper place of the sentences

① A我　　B他　　C一本书　　D看。　　　　　　B
② 请你　　A老师　B打个　　C电话吧　　D!　　　A
③ 我　　　A常常　B朋友　　C发
　　　　　　duǎnxìn
　　　　D短信(message)。　　　　　　　　　　　B
④ A爸爸　B我　　C100块钱　D买衣服。　　　　B
⑤ A请　　B你们　C我　　　D出个主意，好吗?　C
⑥ 昨天　　A我　　B朋友寄　C了　　D一封信。　B

（2）连词成句 Arrange the following words in correct order to form a sentence

① 邮件　我　哥哥　发　给
　　我给哥哥发邮件。
② 姐姐　妹妹　一　件　给　衣服
　　姐姐给妹妹一件衣服。
③ 我　帮忙　给　来　大家
　　我给大家来帮忙。或者:大家给我来帮忙。
④ 常常　妈妈　给　打　我　电话
　　妈妈常常给我打电话。或者:我常常给妈妈打电话。

58. 来 come

4. 练习 Exercises

（1）把"来"放在合适的位置 Please put the character "来" in the proper place of the sentences

① A他　　　B昨天　　C中国　　D了。　　　C
② A一碗　　B米饭　　C。　　　　　　　　　A
③ A我　　　B看　　　C一下　　D。　　　　B

④A 妈妈　　　B 给　　C 我寄　　　D 了一封信。　　　　D

⑤A 他　　　　B 走进　C 房间　　　D 了。　　　　　　　D

(2) 连词成句 Arrange the following words in correct order to form a sentence

①了　妹妹　已经　来

妹妹已经回来了。

②他　来　跑　进　的　我　房间　了

他跑进我的房间来了。

③朋友　我　带　给　来　一件　礼物

朋友给我带来一件礼物。

④这个　太　好吃　菜　了，来　再　一个　吧。

这个菜太好吃了,再来一个吧。

59. 去 go

4. 练习　Exercises

(1) 给下列汉字注音并组词 Write down the phonetic symbols of the following Chinese characters and make up a word for each of them

来(lái) 出来　　　　　去(qù) 回去

买(mǎi) 买卖　　　　　给(gěi) 给他

学(xué) 学习　　　　　打(dǎ) 打电话

做(zuò) 做饭　　　　　看(kàn) 看见

吃(chī) 吃饭　　　　　喝(hē) 喝水

(2) 选择填空 Insert the correct answer in the blanks

来　去

① 现在我在中国,我是上个月来的。

② 我给妈妈寄去了一件衣服。

③ 朋友给我带来了很多水果。

④ 我们买东西去吧。

60. 出 out

4. 练习　Exercises

根据图片选择填空 Insert the correct answer in the blanks according to the pictures

　　　　出来　　　　出去　　　　进来　　　　进去

① 里边太热了,你<u>出来</u>吧。
② 快<u>进来</u>吧,外边下雨了。
③ 你看,大家都<u>进去</u>了,我们也<u>进去</u>吧。
④ 下课了,你们<u>出去</u>休息一下吧。

61. 上 go up

4. 练习　Exercises

(1) 根据英语翻译写出相应的词组。

　　go up a hill　　　　　（上山　）
　　go down stairs　　　 （下楼　）
　　go to work　　　　　（上班　）
　　finish class　　　　　（下课　）
　　above　　　　　　　（上边　）
　　below　　　　　　　（下边　）
　　last time　　　　　　（上一次）
　　next month　　　　　（下个月）
　　last week　　　　　　（上个星期）

(2) 选择填空 Insert the correct answer in the blanks

　　　上班　下课　上楼　下山　上边　下一次

① 我们每天8点<u>上班</u>,下午6点下班。
② 山很高,<u>下山</u>的时候要小心。
③ 这一次没有时间,我们<u>下一次</u>再见面吧。
④ 书没在桌子<u>上边</u>。
⑤ 现在正在上课,<u>下课</u>以后我想回家。
⑥ 孩子<u>上楼</u>去睡觉了。

62. 走 walk

4. 练习 Exercises

(1) 把下列短语与其相对应的意思连线 Link the following expressions and their meanings

走路 ——— leave
走开 ╳ walk
拿走 ╳ passing by this door
走这个门 ——— take sth. away

(2) 选词填空 Insert the correct answer in the blanks

走　　走开　　走路　　拿走

① 他 拿走 了我的笔。
② 走开 ，别听我们说话。
③ 每天 走 那个门进教室。
④ 喜欢 走路 去学校。
⑤ 他刚 走 ，你就来了。

63. 开 open

4. 练习 Exercises

(1) 选择填空 Insert the correct answer in the blanks

开始　　打开　　开会　　开车

① 你开车要小心。
② 今天晚上公司开会。
③ 我们开始上课吧！
④ 太热了，我们打开窗户(chuānghu)(window)吧！

(2) 完成句子 Complete the sentences with the words given in the brackets

① 同学们请打开书，看第56页(yè)(page)。(打开)
② 今天学校开运动会，很多同学准备参加比赛(bǐsài)(match)。(开)

③ 你什么时候开始学习汉语的？(开始)

④ 买东西以后，我要开一张发票。(开)

⑤ 他的爸爸是司机(sījī)(driver)，开车开得很好。(开车)

64. 能 can

4. 练习 Exercises

(1) 把"能"放在合适的位置 Please put the character "能" in the proper place of the sentences

① D ② B ③ C ④ B ⑥ C

(2) 回答问题 Answer the following questions（略）

65. 会 be able to

4. 练习 Exercises

(1) 根据拼音写汉字，并想想它们的意思 Write down the characters according to *pinyin* and think about their meanings

① Māma huì shuō Yīngyǔ.

妈妈会说英语。

② Nǐ huì tī zúqiú ma?

你会踢足球吗？

③ Jīntiān bú huì xià yǔ.

今天不会下雨。

④ Míngtiān yǒu huìyì ma?

明天有会议吗？

⑤ Nǐmen shénme shíhou huìmiàn?

你们什么时候会面？

⑥ Qǐng děng yíhuìr.

请等一会儿。

(2) 选词填空 Insert the correct answer in the blanks

不会　　一会儿　　开会　　会　　会面

① 天气很好,我看今天<u>不会</u>下雨。
② 他学了三年汉语了,他<u>会</u>说汉语。
③ 下课了,我们休息<u>一会儿</u>吧!
④ 昨天我跟朋友<u>会面</u>了。
⑤ 现在我们开始<u>开会</u>吧!

66. 大 big

4. 练习 Exercises

(1) 把下列词语的拼音及意思连线 Link the *pinyin* and their meanings of the following words

大事	dà hào	large size
大哥	lǎo dà	important matter
大号	dà shì	eldest brother
老大	dàgē	eldest child
小孩	xiǎo hào	light rain
小事	xiǎo yǔ	small size
小雨	xiǎo shì	trifle
小号	xiǎo hái	child

(2) 选择填空 Insert the correct answer in the blanks

大雨　　老大　　高大　　小号　　小事

① 这可不是一件<u>小事</u>,很重要(zhòngyào, important)。
② 妹妹的脚(jiǎo, feet)不大,她穿<u>小号</u>的鞋(xié, shoes)。
③ 天气预报(tiānqìyùbào, weather forecast)说明天有<u>大雨</u>。
④ 他有两个弟弟,他是家里的<u>老大</u>。

答案 Key to Exercises

67. 多 many

4. 练习 Exercises

(1) 根据翻译写出词语并注音 Write down the words and *pinyin* according to the English translations

many	(多)	(duō)
few	(少)	(shǎo)
how many	(多少)	(duōshao)
how old	(多大)	(duōdà)
how long	(多长)	(duōcháng)

(2) 选择填空 Insert the correct answer in the blanks

多大　多长　多少　大　小　多　少

① 他今年25岁,我今年22岁,他比我<u>大</u>。
② 昨天来了5个人,今天来了7个人,<u>多</u>了2个人。
③ 那个房间不大,很<u>小</u>。
④ 今天只来了一个人,来的人很<u>少</u>。
⑤ 那条路有<u>多长</u>?
⑥ 今年30岁,你今年<u>多大</u>?
⑦ 的衣服<u>多少</u>钱?

68. 早 early

4. 练习 Exercises

(1) 写一写 Write down the following words and phrases (略)

(2) 完成句子 Complete the following sentences

① A:你早! B:<u>你早</u>!
② A:晚上好! B:<u>晚上好</u>!
③ 我们八点上课,他十点才来,他来<u>晚了</u>。(晚)
④ <u>每天早上</u>你做什么?(早上)
⑤ 你<u>吃早饭</u>了吗?(早饭)

69. 高 tall

4. 练习　Exercises

（1）根据拼音写词语 Write down the words according to *pinyin*

gāo (高)　　　　　ǎi (矮)　　　　　dī (低)

gāoshān (高山)　　shēngāo (身高)

gāojí (高级)　　　gāozhōng (高中)

gāodàng (高档)　　dīdàng (低档)

gāojià (高价)　　　dījià (低价)

（2）选词填空 Insert the correct answer in the blanks

高　　矮　　低

① 她的汉语很好，水平很高。

② 昨天很冷(lěng, cold)，气温很低。

③ 他的爸爸妈妈都很高，可是他很矮。

70. 胖 fat

4. 练习　Exercises

（1）写一写 Write down the following sentences（略）

（2）选词填空 Insert the correct answer in the blanks

瘦　　胖　　肥

① 他吃得很多，所以他很胖。

② 她很瘦，她的衣服也很瘦。

③ 那是一只小肥猪。

71. 老 old

4. 练习　Exercises

（1）请根据英语的意思写出汉字 Write down the Chinese characters according to the English meaning

例如：old (老)

boss (老板)　　　　　teacher (老师)

答案 Key to Exercises

hometown (老家)　　　　tiger (老虎)

husband (老公)　　　　wife (老婆)

always (老是)　　　　mouse (老鼠)

(2) 选词填空 Insert the correct answer in the blanks

　　　　老　老板　老师　老是　老虎　老婆　老家

① 他<u>老是</u>去那个商店买东西。

② 他们家是<u>老婆</u>做饭。

③ <u>老师</u>在教室里上课。

④ 昨天我看见一只<u>老虎</u>。

⑤ 我的奶奶很<u>老</u>了。

⑥ 他是公司的<u>老板</u>。

⑦ 我的<u>老家</u>在山东。

72. 长 long

4. 练习 Exercises

(1) 请将下列形容词中意思相反的词语连线 Please link the adjectives of the opposite meanings

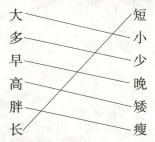

(2) 选词填空 Insert the correct answer in the blanks

　　　　长　短　长期　长度　多长

① 长城有10000里(lǐ, 1/2kilometer)，很<u>长</u>。

② 他要<u>长期</u>住在中国，可能20年。

③ 学完一课要<u>多长</u>时间？

④ 这条路的<u>长度</u>是500米。

⑤ 男孩的头发一般(yībān, usually)都很<u>短</u>。

73. 白 white

4. 练习　Exercises

（1）把与下列词语相对应的意思、拼音和色块进行连线 Link the following words with their correspondent meanings and pronunciations.

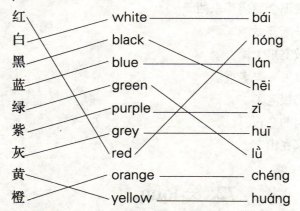

（2）选词填空 Insert the correct answer in the blanks

　　　　　白色　　白天　　明白　　黑色　　白发

① 今天学习的生词(shēngcí)(new words)你都<u>明</u>白了吗？

② 今天<u>白天</u>很热。

③ 妈妈有很多<u>白发</u>了。

④ 黑板(hēibǎn)(blackboard)是<u>黑色</u>的。

⑤ 雪(xuě)(snow)是<u>白色</u>的。

答案 Key to Exercises

74. 高 tall

4. 练习 Exercises

(1) 将下列物品与他们所对应的味道连线 Link the following objects with their corresponding flavors

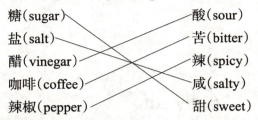

(2) 选词填空 Insert the correct answer in the blanks

  甜食 甜 甜美 甜言蜜语

① 她太胖了,不能再吃<u>甜食</u>了。
② 别说<u>甜言蜜语</u>了,我不喜欢。
③ 那儿有我<u>甜美</u>的回忆(huíyì, memories)。
④ 糖很<u>甜</u>,别吃太多了。

75. 饿 hungry

4. 练习 Exercises

(1) 将下列词语与他们所对应的意思连线 Link the following words and their meanings

(2) 选词填空 Insert the correct answer in the blanks

　　　饿　　　渴　　　饱　　　喝　　　吃

① 我<u>喝</u>了一杯水。

② 今天没吃早饭，现在很<u>饿</u>。

③ 你想<u>吃</u>米饭吗？

④ 你吃<u>饱</u>了吗？

⑤ 我有点儿<u>渴</u>，你有水吗？

76. 热 hot

4. 练习　Exercises

(1) 请给下列词语注音并翻译成英语 Write down the *pinyin* of the following words and translate them into English

热（rè）（hot）

冷（lěng）（cold）

凉（liáng）（cool）

热门（rèmén）（popular, in great demand）

热闹（rènao）（lively）

热情（rèqíng）（warm, warm-hearted）

(2) 连词成句 Arrange the following words in correct order to form a sentence

① 水　　热　　很

水很热。

② 冬天　　冷　　很

冬天很冷。

③ 饭　　凉　　不

饭不凉。

④ 很　　那儿　　热闹

那儿很热闹。

⑤ 是　　音乐（music）　　这　　热门

这是热门音乐。

⑥ 很　他们　热情
他们很热情。

77. 高 tall

4. 练习 Exercises

(1) 略

(2) 连词成句 Arrange the following words in correct order to form a sentence

① 身体　吗　你　好　?
你身体好吗?

② 是　他　一个　不　坏人　。
他不是一个坏人。

③ 菜　这个　了　坏,吃　别　了。
这个菜坏了,别吃了。

④ 晚上　大家　好　!
大家晚上好!

78. 新 new

4. 练习 Exercises

(1) 略。

(2) 选词填空 Insert the correct answer in the blanks

新　旧　老　新鲜　新闻

① 他是<u>新</u>来的老师。

② 妈的这件衣服穿了10年,很<u>旧</u>了。

③ 你看今天的<u>新闻</u>了吗?

④ 我们认识5年了,是<u>老</u>朋友。

⑤ 今天的蔬菜(shūcài, vegetables)很<u>新鲜</u>。

79. 对 correct

4. 练习 Exercises

（1）略。

（2）选择填空 Insert the correct answer in the blanks

    对 错 对不对 不错

① 那儿的菜<u>不错</u>，很好吃。

② 对不起，我做<u>错</u>了。

③ 你是中国人，<u>对不对</u>？

④ 很好，你回答<u>对</u>了。

80. 美 beautiful

4. 练习 Exercises

（1）请把下列词语的拼音和意思连线 Please link the *pinyin* and meanings of the following words

美丽	měihǎo	good wine
美好	měishí	beautiful
美食	měiwèi	happy
美味	měijiǔ	good food
美酒	měilì	delicacy
美景	Měizhōu	Americas
美洲	Měiguó	U.S. dollar
美国	měiyuán	beautiful scene
美元	měijǐng	U.S.

（2）选词填空 Insert the correct answer in the blanks

    美 丑 美酒 美元 美洲 美丽

① 她不漂亮，有点<u>丑</u>。

② 我在那儿喝了很多<u>美酒</u>。

③ 我去过很多<u>美洲</u>的地方。

④ 美国是一个<u>美丽</u>的国家。

⑤ 大家都赞美(zànměi, praise)他，他的心里美极了。
⑥ 我有500美元。

81. 不 no

4. 练习 Exercises

(1) 请用"不"写出下列词语的否定形式 Please write the negative form of the following words using "不"

是(不是)　　看(不看)　　做(不做)
喝(不喝)　　给(不给)　　买(不买)
来(不来)　　会(不会)　　能(不能)
大(不大)　　多(不多)　　甜(不甜)
好(不好)　　对(不对)　　饿(不饿)

(2) 请写出下列句子的否定形式 Please write down the negative form of the following sentences

① 明天我去学校。
　I will go to school tomorrow.
　明天我不去学校。
② 我喜欢打球。
　I like playing balls.
　我不喜欢打球。
③ 他会唱歌。
　He can sing.
　他不会唱歌。
④ 这里的人很多。
　There are a lot of people here.
　这里的人不多。
⑤ 他是美国人。
　He is American.
　他不是美国人。

82. 没 not have

4. 练习 Exercises

（1）看拼音写出句子 Write down the sentences according to *pinyin*
　①妹妹没有钱。
　②没关系。
　③我没去过北京。
　④昨天妈妈没工作。

（2）选词填空 Insert the correct answer in the blanks

　　　　　　　　不　　没

　①下个月我<u>不</u>去美国。
　②去年他<u>没</u>工作，今天他找到了。
　③她<u>不</u>是日本人。
　④我<u>没</u>有这本书。
　⑤她<u>不</u>高。
　⑥我<u>不</u>常常喝酒。

83. 很 very

4. 练习 Exercises

（1）写一写 Write down the following words and phrases（略）

（2）连词成句 Arrange the following words in correct order to form a sentence
　①很　这个　甜　菜
　　这个菜很甜。
　②喜欢　我　不　很　汉字　写
　　我很不喜欢写汉字。
　③的　我　很　哥哥　高
　　我的哥哥很高。
　④吃　日本　很　想　我　菜
　　我很想吃日本菜。

⑤ 今天 的 人 来 多 很
　今天来的人很多。

84. 也 also

4. 练习　Exercises

（1）根据拼音写出句子 Write down the sentences according to *pinyin*
　① 他是中国人，我也是中国人。
　② 我也喜欢喝啤酒。
　③ 妈妈也会说汉语。
　④ 北京也很冷。
　⑤ 这个菜也很好吃。

（2）根据提示，用"也"造句 Make sentences with "也" according to the clues
　① 他是学生，我也是学生。
　② 姐姐很漂亮，妹妹也很漂亮。
　③ 弟弟学习汉语，哥哥也学习汉语。
　④ 他想去商店，我也想去商店。
　⑤ 我一点儿早饭也没吃。
　⑥ 今天一点儿也不热。

85. 都 all

4. 练习　Exercises

（1）用"都"改写句子 Rewrite the sentences using "都"
　例：我去，妈妈也去。→我和妈妈都去。
　① 我和他都是中国人。
　② 我和爸爸都喜欢汉语。
　③ 我和他都很好。
　④ 姐姐和妹妹都很漂亮。

⑤ 哥哥和弟弟都学习英语。

(2) 请把"都"放在合适的位置 Please put "都" in the proper position of the sentences

① A 我们 B 是 C 中国人 D。 (B)

② A 他病了(be sick), B 什么 C 不想 D 吃。(C)

③ A 他 B 连一个字 C 不会 D 写。(C)

④ A 10 点了 B, 你 C 快点儿起床吧 D! (A)

86. 就 just

4. 练习　Exercises

(1) 解释下列句子中"就"的意思 Explain the different meaning of "就" in the following sentences

① 他很快就回来。(at once)

He will come back soon.

② 他们早就结婚了。(already)

They got married long time ago.

③ 我一吃完早饭就去上课。(right after)

I will go to school when I finish my breakfast.

④ 那儿就是我们学校。(exactly)

That is our school.

⑤ 我就一个朋友。(only)

I have just one friend.

(2) 请把"就"放到合适的位置 Please put "就" in the proper position of the sentences

① A 爸爸 B 马上 C 回来 D。 (C)

② A 今天我们 B 7 点 C 上课 D。 (C)

③ A 昨天我 B 看完 C 电视 D 睡觉了。 (D)

④ A 他 B 是 C 我的 D 男朋友。 (B)

⑤ 我 A 有 B 一个 C 弟弟 D。 (A)

414

答案 Key to Exercises

87. 才 only

4. 练习　Exercises

（1）选词填空 Insert the correct answer in the blanks

　　　　　　　　　　才　　就

① 昨天晚上弟弟12点 才 回来,哥哥8点 就 回来了。

② 我6岁 就 上学了,他8岁 才 上学。

③ 我骑自行车10分钟 就 到了,他走路半个小时 才 到。

（2）连词成句 Arrange the following words in correct order to form a sentence

① 他们9点才上课。

② 你怎么这么晚才来？

③ 我才不要他的礼物呢。

④ 弟弟今年才5岁。

88. 和 and

4. 练习　Exercises

（1）看拼音写出句子,并想一想它们的意思 Write down the sentences according to *pinyin* and think about their meanings

① 昨天我和朋友去买东西了。

② 你和谁说话呢？

③ 我和他不是同学。

④ 这件衣服和那件一样漂亮。

⑤ 我喜欢吃饺子、面条、米饭和包子。

（2）选词填空 Insert the correct answer in the blanks

　　　　　　　　　　和　　也

① 妈妈 和 爸爸一起去美国了。

② 我去商店,妹妹 也 去。

③ 我想买水果 和 面包。

④ 我不喜欢吃米饭,他 也 不喜欢。

⑤ 弟弟 和 我一样高了。

89. 在 indicating the position of a person or thing

4. 练习　Exercises

(1) 根据拼音提示写出句子 Write out the sentences according to *pinyin*

① 他们在饭馆吃饭。

② 他坐在椅子上。

③ 他在听音乐。

④ 我们在上午8点开会。

⑤ 他们班的学生在20人以下。

⑥ 你的书在桌子上。

(2) 请把"在"放在合适的位置 Please put "在" in the proper position of the sentences

① A 妈妈 B 不 C 家 D。　（C）

② A 我 B 教室 C 学习 D 汉语。　（B）

③ A 我们 B 吃 C 晚饭 D。　（B）

④ A 朋友 B 住 C 中国 D。　（C）

⑤ A 出发时间 B 明天 C 上午 D 10点。　（B）

90. 向 toward

4. 练习　Exercises

(1)（略）

(2) 选词填空。(Insert the correct answer in the blanks)

　　　　在　　向　　和　　也

① 今天我在家休息。

② 妈妈也会说汉语。

③ 我和朋友一起去吃饭。

④ 他向爸爸问好。

⑤ 我向哥哥借了10块钱。

91. 从 from

4. 练习　Exercises

(1) 略。

(2) 选词填空 Insert the correct answer in the blanks

　　　　　从　　在　　向

① 我在教室学习。
② 向你的妈妈问好。
③ 从这儿向左拐(turn left)就到了。
④ 你从哪儿出发？
⑤ 他在那儿等你。

92. 比 indicating difference in manner, degree or quantity by comparison.

4. 练习　Exercises

根据给出的资料写"比"字句 Make sentences with "比" with given information

(1) 哥哥比弟弟大一岁。
(2) 姐姐比妹妹唱歌唱得好。
(3) 今天比昨天暖和。
(4) 我比他喜欢汉语。
(5) 哥哥比弟弟有钱。

93. 为 for

4. 练习　Exercises

(1) 把"为"放在正确的位置上 Put "为" in the proper position of the sentences

① A我们B他C毕业而D高兴。　　　　　　　　　　　　　B

②A 让 B 我们 C 健康（jiànkāng）(health) D 干杯。　　　　C

③A 我 B 可以 C 你 D 做什么吗？　　　　　　　　　　　C

④A 参加 B 比赛（bǐsài）(match)，C 他们每天练习 D。　　A

（2）选词填空 Insert the correct answer in the blanks

为　　给　　从　　在

① 昨天我<u>给</u>妈妈电话了。

② <u>为</u>找到一个好工作，他努力学习汉语。

③ <u>从</u>我的家到学校，走路10分钟。

④ 我下午<u>在</u>图书馆看书。

⑤ <u>为</u>我们的友谊干杯。

⑥ 请再<u>给</u>我一杯咖啡，好吗？

94. 的 auxiliary word

4. 练习　Exercises

（1）（略）

（2）阅读并回答问题 Read the assay and answer the questions

问题：

①"我"是北京大学的留学生。

②"我"是从英国来的。

③"我"有两位女老师。

④"我"的好朋友是美国人。

⑤"这些东西"是玛丽买的。

95. 得 auxiliary word

4. 练习　Exercises

（1）选词填空 Insert the correct answer in the blanks

的　　地　　得

① 他是我<u>的</u>哥哥。

② 妹妹写汉字写<u>得</u>很漂亮。

③ 我买的衣服很便宜。

④ 我慢慢地习惯(xíguàn be accustomed to)了这儿的生活(shēnghuó life)。

⑤ 老师说得太快了。

⑥ 明天我要早早地起床(get up)。

(2) 选择正确的答案 Choose the correct answer

① 美国太远了，一天 B 。
　A 回得来　　　　B 回不来

② 你要了这么多菜，我们 B 。
　A 吃得完　　　　B 吃不完

③ 你写的字很大，我 A 。
　A 看得清楚（clear）　　B 看不清楚

④ 老师说话的声音(shēngyīn voice)很大，我 A 。
　A 听得见　　　B 听不见

96. 了 auxiliary word

4. 练习 Exercises

(1) 根据拼音写句子 Write down the sentences according to *pinyin*

① 今天我买东西了。

② 我买了一本书。

③ 他吃了饭就去上课。

④ 天气冷了。

⑤ 昨天我没买东西。

⑥ 他不是老师了。

⑦ 她不漂亮了。

(2) 请把下列句子中的时间换为"昨天"并改写句子 Change the words indicating the time in the following sentences into "昨天" and rewrite the sentences

① 昨天我去买东西了。

② 昨天他来了。

③ 昨天我买了一件衣服。

④ 昨天我下课去图书馆了。

97. 着 auxiliary word

4. 练习　Exercises

（1）（略）

（2）看图用"着"造句 Make sentences with "着" according to the pictures

① 门开着。(开)

② 外边下着雨呢。(下雨)

③ 他们骑着自行车去上课。(骑自行车)

④ 他看着看着睡着了。(看)

98. 过 auxiliary word

4. 练习　Exercises

（1）（略）

（2）选词填空 Insert the correct answer in the blanks

过　　了

① 你去过长城吗？

② 昨天我买了一本书。

③ 我没看过那个电影(diànyǐng, movie)。

④ 听说他病了。

⑤ 我下了课就去吃饭。

答案 Key to Exercises

99. 呢 auxiliary word

4. 练习　Exercises

(1) 将问句和正确的答句连线 Link the questions with the correct answers

A:
你写什么呢?
你在哪儿买的这本书呢?
她喜欢谁呢?
王老师呢?
他在哪个房间呢?

B:
他去办公室了。
她喜欢我。
他在211号房间。
我写信呢。
我在学校的书店买的这本书。

(2) 看图说一说"……正在/正/在+动……呢" look at the pictures and make sentences with "……正在/正/在+动……呢"

图1 一个人正在看书呢。

图2 学生们正在上课呢。

图3 两个人正在吃饭呢。

图4 一个人正在听音乐呢。

100. 吗 auxiliary word

4. 练习　Exercises

(1) 选词填空 Insert the correct answer in the blanks

吗　　呢

① 昨天你去商店了<u>吗</u>?

② 我喜欢看电影,你<u>呢</u>?

③ 你不是很喜欢他<u>吗</u>?

④ A: 王老师<u>呢</u>?
　　B: 我也没看见他。

⑤ 他今天来了<u>吗</u>?

421

(2) 把下列句子改为用"吗"的疑问句 Change the following sentence into questions with the character "吗"

① 昨天你写作业了吗？
② 你来过中国吗？
③ 他是你的弟弟吗？
④ 你喜欢吃中国菜吗？
⑤ 他去上海旅行吗？
⑥ 你喜欢听音乐吗？